HELD TOGETHER

A True Story of Love's Victory

Jenny Q

& Friends

Lovely Diane,
what a bright star you
are! Much love

Gratitude and Acknowledgment

To my mama who made me, birthed me and fought for my life.

To my baba who supported me, every step of the way, from adolescence to Dead tour to the hospital bed.

To my siblings who inspire me to be my best, as they are.

To all the contributors, who made it possible for me to tell this story, for so much of the journey was revealed to me through their words.

To Robbi Robb, the mystical boy, without whom I might have been too afraid to ever publish.

To Casey, with his dedication and beautiful eye.

To Rohini Walker and Paul Cullen, who gave their precious time and edited the book.

To Barnett with his gigantic heart, who believes in and holds this entire community.

To Selah, who took care of my family and businesses while I dove into the Universe of Writing.

To Mike Schneider, who was always my big brother's best friend, who I took to prom (even though he was way past high school) because I didn't know any boys my age, and who became our angel at UCI.

To Maria Hess, the world's best therapist, who saw me as whole and helped me recapture that knowing.

To Amanda, Kristen, Isobel and Myshkin who held my store and lab while I was dreaming and rebirthing in a hospital bed.

To Sailor and Felicia who held my wife and child and home.

To Piper who held my hand and gave me courage early on in this journey.

To Patricia, Selah, Tania, Kimberly, Elise, Kristen, Fox and Christina who believe in me and keep my life juicy.

To Georganne Deen, who made the most beautiful legs the world has ever seen.

To Myshkin who held me and holds me, literally and in metaphor. Who stays no matter what the road looks like, and sees my beauty no matter how I have transformed. Who brings me the kind of love I had only dreamed about, and forgotten to believe in, and is so much deeper than I ever really believed possible.

And to Yazzy, who it's all for.

Dedicated to my wife and child,

Myshkin and Yazzy.

My community is my lifeline.

When I fell ill in January 2014, the love of these souls held me together.

In the following pages, this story is told by myself and many of those that gathered me up in their care, kept me alive, and helped me back to joy.

My gratitude, always.

Cast of Characters

Jenny Q: Mama, storyteller, herbalist and witch, owner of Grateful Desert Herb Shoppe.

Myshkin: Jenny's wife, musician, poet and Yazzy's bonus mom.

Barnett: Founder of Joshua Tree Music Festival, organizer for Joshua Tree Living Arts, and papa.

Tania: Drag king, performer, professor and doctor of dance.

Lynne: Co-producer of Joshua Tree Music Festival, teacher and Lola's bonus mom.

Ted: Poet, activist, musician and papa.

Michelle Q: Jenny's younger sister, Yazzy's maternal aunt, naturopathic oncologist, chef and mama.

Maryrose: Artist, musician and mama.

Robbi: Poet, rebel, pioneer of world music and mystic.

Boulos: Jenny's baba (papa), Yazzy's grandfather, pediatric allergist, social activist, patriarch of Q clan.

Felicia: Musician, artist and owner of 31 Beaux coffee house.

Jessie Mae: Photographer, gardener, body worker, sound healer, astrologist and traveler.

Melissa: Lover of music, last person on the dance floor, world traveler.

Katie: Mama of two, homeschooling activist, horse trainer.

Eva: Founder of Harrison House Music, Arts and Ecology, documentary filmmaker, performer and teacher of Bharatanatyam dance.

Erik: Rock climbing guide, musician, teacher and papa.

Kali: Festival organizer, artist, mama.

Stella: Military and family life counselor.

Joyce Q: Jenny's older sister, physician, musician, mama.

Sue: Organizer of We'Moon, witch, mama.

Amritakripa: Mother, artist, musician, lover of nature and Presence.

Marilyn: Yazzy's grandmother, matriarch of Beach family, bird lover.

Michelle: Yazzy's paternal aunt, nurse, mama.

Elise: Shaman, poet, jeweler.

Lena: Owner of Rosemary's Garden, mama.

Cheryl: Founder of Mil-tree: A Veteran's Support Group, producer of Desert Stories, mama.

Susan and David: Psychics, Tai Chi teachers, parents.

Willow: Witch and high priestess of Reclaiming community.

Patricia: Yoga instructor, photographer and yogini.

Maya: Teacher at unschooling camp, homeschooling activist, permaculturist, mama.

Rodney: Dead Head and writer.

Georgina: Painter extraodinaire and dog mama.

Karen: Acupuncturist and poet.

Lisa: Ceremonial drum maker and owner of Bonita Domes.

Liesl: Three stringed bass player, songwriter, poet, activist, general rabble rouser.

Anita: Graduate of the School of Hard Knocks and the University of Life.

Jimmy Q: Youngest brother of the Q clan, lawyer specializing in human right and American Indians, punk rock drummer and baba.

Christa: Artisan, gypsy merchant mama, homeschooling mama.

Selah: Rancher, climber, world traveler and mama.

Ronda: World traveler and merchant trader, off-grid homesteader and mama.

Allison: Astrologer and daughter of the stars, vintage queen and mama.

Mama: Mama and matriarch of Q clan, advocate of music for youth.

Karin: Massage therapist and health activist.

Julia: Happily retired teacher.

Paula: Food stylist, didgeridoo player and sound healer.

Johnny Q: Jenny Q's oldest brother, doctor of pharmacy, musician and baba.

Matt: Writer and photographer.

Julie: Performance artist, dancer, activist, artist.

Nina: Taught the Q clan to belly dance, auntie, mama.

Trinidee: Yazzy's honorary sister and artist.

Yasmin (Yazzy): Jenny Q's daughter, homeschooler, world traveler, musician and creative writer.

jenny

dark, crisp, silent, serene..

bright pins of light everywhere..

stars. faces.. eyes in those faces shining like those stars..

everlasting space that is all the quiet but brilliant with sound..

as if each cell is screaming out with song, yet there is absolute stillness..

clouds too.. wispy clouds of brilliant color.. purple, blue, pink..

there were no thoughts. no conversations.

eyes spoke, perhaps, but without words.

we were

all

being

in indescribable joy..

but without emotion.

absolute presence..

and we were

all

being.

part one

whispers, community, prayers

jenny
intro

a March sunrise in joshua tree is about six-thirty..

most mornings, one could find me greeting our sun's first rays as i ran through the preserve surrounding my home. it was my alarm clock, my business meeting, church.. i would wake with the birds, plan my day and praise the wonder of my earth.. it is what fed my inspiration for the whole day..

that seventh of March, 2013, started like all others, my sweat hitting, then shining, on the passing creosotes as if there was morning dew.

my legs had a little more spring that morning as i anticipated the evening's plans.. kristen, my close friend, was playing a gig and had shown me the poster of her friend who was headlining the show..

'yes, please'..

those were the first words that i remember running through my mind..

the photo on the poster showed a fierce, tough-looking and yes, hot woman glaring at the camera.. i was immediately drawn to myshkin's face and was happy to have plans for the evening..

the morning went like most others.. panting up to the house, finishing my workout, waking my yazzy, feeding and dressing her, then starting our homeschooling for the day.. after our work, i fed her lunch, dropped her at barnett's house for a playdate with lola and got myself to work my shift at the grateful desert..

going to work was like having a long lunch date with most of our local folk and multitudes of tourists.. i provided information on herbs and health, created special essential oil perfume blends, offered a space for emotional catharsis about health and life, and flat-out socialized.. indeed, a dream job..

that day, i happily went into work for some hours, then went to pick up yazzy for our evening together.. we hung out and shared supper and then mama got dressed up to go out! a rare occurrence in my single mama days.. hannah, one of my boarders, really one of the family, watched yazzy as i got dressed up in anticipation and my neighbor piper came over, spiffed up joshua tree style..

as i am piper's self-appointed social coordinator, any time i go any-where, i automatically plan for her to be there as well.. it works out brilliantly for the both of us..

kristen had spoken to me of this myshkin friend and let me know that they would be at the gig early, eating dinner and would be pleased for me to join them.. so, piper and i got there early and as we walked inside the saloon and i saw the table filled with kristen and company- a group of musicians and one of them being this fierce, tough looking woman- i veered sharply, made a hard right and ended up some-where far away from that terrifying table.. thankfully, that turned out to be a table close to the stage so i could be swept away by that talented and fierce woman, that woman who would later save my life.

myshkin

all a dream

I was forty-one, sitting around a wooden table with a crew of Alaskans, in the Redwoods, at a moment before everything changed, when I finally seriously considered the idea: this might all be a dream.

I was twenty-eight, on my first tour, sleeping at a friend's house, when I had a dream. I woke up upset, went downstairs and into the backyard, sat around a cold fire-pit and wrote the dream down, in rhyme, exactly as I dreamed it. It was about a stripper who took it further, and began dismantling her body. A name came with the dream and it was Jenny. It was 1994. I sang the song Jenny for years, its macabre sensibility perfect for myself and my hometown, New Orleans.

I was forty-seven, on tour through the beautiful early spring southwest, at a moment before everything changed, when I went to Joshua Tree and met Jenny. She heard me sing, we took a walk, we wrote notes and sent pictures, I travelled back down a month later and we fell together as if we had always been, together. We planned visits for the summer, and a move in autumn. On October 31, 2013, I came home to my new home, with Jenny and Yazzy. On Thanksgiving we were engaged. In January, the dream changed. Everything changed. But we are still together as if we have always been. Dreaming.

barnett

many nights

The fear in her voice was palpable. Of course I would pick Yaz up from school, I told Jenny; she's always welcome to spend the night at our house. Little did I realize she'd be staying with us for the week, and for many more nights in the months to come.

tania

a bouquet of purple tulips

A bouquet of purple tulips, crinkling inside their clear plastic wrap, was in my hand as I drove steadily up Sunset on the south side of Joshua Tree. The blooms had a white inner core that glowed inside the barely-open flowers. Though off-season (hello corporate grocery), I thought the tulips would be a nice companion to Jenny's bedside as she slept and healed from her minor, out-patient surgery.

The last time Jenny and I had been in contact was the evening prior. Her text message said that her surgery went well and that she was super dehydrated, but happy. "I'm thirsty!!!" the text said. I replied "I love you. DRINK SOME WATER!!" in all caps to push an imaginary water source to her through the phone. Q's spirit felt solid, so I went to work the next day with an easy feeling that my friend was safe.

I had not seen Jenny yet since she returned from her procedure, but I texted her and ran up to her house as quickly as I could after work. It was about five P.M. Bouquet in tow, I parked in her driveway and walked up to the house. The lights were low.

I texted Piper to see if she knew what was happening. I had a strong expectation she would know how Q was, since she and Patricia were as close to Jenny as can be, heartbeats of the same pulse – that kind of thing. Then I turned off my car, walked quietly up the drive and knocked ever-so-lightly. No one came to the door. I knocked again, more delicately than I usually do because now it was obvious that the lights were all off in the house. I opened the door and put the Purple Tulips on the floor, just inside.

Myshkin was Jenny's new girlfriend. She and I were barely acquainted, but Jenny was my long-time friend. I felt ripped between these two realities. What was needed was for me to see my friend, and make sure she had everything she needed. But no one answered. As I turned from the door, I looked back for a second, sending a wish that Myshkin would put the flowers in water soon, so that when Jenny Q awoke the next morning, her soft-focused eyes would be greeted with the gentle bow of the tulip stems, cast against the soft rays of sunrise.

I walked to my car momentary dumbfounded, not sure what to do. A song came to my head: "32 Flavors" by Ani Difranco, one of my favorite artists.

Then my senses clicked into an acute gear. Intuitively, I knew something was wrong. The Ani song left my consciousness, and I texted Patricia asking, "Where is Jenny?" Next, I called Piper, but got a voice mail on which I left a message asking the same question. I sat in my car with one leg dangling, not sure where to go next.

Moments later, I hear the sound of shoes walking on desert sand, and out of the setting dusky shadows comes Piper – walking to the Q house very much in a hurry. I ask her what is up, where is Q, what is going on. She says she cannot tell me, and I then demand she tells me because it is clear I am not going anywhere but with her and everyone else. Piper tells me Q is at the hospital in JT and that something is wrong. A description of shitting glass is all I needed to recognize there was a serious issue at hand. I told her I would be following her down to the hospital after she gathered things. Piper hedged for a second- she may have texted Patricia or Myshkin to ask if I could be included in the hubbub. I felt a piece of my body fall off the moment I heard this news. There was no way I would be anywhere but by the side of my friends; we were a team, a tribe, and this was a fucking emergency.

Lynne

school night

Barnett, Lola and I were excited to have a sleepover with Yazzy. I knew it must be important because it was a school night. The girls crafted, played and read the night away. When we received the call on the second night, I was concerned. My thoughts raced through my head, "What could possibly be going on? Yazzy rarely has a sleepover, let alone on a school night."

ted

the 4th of july

Ten years ago this past July, Monet and I went to the birthing center at the High Desert Hospital in Joshua Tree, for an appointment and to check out the facilities there, our baby Sage due in August. We asked if we could see a room, so a nurse got permission for us to go into one where a baby had been born the day before. Inside that room was Jenny Q - whom we'd known from around town, where the rock climbing world overlaps with the musician refugees in a sort of Hippie Heaven on Earth - and her baby daughter, Yasmin, born, as the song goes, on the fourth of July.

michelle q

rimuoverla!

My four year old son was coming out of anesthesia, throwing his body around and screaming at the top of his lungs. "Rimuoverla! Rimuoverla!" he screamed, clawing at his IV catheter. The nurses refused to remove it due to protocol but after fifteen minutes of listening to him holler while tsk-ing at me, they finally took the damn thing out. After an emotional early morning and late evening in the hospital in Florence, we were finally driving home.

My cell phone rings. "Mom, he is okay. It was all really hard, but he is going to be fine."

"What? Oh, Rafa had his surgery? He is alright? Umm...Michelle, I have to tell you something. Jenny is in trouble. She is in the hospital. All of your siblings are coming."

And everything was turned upside down.

mary rose
finding out

The day that Jenny went into hospital we had been in touch, because we were planning to get our daughters together. Yazzy has always been a wonderful friend to Rosa but we hadn't seen her in a while.

My family met Jenny Q four years before, and immediately I felt safer knowing she was in the world. It's not easy to put into words...both being very busy, we didn't always see each other, although Rosa spent some amazing times with her and Yazzy. She got to make tinctures in her laboratory, have sleepovers. Jenny and I would always look into each others eyes on our brief encounters, picking up or dropping off the girls, and I would feel such a deep shared experience through only that simple exchange.

Life had gotten very busy, so Rosa was extra excited about getting together again. On that day, we had a text from Jenny to say she had a minor medical emergency done and could we put off the playdate for a few days...

Then, on the next appointed day, we had a call from Myshkin. She and I hadn't met, but I had heard some wonderful things about this incredible woman who was Jenny's new love. I will never forget the sound of her voice; it was pure terror. She said that Jenny was not well, that she had been feeling ill since she visited the hospital a few days earlier and that they had to go to the emergency room, so Yazzy wouldn't be free to see us that day.

I hung up the phone feeling very scared.

robbi

distracted

She seemed distracted. Her eyes darted across the room. I naturally followed her line of sight and landed on Tania. Then swift as a black bat she was with me again – her eyes, her dark beautiful eyes staring into me. I rambled on with our conversation, but noticed once again, as if distracted by her thoughts, her eyes had flown across the room as from flower to flower across a garden; then suddenly looking back at me – she listens with her eyes, she is very, very present that way- her dark eyes penetrate right to your soul, as if she sees what you are saying more than she hears you. But that Thanksgiving night she was distracted.

Her eyes darted again across the room – fast as hummingbirds, glancing past Myshkin stirring a pot on the stove, across the room and across Tania's face.

My eyes continued their reconnoitering: there was Patricia chatting away; she often stands as if smoking a cigarette, like an actress in a 1920s black and white movie. Then there was the musical duo, Felicia and Sailor. I was jealous of Sailor's name - I want that stage name. Anyhow, they are lovely, lovely girls, nothing there but sweet- ness. There was Kripa ever curious and ready to laugh or to dance at the drop of a hat. There was Bella, oh and there was Tania. Tania is tuff. Tania crosses the gender line very well, she looks like a guy who owns a small truck and does construction work, and who was once upon a time a Lambretta driving mod. She has all the right rearview mirrors on her scooter, skinny tie, ducktail and all. Yea, Tania is a ducktail as we used to call them back home. On that night she looked very comfortable, she came across more cat-like, leaning lazily into conversations and slouching in the armchair.

The black hummingbirds were back hovering before my eyes, "Where were we?" I returned, gathering my thoughts and continued the conversation.

Anyhow, that was the last time I saw Jenny in that chapter of our lives.

boūloُs

dad

One evening, my wife and I were hosting a party for a local charity organization. During the party, I received a call telling me that my daughter Jenny was at Desert Regional Hospital in Palm Springs. So I told my wife about the call, and we gave our house key and all the alcohol to the party-goers and left.

felicia
vision

Beginnings of friendships are always so interesting. You never know what to expect. Within a few hours of meeting Jenny Q, she told me she had a vision of Sailor and I in Joshua Tree and invited me to do an herbal medicine internship with her. I had been hoping for years to find a teacher in herbal medicine, someone to show me how to identify, harvest and make medicine out of plants. This was the beginning of her magic in my life. Soon enough thereafter, it was settled. The three month internship would begin February 2014.

jessie mae

witchy, coquettish, and fierce

The best souls you'll ever meet never come with a memory of the beginning. You're simply set for a long run of braided lives wafting and weaving the distance with holding hands. A touchstone of growth through time, Jenny becomes your family when she pulls you into her heart, locks eyes with you, making a forever-contract, and feeds your face while you weep. Who hasn't fallen in love with her? No one.

Here's what I know of our beginnings: we met in Joshua Tree at what was, at the time, the only place to eat, drink, and make out: The Crossroads Café. My memories are of Halloweens, parties at various climbers' homes, and her home. Everything about her was witchy, coquettish, and fierce; ingredients for an ideal crush for a twenty-two year old. It was a time when there were no traumas (or if there were, they were buried deep into the psyche, not to come out until after thirty). I dealt lattes and beer, winking twenty dollar tips out of charmed wallets. There was a perpetual spring in the air in those days and the little town felt like your favorite people were with you everyday. I left a year later with a bitter sweetness for all these wonderful folks attached to my heart. Of all of them, Jenny remained dedicated to the long haul of our friendship.

kali

community

Community. It's a powerful thing. A thing I had never experienced before finding my heart in the desert. I quickly followed it and settled here because, well, I had found my people. One of those core people is Jenny Q. We had children that started to grow up together, a handful of them, all born within a month of each other. That brought us parents close together. Jenny became not just a friend to me, but an aunt and a sister, a mentor and a practitioner, someone I could always go to because she is always there... for anybody, at any time. Those kinds of people seem to be an endangered breed these days. I could go on in detail about all the amazing, fun, wonderful times that have permeated our circle, giving momentum to perpetuate the good, decent lives we all wished to live and give to our children; but just know that they are continuous and consistent, a communal Qi that removes the fear that we may be left alone and wanting.

stella

anchor

I moved to Joshua Tree in the Spring of 2014. When I arrived, there were lots of flyers in storefronts and people talking about Jenny Q. I saw requests for prayers and healing thoughts. I began to think of this woman that I did not know and sending good thoughts her way. I kept hearing about the progress being made, the return to home, the food sign-up list, etc.

It was through this connection to Jenny's healing that I met folks in town and got to know people. It was part of what anchored me here in those first months. I continued to think about her and to visit the herb shop.

jessie mae
full moon belly

I would periodically return and witness the depth of Jenny's dedication to life, especially the one that had sprouted in her womb. I saw her read Harry Potter books with full animation to the full moon belly of Yazzy within her. I wouldn't actually meet Yazzy for another few years in the small town of Arcata. The heartache of divorce can swing us into frenzied road trips to find out who does indeed still have our backs when life falls apart and we have no ground, walls or ceiling to contain us. She stayed in a yurt with Yazzy for some months and I witnessed again her dedication to life, despite the brokenness of it and I loved her more for it. She taught Yazzy the proper etiquette for social survival out of the back seat of her car, which Yazzy's brilliant three year old brain shared with me: "Always sneeze into the crook of your arm so you don't spread germs."

jenny
deeply held, holding deeply

this, the community i have always wanted. have always strived for..
deeply held.
holding deeply.
so fulfilling..

melissa

love letter

Here's the thing about you, Jenny. You're one-of-a-kind. There is no one like you. You're badass and you're magical. No one builds community like you. Queue the constant stream of neighbors, family friends dropping by, plugging in, being a part of your scene. See the fanatical admiration you inspire all around you. See your beautiful daughter.

When I met you, way back when in Ocean Beach, I didn't know who you were- a friend of a friend? But I do remember you in your black, boxy glasses (before those were hipster chic, by the way) and such a warm smile! No static, no defensiveness, no posturing. Just…friendliness. Openness. Who is she? Jenny Q! Oh. OK, got it.

As we both know, you would turn out to be my dear friend. And my respite/retreat in the mountains, where we would go to dance and party the night away! Where I would go to connect with nature and remember what we know to be true about the nature of our being. To hang with my girlfriends, tell the truth and laugh together. The good stuff. We were such lovely forest nymph goddesses, weren't we though? Sips of scotch, your records playing…. there were no MP3s! It was the 90s. Classic.

A hoedown was what was on tap.

And through those years, I never wavered in my appreciation or in my enjoyment of you, never underestimated our goodness, despite the challenges that never seemed to stop rolling in.

Then came marriage and Yazzy and the subsequent unfortunate, but not surprising, result which was not seeing you much. You were in Joshua Tree now, doing stuff like being a mom and going to school and starting a business and building a house. But we kept the thread and knew the bullet points of what was going on in each other's lives, more or less. You came to see me in Portland. It was kind of random. Yazzy wasn't feeling well and we didn't have very much time. We couldn't really sink in to our connection.

Shortly after it was divorce time. Looking back, it did seem like there was a shadow. Foreshadowing...

Finally, you were getting your groove on again. Blossoming, yes. Blooming with new ventures. A beautiful homestead, teeming with activity and community. Like some kind of cowgirl ranch in the crazy rocky desert, buzzing with creativity, productivity and possibility. Grounded in powerful feminine energy. I wanted in on that vision of a collective. The dream! Of our commune. Living how we want to be: beautiful, conscious, free, supportive, collaborative, tuned-in, balanced, healthy. Greeting the sunrise and honoring the dark. Real, vital, soft, strong. You know I still hold that dream, girl.

Even my Gavin, bless his heart at twenty years old: immune to the influence of parental guidance or taste, unamused with my alternative world views and impossible to impress from the middle-age bracket. There he was, holding on your every word, soaking in every bit knowledge and wisdom of your craft - healing with herbs, expressing his desire to spend time with you in your lab. To learn. Because he knew, without question, that you are the shit. You were laying down the truth in a way he could hear, and he respected not only your expertise, but simply who you are. I could have cried for the loveliness of the moment.

Next came Myshkin. Your excitement of big yummy love was evident and pervasive. But alas, she was not there for me to meet. Musician on tour. Happy for you. These things are always so acutely all-consuming and wonderful in the beginning. But would this be a lasting lover? Would this sustain.

Then it happened. I got the call, but not much information. I was terribly disturbed but also unable to process.

The message was: life-threatening. You might die. My response was: No Can Be. Cannot. Will not. No. Period. But then.... what if? My adrenaline was up, and it was sickening. Horrific. Not knowing.

katie

horses and thoughts of yazzy

I remember feeling something was wrong. I didn't know quite what was going on, but friends kept acting weird. I was not informed as quickly as everybody else was because you and I had experienced a falling out and hadn't been talking.

Then one day, I think it was Christa that pulled me aside and said,

"Katie, I know that you and Jenny have not been in touch and I know how close you are," and she explained to me what was going on.

And I just couldn't believe it, you know.

Someone that I loved so much. I always assumed that we would come back together again and now I possibly was going to lose you.

And I was stunned.

I held it together because my kids were there and I didn't want to freak them out.

But at some point, I broke away from my family and went down to my horses and cried so hard, just wailed and wailed. I went into a space where I knew you were, and told you I loved you and held you there.

Like I was hugging you. I told you that you were going to get through this.

I wasn't going to let any bad thoughts get in.

And then my thoughts turned to Yazzy and I thought, 'Oh my God!'

I was so terrified and yet I didn't feel comfortable calling to see if I could help, because we hadn't been speaking.

I wanted to offer bringing Yazzy to my house so she could be somewhere she knows, and feels comfortable and safe. I knew there would be people around her, but I wished I could have her at my house. We have so much history.

And it just hurt so bad.

I called a couple of people, just to kind of throw it out there that she was welcome to come stay with me, but I felt awkward because I didn't know Myshkin yet. And it was just so weird to feel like I was so on the outs Everybody was acting so secretive.

eva

chocolate and big hips

As President of the beleaguered Joshua Tree Chamber of Commerce, naturally my interest was piqued when I heard a new business was moving in next to the health food store. Several friends of mine seemed to have the scoop. They said, "You know, Jenny Q is going to open a place to sell tinctures..." Hmmm. The special twinkle in their eyes as the name 'Jenny' rolled off their tongues informed me that she was a person I would want to meet.

Indeed, her bright smile and joie de vivre were immediately infectious! I was surprised and so pleased when Jenny, with great joy, wanted to join the Chamber and have a ribbon cutting ceremony for "The Grateful Desert," her dream-come-true Herb Shoppe and EcoMarket. She was a bright spot on the horizon because so many others in the 'village' of Joshua Tree were anti-Chamber at that moment. It was a clue to her personality... Jenny was her own person. Her opening was a festive occasion with her lovely six-year old daughter Yazzy, the apple of her mother's eye, central to the ceremony.

Soon after, I attended a party at the cozy shop. I remember dancing to some exotic sounds and then squeezing myself onto a comfy couch, in the midst of live music and new people to meet. It was not hard to pick up on her more intimate side—she was a sensual woman, quick to give a warm hug with feeling oozing from her deep, dark eyes.

In the months that followed, I found myself nipping into the Grateful Desert a little too often to feed my addiction to the highest quality and most delicious dark chocolate- with sea salt, cherries or coffee beans- that Jenny would with authority recommend as "medicine." Somehow I suspected there were others like me.

On occasion, when the store was quiet, Jenny and I would chat over the counter about business, life and love. I found her easy to get to know on a personal level because she was so open. Between her introductions to the healthiest facial cleansers and moisturizers one day, she extolled of being attracted to women with big hips. How refreshing, I thought to myself. I would think about how wonderful it was for her daughter to have a mother that taught her by example to love honestly. I admired Jenny for that and sampled another kind of chocolate!

Perhaps the last time I saw Jenny Q in her shop before the dawn of the dark days, she introduced me to her new love. They had just driven down from the north having moved Myshkin lock-stock-and-barrel to Joshua Tree. I felt like I had missed a few chapters in a novel... when did this happen? Jenny was excited to introduce us because her new partner was a musician and I ran an artist residency/music program. I could feel the love they shared and was pleased for them. They seemed so happy together.

When I first began to hear rumors that Jenny Q was not well and was hospitalized, my body filled with a darkness and fear of losing something. It's moments like that when one discovers what's important in life. Jenny was by no means a close friend but her aura of caring, joy, exoticism and sensuality had affected me in a way I hadn't realized.

tania

how i met jenny qaqundah

I was caught instantly by the halo of her smile, the first time I "officially" met Ms. Jenny Qaqundah. I was in Joshua Tree, at her Grateful Desert, the store she owned and managed. On that afternoon, I had no reason to step into a store named "Grateful Desert," for surely I felt I would not live up to the task. I was starvin' like Marvin but hardly a deadhead. Still, I walked into the Shoppe because, as mentioned, I was hungry – and was soon pleased by the awesome fragrances wafting through the cool Shoppe air.

It seemed my body walked before my brain did, and to everyone's good fortune, I found myself staring into the Middle Eastern food section of Grateful Desert, which was at that time against the Western wall. I saw well-oiled dolmas in a can, a large tin of olive oil, and bottles of Cortas Rose Water, clear and light, on her shelves. My heart-rate sped up as my eyes moved down the shelves and read each box and container, salivating at familiar foods that were cuisine staples in my Lebanese-American family, when my brother and I grew up in San Diego. I was raised on good grape leaves and home-made yogurt, touched with lemon and olive oil. My heart began to settle, seeing these familiar brands and foods. I felt at ease. Then, my feeling turned to curiosity. Why was there such an array of Middle Eastern foods in the middle of this tiny store on this tiny block in this giant desert, I wondered.

I looked around for the shop-keeper and spied my eyes on the dark curls and grand smile of the person standing near the counter, Shoppe-owner Jenny Qaqundah. I pointed at the boxes. "Why do you have so many Middle Eastern foods? Are you Arab?" I asked, all at once. I was standing in front of her counter now (which was located in the center of her store), and she said "Yes, I am." And then, also "Are you, too?"

I said I was, and she was delighted instantly.

25

I believe at this point Ms. Q assumed I was a lesbian. Because her next phrase came with a well-spring of tears: "I have never met another lesbian who is Arab. I am so happy!" AND THEN THE TEARS. The tears flowed from her eyes, nose, and it was during this time that, besides falling in love (which was instant), I got to hear the chortle of her nose as this beautiful woman wept and laughed at the same time. SNORT. HONK. HA HA HAAAA HAHAAAA. Then she grabs your arm, and you too, grab hers. Each has a smile that feeds the next onslaught of love-filled adrenalin. I was smitten.

We come to the desert for these kinds of exchanges. We arrive here to slip away from other, mundane, existences— hoping there is another way to live.

erik

singing songs

I knew Jenny was sick but didn't know much else. For some reason the details kept eluding me, like grasping for trout with your bare hands in a rushing creek. Someone mentioned that she was at Desert Regional Hospital in Palm Springs. "I have to go and sing her songs," I kept thinking, so off I went, blithely unaware of the seriousness of her condition. "We'll sing some songs and it will help her feel better," I said to myself. I have long been a believer in the power of music to heal, and besides, Jenny and I like a lot of the same songs.

When I arrived at the hospital, guitar in hand, the nurse informed me that Jenny was too sick to receive guests, and they were concerned about visitors inadvertently bringing in a bug that might latch onto Jenny in her weakened state. That was my first clue that things were more serious than I realized.

So what does a self-respecting hippie do when faced with such a situation? Find a patch of grass and sing some Dead tunes, of course. Not just any patch of grass, mind you, but preferably on a hill under a graceful oak or tall redwood. I settled for a grassy knoll not even ten feet tall in a courtyard outside. Maybe Jenny's room faced the courtyard—she might see me out the window and ask someone to it so that she could hear the music. It could happen, right? It was worth a shot.

I started with Ripple, a song that Jenny and I had sung before that always made me feel a warm glow inside like when you've eaten your last s'more at a campfire with your friends and you don't want the evening to end even though you're really ready for bed. Except this time the feeling was more like saying goodbye to your friend at the airport and you don't know when they're coming back. But I plowed ahead with the song, getting through all five verses and a few choruses, even though the glow felt more like a dim flicker in a dark cave.

Can you hear me Jenny? I didn't notice any windows opening.

I got through the first song with only a small lump in my throat. My second song was going to be tougher. It was a favorite of both Jenny and I—Brokedown Palace. The name says it all.

By the time I got to the first chorus tears were rolling off my cheeks and onto my guitar. You can't imagine a person bursting with more love for all around her than Jenny. A person you want to have in your life. It wasn't fair that this was happening to her. I never did make it to the end of the song. It wasn't just that Jenny and I happened to both like these songs. It was as if Jerry had written them with this occasion in mind. How does he still do this, twenty years after leaving this mortal coil?

Two thirds through the song I was sobbing uncontrollably. I had to stop. It didn't seem like the magic was working. I gathered myself and walked back to the visitors' room. Jenny's partner, Myshkin, walked in and I asked her how Jenny was. She said they were about to transfer her to UC Irvine where she could be closer to her family.

kali

nothing seems to happen

At the start of 2014, I met Myshkin, Jenny's partner, who had moved down from Oregon. We really hadn't gotten to know each other, but that's a great thing about community: if your loved ones love somebody, they instantly become extended family. And while I was busy furthering my education and working hard to create my own life, I indulged every precious moment I got to share in our little slice of heaven here in Joshua Tree. This community makes it work, we are strong, and nothing horrible seems to happen...

boŭloᵣ

first step

Immediately, the receiving doctor told me, "I have to intubate her."

I was astonished and asked, "Why?"

He said, "She is having toxic shock-like symptoms and intubation might save her life. If I don't do it now in the Emergency Room and before she is admitted, it might be impossible."

That was the first step in saving her life.

But from there, everything went downhill.

joyce g
finding out

I was squatted on the floor of the emergency room holding onto Myshkin's hand. This is the scene etched into my brain when I think of the medical calamity that ravaged my sister Jenny in January 2014. That day I received a couple of texts and a phone call from Jenny's girlfriend, Myshkin. Jenny was not feeling well. She was vomiting and having significant pain to her bottom after having a hemorrhoidectomy two days earlier. The surgeon's office said pain was expected and we all assumed the vomiting was from the narcotics. My day in the office was unusually busy seeing my own patients so by the time I called back, Myshkin had taken Jenny to the ER in their small town of Joshua Tree.

It was obvious things were serious when I got a text saying Jenny was being transferred to a higher acuity hospital by ambulance. Jenny lived forever away so I raced home, threw a few things in an overnight bag, kissed my family and made the two hour trek to Palm Springs.

Built up stress during my drive made me not shy about barging into the emergency room ward. Surprisingly, no one blocked my entrance. I wanted to get to Jenny, but a kind and professional ER physician stopped me. She was very concerned about Jenny's condition. Having stated that I was a physician, she explained the details of her labs. Her creatinine was 3.3. I was stunned.

Creatinine measures kidney function and normally runs 0.6-1.0 in a woman. 3.3 meant she was in acute renal failure. Her calcitonin was >50. The ER physician said she had never seen a level this high. Calcitonin is a marker of infection and a level greater than 3 is considered elevated.

Jenny was lying in a stretcher with this wild look in her eyes. She was breathing quickly and trying to get out of the bed but she was restrained. Myshkin was trying to calm her down with soothing words. My heart was sinking. Jenny was delirious. She recognized me but her mind was set on getting up to get bubbly water. Her foot was stuck between the mattress and the bed frame at a strange angle. Mortified, I readjusted her legs. The correction did not last- it was if she had no feeling in her legs. She kept getting her feet readjusted in an awkward position. OK, now I'm scared- what the hell is happening?!

Two weeks earlier, Jenny came to San Diego to celebrate my birthday. It was New Year's Eve but I was sick of always having to host a big party, so instead arranged a daytime picnic and softball game at the park with friends. Of course, Jenny and Myshkin arrived three hours late, as most of my friends were leaving. The main reason I was disappointed was because I was looking forward to showing off my sister. I love introducing Jenny to my friends. She's beautiful, incredibly warmhearted and quite frankly the life of the party. When Jenny arrives the volume is turned up, there is more laughing and depending on the time of day, we'll either start making amazing coffee or cracking open a beer.

I see her striding across the field towards us with a big smile, hair jet black and longer than usual, typical sloppy clothes but with her slightly hippy style. My close friends are still at the party and know her well. I'm slightly irritated some of my newer friends left before meeting my tattooed sister. Steve thinks I'm ridiculous for stereotyping my neighborhood but let's face it, the burbs in San Diego are conservative. Jenny reminds me to keep my style and own lifestyle despite the social norms.

It's hard to believe someone perfectly healthy two weeks ago is lying delirious in a stretcher, septic and in renal failure. This is something I studied in medical school and read about in journals but as a family practitioner and working in an outpatient clinic, I am rarely exposed to this type of severe illness. Even the ER physician was uncomfortable and had already paged the ICU physician and cardiologist. The cardiologist came first and explained he wanted to insert a central line. This is basically a port of entry to a major artery near the clavicle for easily drawing blood and administering medications.

I'm a forty-five year old mature adult but nothing was more comforting than seeing my parents walk through the ER curtain. OK, everything is going to be fine now. Nothing unsettles my dad as he takes charge in any type of difficult situation. Funny enough, the ICU physician was Middle Eastern so my parents and him were chatting away in Arabic. Typical Arabic pleasantries were exchanged as if they were old friends. My dad is a pediatrician so they discussed Jenny's case. My mom was already holding onto his arm, begging for assurances that her daughter will be fine.

I'm not sure what changed but Jenny started decompensating and it was obvious that she needed to be intubated and transferred to the ICU for critical care. Things got chaotic as we were pushed aside and I remember my dad saying, "Goddamn it, we might lose Jenny!" This was when I suddenly felt my blood pressure drop and I needed to squat on the ER floor holding onto Myshkin for support. I heard Myshkin make a sharp cry and my mom started wailing in Arabic.

ﺲ ﻮ ﻋ

keep her here

"Is she going to make it?" I asked Myshkin, sobbing on the other end of the phone.

"I don't know! She has to! Pray for her. Do what you do. Please, Sue, keep her here!" came her tearful, pleading answer.

In thirteen years of deep friendship, I'd seen Myshkin in love and in anguish, but never like this. This was another level, another world, a deeper understanding of love and anguish.

Loving Myshkin gave me access to love Jenny, but I would have anyway. In fact, I found her first. When Mysh returned from tour that Spring, she told me that she had found an herbalist and she might make out with her. "I found a version of you that I can date," she said. I had sold We'Moons to the Grateful Desert the previous Autumn. That phone order was a memorable conversation. We easily chatted about herbalists and conferences and home. And although Jenny is thoroughly herself, as am I, our commonground- motherhood, herbalism, feminism, spirituality, love of nature, love of Myshkin- is an uncanny comfort to me.

So, it was that night, the night we almost lost the bright light that is Jenny, and I knew I had to find and be the calm in the storm. I'd only prayed overnight one other time, and I had no idea what was ahead of me, but I prepared myself. My family was already asleep; I had the downstairs to myself. I turned out the lights, stoked the fire and sat in meditation.

And suddenly, I was lifted, out of my body, out of this world and I was floating in space and there was Jenny. Happy, whole contented Jenny. She sees me and is so excited! I say, "Jenny, where are you going?" She tells me of this place, she's seen it before, and it's better than here and she can work from the other side to make here better. And I believe her. And I cry. I cry because I think we are going to lose her and because of Yazzy. Yazzy, I scream. My heart breaks and I feel my energy rush out of my hands and, root-like, wind around Jenny's legs, keeping her here.

"When the going gets rough, the restless split

That's what I always done, I fear that's what I always

Will you grab me by the ankle, wrap around my thigh

Plant my feet in fertile soil, I get that faraway look in my eye"

—Myshkin, from "Bywater"

Jenny allows me to keep her here and we talk and commune and love for so long, but I realize somewhere in the night, that it has to be her choice. I tell her how much we love her and how much we need her and how my heart is broken for Yazzy. That Yazzy still needs her.

jenny
wanting to do it right

i wanted a baby girl for fifteen years.. i dreamed for over a decade of her and even experienced birthing her long before her physical entrance into my life..

i waited.. i wanted to do it right.. when i think back, i am amazed at the restraint i had.. i was ready at eighteen.. i was silently wishing for pregnancy until my mid-twenties, after that not so silently..

i knew i wanted to finish my bachelors degree first and exactly nine months before i graduated, i got a call from my beloved friend christina, who told me that i was officially free to get knocked up..

but i waited.. i wanted to do it right..

barnett

friends and neighbors

Yaz and Lola were born fourteen days apart, and our families' lives have been intertwined ever since. Learning to be good parents, helping each other out, starting a school together, homeschooling together; living, loving, laughing and crying. Raising an only child as a single mom means that your friends are more family than friends, and working together is a necessity, not an option. 'It takes a village' is not a cliché to most folks in our community.

ted

ashram for children

The summer of 2005 was a bit of a baby boom in Joshua Tree. Weeks after Yazzy's birth, my son Sage was born and between songs on stage at Pappy & Harriet's, word came from down under that Lola was born.

A couple years later, we all started taking our kids to Sharron's Ashram for Children, to play, to make arts and crafts, listen to music and stories, and to learn to socialize with other children. The group of children continued to grow in number and Sharron, from Woodstock, New York, became all of the kids' Hippie Godmother.

jenny

dig and dig to the roots

someone told me today that i need not ever argue with myshkin.. that there is never anything in life or relationship to get upset about.. that nothing is worth a fight..

i was quiet for a moment.. they were right of course.. there is nothing wrong.. all is perfect.. my goddess, we have been through so much, why on earth would we ever- even once- get upset?

dang, i used to be so polite. i used to just let things go and not contradict. but not today. today i said-

"yes, indeed.. it seems ridiculous to ever argue with anyone again..

that goes for anyone and especially me, who knows that all is not just well, but amazing! our lives are a gift and when we pass, it is as though we never left..

all is back to oneness and serenity and being..

so why ever go there? why ever allow disharmony?"

then i said, "but i want to get to the root of things! i want to dig and dig and not stop till we reach the deepest truth!

i want to truly be heard and to listen with utter clarity and attention. i want to stand by my woman in the circle at our wedding altar and look deep into her eyes and know her truth. and know she knows mine.

and know that we hold so tenderly the most intimate parts of each other!"

i told her that, for me, if it is not deep and true and right down to the roots, it is just not worth it. life is too short. and too precious. and too damn juicy.

perhaps my friend is right. perhaps life is too short to ever have a disagreement. perhaps my passionate way is really just a tendency toward discord.

maybe i should have just been polite and agreed with my friend.

robbï

making shit up

It was early morning when Piper called her yoohoo through the door, asking if Kripa was in, No, Kripa was on her early morning walk..or in the shower.. "I just wanted to come tell her that Jenny is sick and has gone to the hospital"

"I knew it!!" I blurted out. I quickly reigned myself in.

Silly me! I didn't know anything, you see, my mind just makes shit up. Godammit!

myshkin
boots

Jenny's pain had increased to the point where she couldn't take care of Yazzy, to the point where she had decided to go and find a surgeon to take care of her. She didn't want to see anyone in the desert. She was feeling shy about the part of her body that hurt and knew she would see people she had worked with during nursing school in this small community. So, the next morning we began looking up and calling specialists in Orange County. We made an appointment with Dr. Mills- a doctor Jenny would later come to know well, someone who would in the near future save her life in emergency surgery- but the earliest appointment was for later in the week, and she was in extreme pain. She kept calling and found Dr. Gregory, someone who had an immediate appointment available, so we got in the car and drove. I remember parts of that two and a half hour drive so clearly, a route I would soon be driving every week for many months, but who could know that then? If nothing tragic had happened, it would have slipped into the deep waters of my memory, but when something goes crazy, so many moments around it becomes blinding-bright and etched in us. I talked to Sue for a bit, Jenny talked to her mom. Her mom asked her to come stay at the house.

Jenny said, "What about Myshkin? She is not my chauffeur."

"Impossible," said Mrs. Q.

Not surprising, as it was only three weeks after we had not been allowed to join her family at her childhood home for Christmas. It was the second time Jenny had ever missed a family Christmas and it had cut her deeply. We called Ambrosia and arranged to stay with her in Long Beach. I felt protective, sad for Jenny.

Dr. Gregory had snake eyes and good boots, a matter-of-fact demeanor that inspired confidence. We liked her. She didn't spend much time, wrote a bunch of scripts, scheduled surgery for the following day. We went to Whole Foods, cooked and hung out with Ambrosia, told her we were engaged. Jenny was working all night, trying to pin down a few things for the business she had been working on for a while. LLC registration and an Amex card. The card came through, the LLC did not. It was the last bit of business she did for half a year.

In the morning we took a walk, poked around some junk shops, took some photos. Jenny was thirsty, but wasn't allowed to eat or drink before surgery. During surgery, I was reading East Of Eden in the waiting room, not scared. Maybe I should have been scared? When they took me back to see her after, she was groggy. Slowly waking, then slowly dressing. The nurse liked her boots. It was a theme.

We cruised back to the desert, ate chicken soup, watched something, slept. And that was the last time I saw my love out of pain for a very long time.

jenny
dependency

in the past, i have prided myself on being independent, tough.

i could handle large amounts of work, extreme pressure, immense pain.

i was a single mom, nursing student and business owner.

i made it work in even the most dire situations. during nursing school, yazzy and i yet again shared a bed as i rented out every room in my house other than my own so that i could pay the mortgage. i had people living in trailers on our property in order to pay the bills and keep my businesses afloat.

i was a founding member of yazzy's cooperative school and was joyfully immersed in my community.

yes, i thought i could handle a lot. i thought that i had life under my belt, that i was, indeed, totally autonomous.

little did i know, i was about to become totally and in the most extreme way, dependent.

felicia

terribly wrong

Little did I know that the journey I was about to embark on would be so different, important, intense and life changing. Things were planned perfectly. I was to go to Myshkin and Jenny's place and do my three month long internship.

It was January 2014 and Sailor and I were at my sister's in Flagstaff, helping her family pack for their big move across the country. It was hard to imagine them leaving the West. My sister and I are very close and I had the privilege of nannying her two precious daughters as they began life. I was going to miss them badly.

One night while we were there, Sailor received some strange texts from Myshkin and decided that she had better step out and give her a call. When Sailor came back into the room, it was clear by her face and her tears that something had gone terribly wrong. It was so scary. Jenny was in the hospital and no one knew what was going to happen.

tania

premier

We went to JT hospital and within less than an hour, I guess, it was clear that Jenny would be transferred to Desert Regional Hospital. We all got on the same page– Patricia, Piper, Myshkin, and I- that we would stay in text message contact. There was discussion on how to support Myshkin. I volunteered to go to the hospital and would gather up anything she needed from their house because Myshkin would be with the ambulance, following in her car.

As far as I could tell, everyone was in shock. I certainly was. But on the other hand, crisis response was definitely in my skill set. Keeping watch for long stretches of time was second nature, learned while working for the U.S. Forest Service as a premier fire fighter.

amritakripa

hearing the news

The words that assaulted my ears were a stark contrast to the sunny softness of that warm winter's day in January, 2014. They came at me like the unwelcome slap of a hitherto unimagined and unfathomable possibility, shocking me out of my languid flow and into a state of single pointed focus with only Jenny Q as the object of my inward attention. "Jenny is on life support at Desert Regional, she might not make it," were the words that scrambled around my brain, looking for a place to land. "What? Who? Our Jenny? Jenny Q?" I was told the news had been delivered by my neighbor, Piper, a few minutes earlier. Needing to get more information, I went running down the road to catch up with her. I had to clarify, to find out perhaps that this was all some weird misunderstanding- a dramatic misinterpretation of something far less serious- as in a game of Chinese whispers. Piper confirmed the worst and let me know that Jenny was in fact in the ICU with a serious case of sepsis. Her body had been overrun with infection after a minor outpatient surgery. She had already been in the hospital for a couple of days, her organs were shutting down and her chances of pulling through were slender at this point. Piper agreed that I should go down there, and provided Jenny's ICU room number, encouraging me to try to get in, even though it might be difficult because only a small number of visitors were allowed at any given time. As though being pulled by a magnetic force to Jenny's side, I rushed home, shared the update with my husband Robbi, grabbed the car keys and headed to the lower desert.

myshkin

frozen

Some months later, March probably, Jimmy asked me to write about the two days after the surgery, that initial surgery with Dr. Gregory, before it was forgotten, in case of legal necessity. I wrote all I could remember, coldly, clearly, of Jenny's increasing pain, her inability to keep anything down, her weird lack of fever, my calls to the surgeon's office, only to be told: don't worry, it's just painful, don't worry, don't even look at the wound. These wounds are ugly, we tell people not to look at them. Much later, we saw what the assistant who took those calls had written about them. What she had written about the day I called to plead for help, to tell them that her wound was spreading, was that she advised me to take Jenny to the ER. She lied.

By Thursday morning, Jenny was going inward. I had almost lost sight of her; I was terrified, and also frozen. I just recently learned that our old brain panic responses of fight or flight have a third possibility— freeze. I am prone to flight, but even more prone to freeze. Jenny had called her family, I had gone out to buy a new thermometer because I couldn't believe she didn't have a fever, and the post-op papers said to worry if there is fever. I kept reading those post-op instructions, I kept telling her, don't strain, don't throw up your meds, it says that here, what can I do? How can I help you? I was terrified. Fuzzy from lack of sleep and a slow cold panic, never even thinking that I should just take her to the ER. I would have gone the moment someone said go. It is something I sit with and always will, this knowledge of what might have been different if I had been less frozen, if I had not waited to hear it from someone else's lips. If I had just gone for help at the first sign of trouble. Patricia—who knows Jenny better than most people, who has seen her every kind of way, but never THIS way— came over towards noon on Thursday, and said GO. And the sea ice cracked and my big slow ice-locked ship of a brain came unstuck, and I raced Jenny to the Joshua Tree ER.

Her blood pressure was 55/20 when we arrived. She was in shock and could barely stand. We began another long wait, while they pumped her full of fluids and she cried in pain, and the wound spread, and the tests showed only that they could not help her there. There was no ambulance available to take her elsewhere. When I finally reached Dr. Gregory looking for answers, help, anything at all, she only said, "This can't have anything to do with me."

They would not let me drive her to a bigger hospital, so we waited. We were there much too long, and the infection raced through her, and they finally gave her something for pain, and the nurses looked horrified, and the ambulance still did not come. For eight hours we waited. It was as if the whole world was frozen.

Finally, the ambulance came. Tania, Patricia and Piper brought me some things from home and I followed her down to Palm Springs. From the waiting room at Desert Regional Medical Center, I called Yazzy. Don't worry, Baby, don't worry, Mama's in the hospital but she's going to be ok. Don't. You. Worry. And then they let us into the ER with Jenny, her mom and dad, Joyce and me, and the doctors were looking gravely at Dr. Q, saying: your daughter is very, very sick.

joyce 9
illness details

It took six days of ridiculously perilous near death tragedies before Jenny was stable. Her six-day ICU chart could probably shelve a small library. There were seven different consultants that visited Jenny daily. The one-to-one ICU nurse was constantly attending to her needs. They gave her an amp of D 50 every thirty minutes as her blood sugar kept plunging down below ten. Multiple antibiotics coursing through her veins, dialysis to filter her blood as her kidneys were failing, pressors to keep her blood pressure up, serial platelet and blood transfusions, ventilator for breathing to name a few.

Luckily, her heart and lungs were holding up, but Jenny was in a coma and we had no idea if she had brain damage. Just as distressing was watching her hands and feet start to discolor to bright red and become stiff. Jenny was in a life threatening state called DIC (disseminated intravascular coagulation). This is when platelets and other clotting factors clump, which greatly increases risk of bleeding. Red blood cells break up and blood clots form in small arteries, clogging the vessels and cutting off blood supply to extremities and other organs.

Thankfully, we were not alone. My mom had called my two brothers, John and Jimmy, at two a.m. that first hospital night. They both were on the first flight to Palm Springs that morning. My other sister Michelle was contacted, but as a mother of a four year old living in Italy, she needed a few days to arrange her trip. Word spread rapidly and the waiting room was packed with Jenny's friends from Joshua Tree. Soon, relatives and friends from Orange County joined our group. There was a constant vigil praying, singing and waiting outside the ICU.

jenny
life-saving line

there was always a voice in my head when i was doing crazy things as a young adult. my palestinian parents had been so strict, terrified of the foreign culture they found themselves in, fear continuously seeping in as their children became teenagers.

my parents held such a tight leash in order to protect us from what they saw as a dangerous culture for kids to grow up in, yet we were all a bit nuts. i don't know if their strictness added to our unruly behavior, or if it is just the way things went, but go a bit wild we all did. maybe it was because of some hard history for me, but i was by far the worst.

even so, no matter what trouble i found myself in, i always had the counsel of my parents. in my head.

my two closest friends didn't have that irritating yet life-saving line to reel them back to safety. one has already died. as for the other, i am always on alert for a phone call telling me of his departure.

my folks, though they didn't know it, continued to guide and parent me through the darkest of journeys.

so many times, they saved my life.

marilyn
desired coveralls

Before Jenny Q became my daughter-in-law, she had joined us for a family gathering during the month of August at our vacation home in Utah. That day, all of us gals were perusing the stores in town and discovered the Mormon thrift store. Chatting while looking, we discovered that Jenny Q's birthday was just a few days away. Of course we immediately wanted to take her to any store in town and buy her a gift. She just smiled and said no, she was fine. We didn't give up. The following day, she did admit she would like to go back to the thrift store and buy some coveralls she saw. Joyfully, we took her back, found the coveralls then started asking her what else she could use. Well... maybe some silverware for her new place. So we stocked her up with those and anything else we could cram into the cart. Later, as we met her parents and relatives, we had to laugh. It looked as though she could have had most anything she needed from any store! We apologized for not knowing. She laughed and said she loved her special gifts.

And that is 'my' Jenny Q. Sorry. I know everyone else claims her too! And as anyone else would also agree, Jenny has a contagious smile. She walks into a room and immediately knows no strangers. She taught me much about a new type of music that I had never heard before. Cesoria Evora became one of my favorites. And then Jenny Q and Todd gave us all the gift of Yazzy, a priceless gem.

The journey of life goes through many changes. Jenny and Todd split up and I could not call her daughter-in-law anymore, but life moved on. Jenny Q was always tucked deep within my heart. And then the day came that I will never forget. The call: Jenny is in the hospital and might not make it. Time stood still.

michelle baum
facebook messages

It is so awesome to see all those who love you gathering together to pray, send positive thoughts of healing, and love to you. Never ever question your worth my dear!! You have impacted so many lives with your love, giving spirit and your awesome kind, loving heart. There is no other Jenny and we need you among us.

myshkin
little torches

Jenny's family started arriving the first hospital night. I was so grateful. A family full of doctors, to try and understand what was happening and advocate for Jenny. To hold her and each other. To have names and explanations for things, to battle the big fears with these little torches of knowledge. We never did find out what the culprit was, really. Just that it happened- so quickly- after a tiny surgery that should have been so simple. Quickly over, easily healed. But instead, something dark raced through her body, shutting out the lights behind it as it terrorized her, from room to room within her. Her body was shutting down. The docs said "renal failure" and "DIC" and I was looking these things up on my phone. I am not a medical person. I knew nothing. I learned much in the following months. Names and parts and processes. Torches in the big big dark night that shine a feeble light on us when our bodies- usually so sturdy, so reliable- just falter.

mary rose

deep and shared

I was worried about what was happening with Jenny, but I was hoping that this would turn out to be a simple problem, easily solved, and that we'd see her again very soon.

I'm not sure how many days passed before I had a frightening email, simply asking if we could say a prayer for Jenny Q.

myshkin

light people

I was four, kneeling on my bed in terror, a ball of light streaking through my bedroom. Many years later, I remembered it.

Later still, I asked what it was, and got a crazy dream answer:

Jenny on her way in, asking me to come find her.

jenny
courage

we knew it from the beginning. we somehow knew we would need to have trust. that our relationship would bring the need for deep courage.

i bought a book of stamps during myshkin's first trip down to the desert to visit me.

the big sticker that came with it was the word

C O U R A G E.

we were brand new. we had only spent a handful of days in each other's physical presence, but we knew. and we dreamed. and we planned.

but that sticker, that was to be our mascot in those early days. we must have both intuited that ours was not to be a path of ease. even in our bliss, we must have known.

we stuck that courage sticker on bertha, my car. it stayed on the dashboard for years.

all through the hospital stay..

myshkin
highwire

Not pulling stakes up from this ground
it is my heart, I'd hemorrhage
Packing my bags and traveling south
and all for love
and still there is
some kind of blue, like robin's egg
so delicate, so delicate
Come take me in your tender mouth
untie my tangles
fly me south
Enter the journey no one knows
but I propose it never ends
I'll cross the sand you cross the ocean
boats and bridges roads and bends
And each time we meet it opens wider
aperture, our aperture
Let more light in each other's eyes
to live less blind
to love more wise
And we're dancing up here on the highwire
little white gloves
and our hearts on fire
What of these shades that paint your days
these hues that you go swimming in

Some kind of blue that never fades
you kiss the bottom yet again
But each load you lose you lift a bit more
helium, like helium
Closer into the pith
the core
leave all your tangles on the shore
And we're dancing up here on the highwire
little white gloves and our hearts on fire
So I'm not pulling stakes up from this ground
pull one foot out
you put yours in
I'll take a giant step all the way south
put mine where yours has lately been
And that's how we'll move, in tango arcs
all parabolic
one burning heart
Somewhere where there's no ends or starts
a tightrope's strung between two stars
And we're dancing up here on the highwire
little white gloves and our hearts on fire …

elise

visioned and held and wept

Had I known..... I would have..... I could have.... maybe........

I had seen Jenny a few days before she was admitted to the hospital. She wasn't well, in a way I had never seen in the fifteen years of our friendship. We made plans to see each other the following week.

On my birthday, I was informed that she was in the ICU after a minor surgery had gone awry.

When I arrived at the hospital, everyone was serious. Jenny's entire family was there, her partner and a couple close friends. We weren't allowed to see her: family only. She was unconscious and unstable. All we could do was pray. And we did. A lot. I played my angelic thumb piano, hoping the song would lift her soul into peace and whisper to her that it was safe to come back, that we were here, that she wasn't alone. I visioned and visioned and visioned her in whole, balanced, beautiful health.

Jenny's Arab family is stoic and understandably holds their family matters close, but I couldn't accept not knowing anything. We were desperate to help, and we felt we couldn't do that without knowing what Jenny most needed.

I found the opening in her sister Joyce and brother Johnny, who both warmly shared when I inquired- entrusting me to keep details close and tight among only those of us at the hospital. For many days.... every day....Life was busy as usual, but somehow the only thing I thought of and worked with was Jenny- doing long distance energy work every day. I didn't eat much so that I could better sense what was happening with her. I was focused. My warrior training and my energy medicine training kicked in and merged, something that I had thus far not experienced in such a way.

Kristen and Fox, two dear friends of Jenny's, whom she'd been wanting me to get to know, live near me and we carpooled every day to the hospital- and we got to know each other and love each other during this time. We prayed together and sat in stillness and vision. We wept and held each other. We were patient and impatient, fierce, soft and surrendering. A couple other friends came and went, some stayed and stayed. We held and held and held with all certainty that our Jenny would emerge any moment. But....she didn't.

tania

arriving to desert regional

My heart was racing to keep apace of my friend Jenny Q. I knew I would be on my own for this emergency – there was no one to lean on as I pushed my way through the huge pulses of emotion pouring out of my body. This is the Life Force: this is the thing that pushes us further and further into the great unknown. We follow it because we know we can help. Being in service to the Life Force is a gift to warriors.

jenny
adolescent self-esteem, psych institute

my adolescence was a struggle.. i have felt embarrassment and remorse for the strain i put my parents through on many occasions, but it was only when i had a child of my own that i realized how terrified my immigrant parents must have been..

of course, i never meant any harm.. i was riding my own turbulent waters, traveling treacherous roads and searching for safe lands and stable ground..

but i think of the messiness i created and feel humbled..

as a teenager, i was hospitalized for a short time for emotional turmoil.. i remember being stuck in a room with three counsellors grilling me about my low self-esteem.. finally, they told me they wouldn't let me out of the room until i could tell them one positive thing about myself..

no.

but they wouldn't take that as an answer.. one good thing.

no.

damn, being a teenager was tough work.. i finally came up with an answer..

i am the luckiest person alive because i have the best friends! i somehow have the best people around me!

even though the counsellors refused to take that as a satisfactory answer to their question, i still to this day take that as the best compliment i can come up with for myself.

tania

diaspora in the kitchen

Jenny says to me, "It's because you're Arab" when I pose food or hospitality-related questions to her in the kitchen. I love it when she says this, because it reminds me to claim my spot in the Arab-American diaspora who form community and a shared sense of belonging when creating in the kitchen.

felicia

germs

Coincidentally my sister, like Jenny, had just undergone surgery. While helping her wash and dress her giant wounds, I found myself thinking of Jenny clinging to life, quite possibly because of some mistake in cleanliness. I hoped with all hopes that my hands were scrubbed clean enough and tried to overcome self-doubt and fear.

What if I didn't wash long enough or well enough? Was it the right soap? What if there was some terrible contaminate on the handle of the sink? What about the hand towel? Was it clean?

Simultaneously, my dog was dying and Sailor, my partner, was very ill..

It was one of those times where everything around was in flux. It all felt so surreal.

myshkin

never lost track

Back on that first night in Palm Springs in January 2014, I called my family and they made plans. My sisters Sunny and Ingrid drove down the next day from Northern California to be with Yazzy in the house for as long as they could. They stayed about a week, my mother came from Indiana to stay for three or four, then my dear friends Sailor and Felicia came for the duration. I never went home while my sisters were there. Everything was so tenuous that first week, and I could not even think about being sixty miles away from her. It was hard enough sleeping across the street.

John and Jimmy, Jenny's brothers arrived from up north, Joyce and her mom and dad were still here, and then there was me. All in this tiny ICU room with doctors and nurses scurrying around us, trying— and continuously failing—to limit the amount of people in the room, and dealing with a family full of medical professionals. Jenny was put on continuous dialysis. The machine was temperamental and horrible, gave off a fire type alarm anytime it got bumped, or didn't. They brought in an easy-chair for Jenny's mother to sleep in, as she would not leave her side. Once Jenny's mom and I were alone with Jenny, on either side of her and holding her hands. Jenny, from her faraway/ right/there coma state, raised our hands up to meet, and moved them up and down a little as if asking us to shake hands. She continued to do this for five minutes. Suad, her mom, kept saying, "What do you need, Habibti?"

I kept thinking, "I know you want us to get along, Jenny. It won't happen right now, but someday, don't worry."

I was sure Suad would accept me someday, and even if not, Jenny needed to believe so.

joyce q
arab parents

My parents are Palestinian and moved to LA when they got married. Strict Middle Eastern parenting clashed hard with the five Huntington Beach kids they raised. I was probably the most disciplined but there was plenty of sneaking and lying. Jenny gave my folks the most grief. Dropping out of college to follow the Grateful Dead was disastrous for my parents. Regardless of the number of times Jenny needed a line during her wandering years, my dad always came to the rescue.

Despite my parent's high expectations and periodic disapproval, they were always very involved and supportive in their kids' lives. At this point we're all well adjusted with careers and family but they weathered drugs, career changes, rejection of their religion and divorce to name a few. I believe their unconditional love plays a big part in making us a close-knit family.

I describe my dad as a fixer. Even now if I have a hard medical case, I call my dad to discuss symptoms and diagnosis. I don't think any of his kids have made a big decision, such as buying a house or changing jobs, without his advice. As dire as a situation may feel, my dad never falters and always finds solutions. My pillar faltered when my dad lost faith in Jenny's ability to survive this ordeal, making us realize the unthinkable was a real possibility.

jenny
how the dead changed my life

the grateful dead changed my life.. not always easily and certainly not attractively in my parent's eyes..

it didn't look pretty to the outsider.. dreadlocks, clothes that could use a good wash and serious mending, eyes too red to be from fatigue alone. also, the substances.. they did their work on me and set me on a long and arduous journey of recovery and self-realization..

but dead land was a magical place..

picture a large community of misfits, uncool people, sensitives that wanted nothing more than to be seen and to love the ones around them.. those of us who were never in the "in" crowd at school, those who would be laughed at for their inch-thick glasses, or their weight or their unruly hair.. here was a group of people who were finally adored for their differences, savored for their quirks and accepted as family..

you were never the weirdest one in the room..

during a show, you could dance so openly and joyously. you could shed your insecurity, stomp and shake and look like a fool, only to open your eyes and catch the glance of the dancing fool next to you.. love and light would pour between the two of you in an unabashed sharing of a magic moment..

this happened to me regularly, and though i knew few of them, i would recognize so many as i moved from city to city and state to state to satisfy the hunger of that shared love and ecstasy.

i suffered from states of depression and jubilance as a teenager on a planet known as adolescence.. i was an adept brooder and often cried myself to sleep to pink floyd, stunned by the inconceivable depth of despair and the brilliance of deep emotion..

when i found the grateful dead, it was an opening like the cracking of an egg, a bright light being shone on me..

i can feel this much emotion and have it be joy?!

maybe choosing to be happy is a simplistic concept that most just inherently know.

i did not..

and i grasped onto that knowledge and clung to that world,

finding the joy and gratitude that would finally become the greatest guide for my journey on this earth,

the saving grace for every breath as i glide through the tale of this life..

tania

the first night at desert regional

Four a.m. I sat down in a set of three chairs off-set in low light, stationed close to restrooms and drink station, a hallway away from
the ICU. After being turned away from Jenny's room by Myshkin,
I felt unsure where to step. Turned down porch lights? It's okay, I
can see in the dark. Closed door? It's okay, I can see that it swings
open every time a staff person walks in or out the ICU area. The
space determined a new game plan. I found a place to sit not far
away and had a sip of water. As being alone was not new to me,
I sat and listened to time pass. The hospital area was friendly at
this time of night, because there were only a few people there.
It looked as though they all were overnighters, concerned about
loved ones who were also in ICU.

In the beginning of the emergency, I put my active intuition to use.
I put my ears and nose up like a fox in the wind, sniffing the air for
information to put the puzzle together of what was going on, and
what the moment called for. I was ready. My brain conjured up an
image of Q's smile and the twinkle of her eyes. My ears were open
— everything needed to be heard; my brain was open -- everything
needed to be memorized. I kept my muscles warm, my heart pulsing and regulated. Whatever it was, I was down with it. Jenny's life
was at stake.

It was too early in my emotions to speak with anyone. Overnighters
found seats and areas in the hospital to sleep or pace in, for the
long wait ahead – some got unhealthy snacks from the food
machine, others kept quiet conversation, or slept. I was facing forward, towards the ICU hallway.

I crawled around under the cubicles, searching for a plug for my
phone. Other visitors did the same. This kind of "making home" in
unfamiliar places is part of how most people cope with being away
from home. I began to rely on the familiar movements of strangers, their specific gestures that marked them as "the daughter and

mother who were down for the count," or "the family of fourteen who were out in the front." I took in the energy of those around me; and when all seemed safe, I dozed off or took a minute to breathe. For peacefulness, the waiting areas of Desert Regional were just fine. No one was offensive; in fact, it was a very respectable place to be stationed.

Hours later, I glimpsed a nurse passing by me, and instantly recognized her. As she saw me, a smile came across her face and she stopped to speak to me. I can't remember the dialogue, but she was that beautiful South Asian woman whose family owns Sam's Restaurant and Market in Joshua Tree.

I cried into her arms, "What does it mean that she is in the ICU?" I asked. She answered the basics about what the ICU unit did. I told her it was you, Jenny Q, who was in there. She knew who you were! She was surprised and concerned too. I cried some more. I, grasping for a gear to hold onto, like a dog swimming in waters too high for her tiny head, felt relieved at having made a new friend (and such a fine looking one).

After some additional weeping and also casual conversation, we left each other, both feeling much better it seemed to me.

a mritakripa
hospital visit

When I moved to Joshua Tree in 2014 with Robbi and my daughter, Bella, we knew that we were in the right place at the right time in our lives. There was a strong sense that we had found our 'tribe' so to speak. Here was a community of open, loving, unique and creative beings who embraced us as though we were family. For me, Jenny was one of the first amongst that tribe. She was a holistic sister, herbalist and goddess with a brilliant smile, easy laugh and eyes that you could simply take a refreshing dip into on a hot desert day. Just knowing that she was there, a neighbor within walking distance, made everything perfectly fine. That's how it had been since we arrived. She was an integral piece of this beautiful puzzle, which is the weird and wonderful world of Joshua Tree. Any and every interaction with Jenny left me with a feeling akin to having walked through a vast field of wild flowers - many colored, beautifully fragrant and inherently healing.

Driving down the grade toward Desert Regional, my mind traveled in circles. How could this be? What about Yazzy? Joshua Tree without Jenny - No! Hang in there - Please God! And again back to, How could this be?

Not having a clue who would be there at the hospital and feeling as though some sister energy would be helpful, I reached out to our dear mutual friend, Paula. No answer on her cell, so I left a message for her to call me back as soon as she could. It so happened that when she did call back, she told me that she was driving home from a job in Orange County and hadn't picked up because she had been on a call to another friend, explaining that she was feeling 'toxic' and was in need of some herbal cleansing. She knew just who she was going to speak to for advice when she got back to Joshua Tree - Jenny Q. We agreed that it was an odd conversation in light of Jenny's situation - a tuning of sorts into the universal intelligence around this unique circumstance. Paula and I agreed to meet up and go to the hospital together and it seemed as though our schedules had been perfectly managed by an unseen hand that flowed us in Jenny's direction seamlessly.

When we connected at the appointed gas station just off the 10 freeway, we took a few moments to consider our plan. We spoke about the likelihood that we might not get into Jenny's room. Obviously, her family and Myshkin would be at her side and it was possible that they would be the only ones allowed in, given the seriousness of the situation. We just felt the urge to be close enough to feel connected to what was going on, without in any way wishing to impose our desires upon that powerful circle of close ones who were already holding space for our beloved friend. Detaching from any specific outcome, we decided there and then that Jenny's angels would get us as close to her as needed, and that, wherever it turned out to be, would be just perfect.

Arriving at the hospital reception, we announced that we were there to visit Jenny Q in ICU and were naturally told to wait in the waiting room until called. For some reason though, neither of us saw the sign to the waiting room, so we turned in the opposite direction and arrived at the first set of locked doors leading to the ICU. We pressed the buzzer to request entrance and were greeted by a voice through the intercom, "You'll have to wait in the waiting room until called," it said before abruptly hanging up. At that very moment, the doors opened before us and, without hesitating, we took the opportunity to step through, knowing that Jenny's angels would take us as close as we needed to be. Once on the other side, in that faceless white corridor, we noticed a window with a wide ledge, perfectly sized for the two of us to sit on comfortably side by side. For some strange reason, it seemed natural for us to take off our shoes and sit quietly. Eyes closed and cross-legged, we became absorbed into thoughts of Jenny and prayers for her wellbeing. For quite some time, we sat there in silence, undisturbed, despite the movement of people up and down the corridor before us. People came and went, nobody said anything and it felt perfectly fine to sit in meditation - just as we would in any temple of the Goddess.

Within moments of opening our eyes and reconnecting with one another, a nurse, wheeling a gurney past, paused before Paula and I and respectfully let us know that we would need to wait in the waiting room. Of course we would. As we re-shoed ourselves, and readied to move on, the nurse disappeared through the automatic doors and the corridor was once again empty. For some reason, perhaps having to do with the magnetic pull toward Jenny, neither Paula nor myself turned to exit those same doors, but instead turned in the opposite direction and started walking toward the unit we knew to be her abode at that moment. I took the scrap of paper out of my pocket that held the scribbled room number that had been provided by Piper, and, soon enough, we two irreverent sisters found ourselves standing outside the final locked door. Jenny's angels would get us as close as we needed to be. We could just stand there and say our prayers or we could let the nurses know that we had 'arrived' and were hoping to visit with Jenny. Fortunately, without much encouragement needed, Paula picked up the intercom and announced our intention. "You'll have to wait in the waiting room until you're called." came the all too familiar response. Paula hung up the phone and, at that very same instant, the door swung open before us. We sideways glanced at one another and knew that Jenny's angels were making it pretty obvious where we should be, and so we stepped through.

In the main room, there was a central island, the nurse's station, with perhaps three or four cubicles around the periphery, each with a patient in need of critical care. As we stepped in, a nurse looked toward us and, while she might have been expected to admonish us for entering or to tell us to wait in the waiting room until called, she instead silently pointed us in Jenny's direction. There was our beautiful sister, hooked up to a multitude of tubes and monitors, eyes open but not there, you could say. Her vast spirit had clearly loosened the 'grip' on its earthly form. Our Jenny was on walkabout, visiting realms that most of us can only speculate about during our sojourn in this physical play of existence. Jenny's mom was at her head and dear Myshkin at her feet. There was a holding on, a feeling of a powerful desire to be the anchors that Jenny so desperately needed if she was going to return to 'this reality' and play with us for a while longer. Paula and I automatically scooted to Jenny's feet, one on either side of Myshkin. We each placed one hand on Myshkin's back and the other on Jenny's legs. My eyes closed and breath became my friend.

I remember reading the story of a young boy who was standing on a similar precipice between form and formless upon which Jenny was now resting. The father of the young boy wrote of how he had invited friends and family to visit and offer energy to be used freely for the purpose of the patient to draw on as needed. Standing at Jenny's feet, knowing that energy comes from source and was not truly mine to give, I nonetheless let go - hoping that I could be a channel in some way for that precious elixir of life. Here it is - take as you need, drink from this cup, was the feeling of my prayer. At the moment of contact with Jenny, I was consumed with a wave of energy - no, rather a bolt. It was good energy, light, the force of life. I cannot say for sure what the experience was but the pulse was so strong that I felt my body sway, almost topple in fact. It felt warm, positive, delicious - there was a feeling that all was well. I remember sensing the presence of many beings of light, all there, offering themselves to Jenny, some-how working on her behalf in the invisible world where the unmanifest threads of light become woven into the very fabric of this existence. After a few minutes, we heard our marching orders, "You'll have to wait in the waiting room," came the voice of the nurse. This time, we obliged. Holding one another, Paula and I retraced our steps into the world of waiting and wondering.

jenny
third person

this process of writing a book about myself has been so challenging and interesting to me.

writing about the most traumatic time i have ever experienced,

could have imagined..

how is it that i handle going into each memory? pain. despair. fear. yazzy. myshkin. yazzy. yazzy. yazzy.

i often find myself referring to jenny in the third person.

i speak of the main character, this jenny person..

"how am i to develop a sense of who she is?"

"how am i to communicate the pain she was feeling?"

"should i speak of her past to give people a sense of her history or should i remain on topic to allow for a smoother flow?"

we creatures are so amazing.. we have the most amazing tools for self-preservation.

Lena

habibti

First, I must go back to year 1995. You and I sat in the garden behind my shop, Rosemary's Garden, for your interview. I loved you instantly. The connection was based on our Middle Eastern background. You, Palestinian and me having been married to a Syrian man for many years. As we worked together, we called each other "Habibti" meaning sweetheart in Arabic. Then you graduated from Sonoma State and that's when I met your family. Ah, the Arabs!

You had gatherings or "parties" at your place, where I remember you kept quart jars of herbal tinctures in the window. The other deep connection was that you loved The Grateful Dead and my late husband was a Deadhead, just like yourself.

Then you left Rosemary's Garden, moved on, started your own shop and became an RN. We kept contact. Called each other on occasion and sent love via Facebook. You came by to visit a couple of times with your sweet Yazzy.

ted

unconscious

I picked up flowers from the Farmer's Market and drove to Desert Regional.

I took a photo of the flowers, where I left them outside, before going into the ICU.

I saw her lying there, hooked up to all the life-saving machinery. Her father gently expressed his gratitude for all the warmth being felt from Jenny's community of friends in Joshua Tree. Jenny's mother, on the other hand, said nothing. Both of them looked sick with worry.

tania

meeting mrs. Q

Late into the second night of your arrival at Desert Regional, some-one convinced your mom to get some sleep in a real bed. I was not privy to the convo, and I could be off by one day, but the point is: your mom was leaving the hospital.

Your mom was walking out with Joyce, and slowed as she came near the chairs where I sat. Curious, but unexpectant, I looked up. Joyce's mind was somewhere else. Mrs. Q asked me my name, and inquired if I was one of Jenny's friends. I told her my name and I said I was. It seemed that Mrs. Q saw in me a person who had matched her own endurance stamina. I had been at the hospital for a very long time.

Then, Mrs. Q reached her arms out and hugged me. "Go home," she said, and she gave me a firm and fond embrace. "Go home, get some sleep," she said again, motioning to the door. For her, I wanted to do exactly that. Instead, I gave her acknowledgement with my eyes, and said something like "I am going to sit here for a while, but thank you. I hope you sleep well. Good night."

käli

we find out

Details were pretty hush-hush. I was told that we were to keep it that way. This was mostly to keep her daughter from hearing how serious the situation actually was. There seemed to be lots of confusion and the doctors were just trying to keep her alive... What? She was in perfect health when I saw her last week! How could this be?

One day, while picking up my daughter Trinidee from school, I remember how sad Yazzy was and how all her friends surrounded her with a group hug. This occurred frequently over the next six months, those group hugs. These kids are really wonderful little humans and know how to lift a friend up.

cheryl
whispers

I remember the whispers; Jenny was in the hospital, almost lost her life, would be there for some time . . .

Things were very hush hush. I would go into the Grateful Desert and ask, "What's going on? How's Jenny?" Whoever was working behind the counter would take a breath, and with a nod, acknowledging my concern, or with a serious expression, just reply something to the effect of, "She is slowly but surely getting better." No details.

I felt sad and helpless. I chanted my Buddhist prayers, and sent light and love, knowing nothing about her health situation except that whatever she was going through was serious.

susan and david
jenny's odyssey

Susan - We didn't know what was going on. The story we heard was that Jenny had 'a procedure' done. Later in the night, she wasn't feeling well and went to the hospital. Time went by and she didn't come back to the store. Rumors were running through town, but nobody who actually knew anything was talking. It was frustrating and created more fear. I asked David to lucid dream and ask Jenny what was happening.

David- I set my intention to find Jenny in a separate reality and fell asleep. When I became conscious in my dream, I was somewhere foggy and misty white all around. It was like we were inside a bank of clouds.

I saw Jenny. She was lying down as though on a bed. She was so far into this alternative realm that she couldn't communicate with me, so I just sat with her and radiated calm from my heart.

When I journey during lucid dreaming, Susan wakes with the same memories of the experience that I have. We talked about what Susan could find out in this realm, at Grateful Desert, and from Jenny's other friends.

Susan- Rumors were getting crazy. I was told that Jenny's family didn't want anyone talking about what was going on and that her friends were going to honor that request. Jenny's family of origin doesn't live in Joshua Tree. Most of us who know Jenny feel like she is our relative, and we think Jenny feels that way, too. And Jenny herself is the opposite of secretive. She's the most wide open person we know. We did realize that the friends who were in her inner circle were dealing with a tough situation with her family, and everyone was doing the best they could.

Eventually a notice was put on the door of the shop telling us to quit asking questions and just put Jenny in the light and pray for her, or something to that effect. David and I do pray, but our prayer is 'Thy will be done', and I don't think that is what the directive meant. We knew that people were setting up prayer circles and that powerful people were working towards helping her heal.

jenny

co-incidents, gratitude

i don't believe that there are accidents.. coincidences are just that- two incidents happening at once.

to think of the world as random is much stranger to me than thinking that things happen just as they are meant to..

i also believe that we can't know everything, as the cosmos is vast

and we are tiny

and we are large and infinite

and flesh is fleeting

and the more i know, the less i hold onto..

nothing will surprise me too much, as the only real wisdom to me is that it is all possible, all happening..

but some things i do know..

i know this..

i had just finished teaching a three-month internship to isobel and decided to hire her to work with me in my lab..

i had just hired amanda, my dream bookkeeper, as she was more inspiration soundboard and creative, box-breaking visionary than any bookkeeper i have ever met and still..

i had just asked kristen to manage my shoppe, in the knowledge that i was the luckiest person to have her and wanted her energy in the grateful desert as much as i could get it..

these things did line up coincidentally- at the moment that myshkin moved to joshua tree..

on the precipice of the illness that would result in me being totally absent from my businesses for months..

and those people ran everything, with myshkin's voice, and later mine through hers;

and the community gave copious donations and shopped voraciously at grateful desert to support our family..

tañia

what inspires, awakens

I often have conversations throughout the day with Jenny Q silently in my mind. I share successes and highlights of the day. Bed made- check. Dishes washed- check. Teeth– check. Play with dog– check! If a cactus flower blossoms, I take in the startling burst of color with everything I've got, because I don't want to miss a minute of its magnificence, so I can tell JQ about it later.

Jenny Q makes me laugh, oh yes she does. I feel lucky to know her – for as the jewel of this Mojave Desert, she is in high demand. She is Palestinian and has a degree in nursing, which is really hot. Besides a head of dark curls, which cascade off her head, my friend has a sharp sense of humor and is notorious for giving good hugs.

Why live unless you are ecstatic, right? That's one of the lessons the witch part of Mama Q has offered. She has us all within her grip.

felicia

precious and unexpectedly fragile

News over the next few days didn't get any better. Jenny was in a coma, had a machine breathing for her and no one knew if she was going to make it. What??? None of it made any sense! She was so strong and healthy and full of life and love! What??? One moment all is well, and then the next moment our new, beautiful friend was suddenly teetering precariously between life and death.

Life is so precious and unexpectedly fragile. Sometimes it all just seems so chaotic and so quick to change course, leaving such a feeling of helplessness to the will of chaos. This was one of those moments.

robbï

godammit!

"Godammit," I would shake my head and mutter under my breath. Everyday, the same route through the Highlands neighborhood past her house, and every day the same muttering under my breath "Godammit, Jenny, how the fuck could this have happened? Godammit!"

jenny
the older i get

we grow and we live

we learn, we seek.

we ask for wisdom.

so it seems to me that the older i get, the less i seem to know

the less certain i am of anything

the more open i am to everybody else's ideas…

don't get me wrong..

i feel pretty certain about some things…

that hurting our planet is not just suicide but homicide,

that judging somebody for living the way they choose and loving the way they do is comedy and tragedy,

that love is the ultimate way to heal, to see anyone.

but knowledge of the great state of things tends to elude me;

wisdom changes for me every day.

people ask me what happened when i was out of my body, hoping that i may have some secret about death and beyond.

yes, i got to have that experience.

but would that experience be the same for everybody?

was the journey i took the same that we all take when we go? did i get all that light and love, laughter and beauty, because it is what i expected would happen?

i don't know. i question myself; i wonder.

i can get swayed by other people's perception of where i went.

my feeling of certainty changes with the tides.

my ideas and bits of knowledge are like clay, shaping beneath my hands, but never seeing the kiln.

they change and mold and change again.

my certainty about my journey hardens and softens, giving me gifts and bits of wisdom that blow away with the desert wind.

when i remember floating in space, no conjecture, no thoughts, no questions,

it just was.

my brain wasn't asking, "is this real?"

there was nobody saying, "isn't this amazing?"

it just was.

i just was.

and it was indeed mind-lovingly beautiful.

but was this just mine? or was this the in-between or the pass-through or the great being?

i realize as i grow older that for me wisdom comes in the form of not knowing.

nothing is attached to anything that i hold as truth.

it's probably all true. and all not true.

elise

black and vacant

Sitting in uncertainty, holding tight to our trust. Slowly, we were allowed permission to see her, one at a time, for a few minutes only.

I was strictly instructed to wash my hands with sanitizer before touching her. It was such a shock to see her that her brother had to put the sanitizer on my hands for me. The Jenny I knew was not there.

Her body expressed only subtle, jerky movements, her eyes black and vacant. In that moment, the world changed.

I have seen pain and suffering and even death, but I had not seen this- someone with a foot in both worlds- and that someone was one of my dearest friends.

tania

the qaqundahs arrive,
one after the other

The Qaqundah Clan cherishes connection and the gifts of life. As a family, they cook and eat and chitter-chatter their way about the universe- laughing, dancing, discussing ideas, babies, food, watching TV etc.- in packs and teams and tribes.

To me, Jenny's biological family came first. A biological family belongs to each other in very specific ways that are deep, complex, and necessary for the psyche to stay balanced when the boat rocks hard. To support the Qaqundah family as one body meant to support Jenny – for me this was how I saw the situation. This is a primal bond. I understood without question that the Qaqundahs needed each other very, very much. They, like we, were beyond language – confronting the impossible -- in those first hours, days, months when it was unclear if Jenny Q would survive this MEAN face-off with death, and return to our arms.

I felt it was unjust that Patricia and Piper were not invited in immediately to be at Jenny's side as advocates and liaisons for Jenny's tribe and family in Joshua Tree. Patricia knew Jenny emotionally and physically like the back of her hand; Piper did as well and is a nurse so would be able to absorb and translate information to the community. These shocks to the tribe-family internal organization sent a worry through the JT community, and certainly to those of us at the hospital door wondering how we were going to help save her life if no one would let us in!

I think everyone knew at different levels of consciousness that Jenny's life was passing before our very eyes. The horror of that remains indisputable. It was a fucking nightmare. All of us responded to the universe: HELL NO!

The entire hospital quickly became aware that The Village of Joshua Tree had arrived to tend to Jenny Q. Some stayed for an hour, some for three hours, some for longer. With Kristen, Fox, Elise and Patricia,

I remember we prayed together for the first time, out loud in Desert Regional. Although Kristen and Fox had been at Desert Regional several times, they never got to see Jenny. So, the chanting and praying together with Kristen and Fox was especially meaningful to me. Elise smelled like Palo Santo and made rich sounds on a music box she brought.

ted

love, trust and respect

As our children grew from toddlers to pre-school age, the kids started learning "People and Plants" from some of the artist Andrea Zittel's interns, doing organic gardening behind the High Desert Test Sites headquarters, leading to the formation of a free-school/home-school co-op we called the Livingschool.

At Livingschool, Yazzy, Lola, Sage, Andrea's son Emmett and several other high desert children started the day with yoga and Woody Guthrie songs, before beginning their Waldorf-inspired curriculum, and playing, making art and gardening, with visitors ranging from next door neighbor, artist musician, Shari Elf to a Tibetan monk who is the great-nephew of author Aldous Huxley, with field trips to see live theatre and to visit Jenny Q in her laboratory, while she made healing tinctures for customers of her shop, the Grateful Desert. This experimental school, funded by the parents and generous local supporters, through creative benefit events, lasted for a solid three years, before shrinking enrollment and increasing time commitments, along with natural disasters, a flood, to be exact, causing damage to our schoolhouse, finally brought this beginning phase of our children's education to an end.

Through those early years of the kids lives, all of the parents who went through that experimental phase together became bonded by the experience. To say that Jenny and I became close is not an overstatement. Some friends, noting that each of us was no longer with the other parent of our children, even made lovely projections about romantic possibilities!! And though Sage and I rang in a New Year or two with Jenny and Yazzy, and some of their loved ones, our love for each other has been that of a brother and a sister. With humor, trust and respect at its loving core.

joyce 9
of yazzy

Yazzy was seven at the time. She is Jenny's only child and they have always had an intense bond. Jenny practiced 'in arms' parenting. This is when a child is literally never put out of her parent's arms for the first year of life. For the first seven years, she never used a babysitter. Yazzy would be snuggled in a sling on Jenny's front or back for any occasion. Wearing large ear muffs to muffle out loud noises, Yazzy went to music festivals and movies.

Yazzy was three years old when her parents divorced. Thankfully for Jenny, it was decided that Yazzy would spend most of her time with her mom but still, their separation every other Saturday was difficult for both. Possibly this separation was good practice as it would be a good month until Yazzy would see her mom after she went into shock and then it was only occasionally for a good six months.

willow

altar

On my altar in front of me is a picture of you, sculptures of Gaia and Kwan Yin, and an angel holding a lit candle. Sacred space to tell a sacred story.

We met when Yazzy was still a baby. My daughter, Maya, was your assistant while you were working your business from home and I picked her up from work on one of my visits with her and Damian in Joshua Tree. Right away, I was struck by your genuine demeanor; you seemed to be radiating happiness and, most of all, you were so present! I think I fell in love with you at that moment.

It was January 19, 2014, when I read a post by Kripa on Facebook that asked us to pray for you. I immediately burst into tears and my heart felt heavy. I felt as if a loved, close family member of mine was in trouble and it allowed me to see how connected I felt to your spirit, in spite of our rather distant relationship. Still sobbing, I phoned Maya. She told me that you were gravely ill and in a coma. There seemed to be very little information available at that time. Meanwhile, I lit a candle and leaned my favorite picture of Kwan Yin against it.

On January 20th, Kripa posted a picture of a healing altar for you. I was so grateful for that because I hadn't thought of doing that and scolded myself for not thinking of it myself. After printing out a picture of you, I closed my computer and called in a circle of sacred space. As if in a trance, I collected different items and created my healing altar for you. My movements were deliberate, yet it was as if a divine hand guided me, and all actions and thoughts flowed through me from a different realm. It didn't take very long before I knelt in front of the completed altar, praying for your healing, calm and centered, with a very strong and grounded intention that I have no words for.

I felt very present and had a sense of achievement. Slowly I returned to the everyday life around me. I returned to my desk and for an hour or two and took care of some bills, my budget, answering emails, making phone calls... my mind on that aspect of my life.

What happened next is very difficult to describe.

Suddenly, I felt as if a lightning bolt had struck me. I jumped off my chair and from a deep place within me, a primal cry moved through my body as a rumbling very loud "NOOOO" escaped from my mouth. I collapsed in front of the altar, tears streaming down my face now, and started bargaining with the Goddess. I yelled and cried, I banged my fists onto the floor, and threw my hands toward the heavens. The intensity was unparalleled to anything I had ever experienced. I don't remember everything I roared, whispered, screamed, spoke, uttered, but I will never forget how it felt.

NO, NO, YOU CAN NOT LET HER DIE!

NO, NO, YOU ARE WRONG, IT IS NOT TIME FOR HER YET!

PLEASE, PLEASE DO NOT TAKE HER FROM US, WE NEED HER, YAZZY NEEDS HER!

PLEASE, YOU MUST LET HER LIVE!

Dearest Goddess, I would never dare to go against your Will, but this one time, please, please don't let this happen, please change your mind, I beg you, please, please, please don't take Jenny from us, not now, not for a long time, you must let her live, she still has so, so much to give to us, HER WORK ON EARTH IS NOT DONE, please, please don't let her die, please, please help her heal, help us all to help her heal, please do not let her die!

Never before or after have I prayed like that, nor felt such intensity of desire, passion and power to change what is.

Finally, I collapsed into a curled-up ball on the carpet and just wept quietly, releasing the tension that had build up during this outburst. I felt very calm and alive. I could clearly see that I was not alone, but surrounded by many souls who were part of this extraordinary plea for divine intervention. I was connected to the deepest most sacred space I can imagine.

michelle

consulate

From Italy, I talked to the medical folks in my family and quickly understood what was happening as best as could be understood. I knew that I needed to be there. I knew that my son needed me. I knew that I had just turned my passport in to the Consulate one day ago as it was about to expire and had to wait for the new one to arrive in order to travel to the States.

An excruciating week of waiting followed while I talked to the Consulate twice per day and talked or texted with my family continuously. With a nine-hour difference, the late mornings in Italy were torture, waiting until the morning in California to hear the latest news. It changed drastically throughout the day. She is awake from her coma! She had to be sedated and is under again. Is her brain going to make it through this? Will we still have Jenny's precious beautiful spirit? What if she doesn't make it and I am not there?!

boūloس

ten percent

My daughter was in a coma for six days. I watched her wounds get worse and worse. The ICU was keeping her alive but her legs and fingers were turning blue, then black.

I took a picture of one of her wounds and sent it to Dr. Joe, a renowned wound care specialist. He urged me to have Jenny sent via helicopter to his facility as soon as she awoke from the coma.

As my wife and I were leaving the hospital in Palm Springs to head to UCI, Jenny's doctors wished us luck and told us she had a ten percent chance of survival. When I called a week later and spoke to one of her doctors, he told me that he was shocked to hear that Jenny was alive; that he had given her a small percent chance of survival to give us at least some hope to hold onto.

tania

the cascading effect

It was when John used the word "cascade" that I fully understood what was going on with Jenny Q. We were in the surgical waiting room- you know, the one with a desk where they give you a buzzer for when there is news of your loved one's surgery progress. He was discussing the situation with Joyce- that Jenny's body was shutting down, one part after another.. like the cascading of a set of dominos.

patricïa
animal

It's rare that you get the opportunity to see someone's animal. The animal that resides in each of us is elusive... a secret even to ourselves, until the day that Life forces that wildness to the surface...

I was there the day Jenny Q's animal appeared. That dark day lives in my memory in slow motion...

She looked up at me, startled, unaware that I had entered the room. Her raven hair tangled, her eyes wide and wild. Two days in a bed, pummeled by relentless pain had taken my best friend to someplace far away.

And all that remained was her animal... she feverishly regarded me as yet another human that didn't know how to help. Her fear, desperation, and exhaustion had transformed the sweet and once familiar room we were in to a scene from a movie I didn't want to see.

jenny

pain

each human has the capacity to handle a certain amount of pain.

we even have classes designed to teach us how to endure sensation that is on the outer limit of that capacity.

lamaze, the bradley method… these courses help us navigate the times in our lives when we have an intensity of sensation that we don't normally feel. it is true that birthing a baby brings us to those outer limits, but knowing that there will be the ultimate gift on the other side of it often helps women survive.

but there are different kinds of pain. the kind that doesn't hold the promise of a beautiful outcome. the kind that can be the result of trauma or aggression. or necrosis.

i learned that we can survive the extremity of pain that we are not meant to handle. the kind of acuteness that is meant for one thing only—

to warn against extreme danger.

myshkin

believed

I never pray. I sing, and write, and pull tarot cards, and sit in awe in nature and give thanks for what is. But I never ask. Plead, beg. Until Jenny was in the ICU in Palm Springs, and I was across the street, in the most impossibly beautiful setting: palm trees and bougainvillea, big mountains backdrop to a mission style building where one can stay when one's family member is near-death. Impossibly beautiful stage-set for a nightmare. I prayed. Asked, begged and pleaded. Promised. Believed. Because I had to.

felicia

witchy gathering

We continued to get group update texts over the next few days from Myshkin. In one of them, she implored all of us to energetically do anything we could to help. She asked us all to use our witchy powers to send healing to Jenny. I thought, yes I'm some kind of witch. This is something I can do, even though I have never tried anything like it before. I needed to do something, anything.

So I went outside in the sun and sat down on the back steps away from everyone. It was quiet save for the rustle of leaves and occasional chirping bird. I closed my eyes and thought of Jenny. Then, suddenly I was there. I have never experienced anything quite like this before, but I was there. I was in the hospital room, and I wasn't alone. I could feel that the whole room was full of other presences as well. Beautiful, powerful, loving beings...maybe you are reading this now. Some presences I seemed to know, and some I hadn't met yet. I had just joined some sort of other-worldly energetic witch gathering! The mood was radiant with happiness and I knew that we were all there for the same reason. To give Jenny love.

Jenny was there too! She was outside her body, but there in the room with us.

It was all so amazing.

She greeted me and took time to talk to me even in this other existence. Of course Jenny would! I looked at her and said without sound, "What is happening Jenny?" She just looked at me and smiled her smile and shrugged her shoulders. Her body was in a fight for life. She didn't know why. It just was.

Then we got to work. Light and warmth and love from everywhere.

I came back from that incredible experience, back to my body, back under the sun, back to the backyard steps I was sitting on, with tear-soaked eyes filled with tenderness and awe. I had hope. Jenny was still there. And in addition to the physical world of loving family, friends and medical staff around her, she was also being looked after by a whole pack of powerful beings and loving spirits interweaving between realms.

Jenny you are so loved.

maya

"written the day i found out"

My friend Jenny is one of those people who have several dozen friends who count her as their 'best' friend. When I worked for her, she always insisted on feeding me a delicious lunch before I went home. When I go into her little shop, she calls me sweetheart, kisses me and feeds me chocolate. When I became pregnant, she cried and made me a special oil blend for my belly. Jenny is what I call a juicy woman. She literally radiates light and everyone wants to be around her.

I've always been impressed by her warmth and extroverted nature. I tend to feel pretty shy and introverted most of the time. But there's a specific lesson I want to learn from Jenny- live life fully, reach out, love people up. We don't all have to be as extroverted as she is to do that. It gets really obvious to me in times of crisis. Right now, Jenny is in the hospital and there are literally hundreds of people praying round the clock, and offering to help in any way that they can think of. It's very clear to me that all those people would not be there if Jenny were not as generous as she is. So I suppose it's for selfish reasons that I want to be more generous. I want to give myself to others so that if I ever need something, people will feel generous with me. I hope it's clear that when I say 'generous' I don't mean money. I mean attention and caring.

Thanks for being who you are, mama. Can't wait until you are healed up and back home.

lynne
resiliency

No one's life is a smooth sail; we all come into stormy weather. But it's this adversity - and more specifically, our resilience - that makes us strong and successful.

jenny
little narrator

so many thoughts are moving through my mind.. everyday, i feel like i have a little narrator perched on my shoulder, narrating the story as it unfolds. these last couple of years are so surreal, this part of my life story..

did i really just leave my life for a full seven months? my daughter, my businesses, my partner, my community? is it really true that my stunning friends and new girlfriend kept my businesses alive and thriving while i was away? did my new girlfriend nurture my daughter through this ordeal only two months after moving in with us?

so many people worked incredibly hard to support my family and to help keep my mortgage paid so that i could come back to a home if i did make it.. i can't even fathom a way to express my gratitude for the magnificence of what my community did for me..

i couldn't even make up a story so brilliant, i've never read a novel so captivating and full of magic.. i am indeed keeping my narrator hard at work..

kali

myshkin stayed

Myshkin, who was new to the community, who barely knew anyone, who was fighting to be next to her lover's side through all this.

What a woman! Hardly skipping a beat she stepped right in, making sure Jenny's business still operated and seeing that Yazzy got to school each day, so that life stayed as uninterrupted as possible. Her strength and courageousness left me awed and inspired. That is TRUE love. Most people I know would have just taken off and been unable to deal with it.

myshkin

slipping

Both Jenny's extended family and their Arab community, and her Joshua Tree community were very present in the waiting room in Palm Springs, though strangely encamped on opposite ends of the small waiting room. Fox, Kristen and Elise came together every day, and others when they could. I reached out to some long distance healers in my life: Sue, Raven, Rozz. They all did their work, and found her somewhere in their journeys, and told me things that were true and that I hadn't shared with them yet. I spoke to Sue often, and towards the end of the week, she told me she had had such a sweet session, working long distance Reiki with Jenny. They were swimming, swimming in the air….. I said, "Enough! Stop swimming, it is time to bring her back to Earth, please bring her back to Earth now."

She had been slipping further away, not getting better. And the docs were giving signals that they were at a loss, and didn't know if she would, and maybe we should think about letting her…I could not hear it. John said it and I could not hear it. I did not believe we would lose her. I had my talks with whatever powers there are, prayed, begged and promised.

robbï

poor jenny

Poor girl, oh, I am doing this for Jenny, Jenny spoke with me, I own Jenny, no you don't, she is owned by me, no, she owns Jenny, who knows about Jenny, she speaks for Jenny, why is Myshkin closing the curtains, we can't see now, who said that, oh that person got let in and this person didn't, oh she really got left out, oh I am doing this, I can't believe it, oh you weren't told, mind Yazzy doesn't find out, poor girl, I visited Jenny, you didn't? This is gonna cost a fortune. Poor Jenny, I am sending healing, I am a healer, healer, healer, healer, oh god, don't think like that, don't think this, oh no you can't do that, a fund-raiser, cash mob, who said that, Jenny called, yes me, she didn't call you? Have you heard the news? Hmm.. who said this, your idea? No hers, poor girl – poor, poor girl…. I turned onto Joshua Lane in silence and cried out, Godammit!

jenny
how i started grateful desert

there were many roads that led me to owning an apothecary..

from the time that i was twenty, i worked for myself.. it was rare that i made a paycheck as i was a classic deadhead ..

we made it work from what was in our pockets and the dreams that carried us forward..

i dabbled in herbs when i became a vegetarian at eighteen, started studying holistic health care in earnest in the early 90s and graduated from a therapeutic herbal program before the turn of the century.. several farmers' markets and herb fairs later, my business became a legal venture ..

i had started my dream of becoming an herbal medicine maker.

in 2000, upon moving to joshua tree, i sold my herbal line to local shops while substitute teaching, working at joshua tree's health food store and filling in at coyote corner, our town's first souvenir and head shop. i also developed the joshua tree climbing salve, a healing balm that i marketed to the climbing industry, and it got me so busy that i rarely had time to climb anymore.

after i had yazzy, i couldn't focus on anything but her shining face. my orders piled up and i decided to sell a portion of my business. while i kept the tincture line, i sold the climbing salve, lip balm, aromatherapy chalk, belly butter and tea lines. i nested the money away, which would later become my future ..

when i became a single mom, i went back to school.. fulfilling my dream of an apothecary was not an option until i had the stability of a back-up plan.. little did i know that studying nursing would develop my herbal knowledge to a depth i had not imagined..

so, RN in hand, and with a golden egg in my pocket, i opened the grateful desert, a store filled with herbs, essential oils, local art and lots of chocolate..

it was my dream job, a store filled with everything i loved and wanted to share..

rodney

mayberry

I can't remember who called my brother. I guess a mutual friend from college. Rick was visibly shaken as he told me we may never see Jennifer again. There was a good bit of silence and then a lot of prayer.

Jennifer had fallen for my brother. That was almost thirty years ago. She fell for his looks, his gregarious nature and his Southern accent. They started dating and we all became very close. Family close. It was a time when the next concert was all that mattered to us.

My brother and I were from North Carolina and grew up in a kind of Mayberry-like way even though we are from Charlotte, a way bigger town. Jennifer loved that and we came to love her. Anyway, when we heard about Jennifer, Rick was having some health problems and they were both hospitalized at the same time for six days. The whole time he was in the hospital, I was taking care of my ninety-six year old grandmother we call Gammy. This was the lowest time of all and I truly didn't know if either of them would make it. I had to go on even though I knew I was helpless. As bad as we felt for Jennifer, it was Yazzy we kept thinking of. We knew she would be well cared for, but emotionally it must have been devastating. We prayed a lot for her. In North Carolina, what else could we do but wait and wait and wait. When they were in the hospital at the same time, I couldn't help thinking about those traveling days.

It was almost thirty years ago that a friend of mine, my brother, Jennifer, my girlfriend and I had been in Sacramento for three Dead shows. Then, we went to two more in San Francisco. After that, it was three more shows near Palo Alto.

That last night before we headed up to Eugene for some more shows, we decided to camp to save money. There was one more concert near Palo Alto to attend. Some Deadheads told us about a great camping spot at what they called The Point. Presumably, it was near the water. The problem was with our vague directions. We had five of us crammed in a little Nissan Pulsar. By three in the morning, we gave up. We pulled up to an overlook, which was probably not a legal campsite. All we had were two sleeping bags between the five of us. We unzipped them and spread them out under us. We had one tarp over the top of us. It didn't quite cover all five of us. I know because I was awakened thirty minutes later by raindrops on my forehead. I pulled the tarp towards me. Mike on the other end was now getting rained on. Patrice, Jennifer and Rick slept in the middle oblivious to Mike and me playing tug-of-war with the tarp.

The five of us must have made a pathetic site huddled under that tarp in the rain. But you know what? We were as happy as humans could possibly be. Truly care-free and celebrating life each and every day with our friends and loved ones.

tania

trader joe's freezer bags,
chocolate and chewing gum

There was so much good food eaten and shared while you were in the hospital, Ms. Jenny Q. Being Arab, I understood the language that was unfolding before me in the waiting room at Desert Regional Medical Center immediately.

To get along with everyone, I just followed my nose – as light-hearted as that sounds, that's what I did: because that is what my loyal friend and fellow Ishta, Jenny Q, had taught me to do. Even while you were under the hold of dialysis- and had tubes for food and a lot of nausea once you were conscious- it was imperative that I eat well; because as a family we needed to stay nourished even under the most stressful of circumstances.

Jimmy snuck me into the ICU room at Desert Regional on the third night you were there. It was late– around 2:30 A.M.- and I had been lurking for hours down the waxed hallway, experiencing the slowness of time passing by and studying the portraits of fifty or so medical directors who had run the hospital over the years. There was only one female director as I recall, FYI. Yet, the hospital's interiors, as many of us know, are not quiet mausoleums where a person could get a full night of sleep without bother. The opening and closing of automatic doors as various staff entered/ exited the ICU became a familiar sound. Though it was never regular, it was as if the door opened and closed at pre-determined intervals.

felicia

life is ever changing

We came to Joshua Tree earlier than planned, deciding to leave straight from my sister's house. After the moving trucks were packed, we loaded ourselves up and headed over. We had the three months already open for the herbal internship I was supposed to do with Jenny and wanted to come and help in any way we could. So off Sailor, Tobin the dog, Olive the cat, and I went with a trailer full of memories from my sister's old home... knowing that when we returned, my sister, brother-in-law and baby nieces would be far away on to their next adventure.

Life is ever changing, ever continuing.

tania

meeting jenny's dad, Dr. Q

Dr. Q falls asleep very occasionally, which I learned on approximately Day Seven. It was on that first night that you were at the third hospital, UC Irvine. There, Dr. Q dozed off at least two times, a fact that is only to say that I was there long enough to notice. I got to watch his special way and it made me feel more familiar with him. When he woke up the second time, he offered me a coffee. I accepted, and off he went to get us both some coffee and cream from UCI Hospital Cafeteria. He returned shortly, and we talked about his iPad while we both drank our coffee.

Eventually, Dr. Q started getting up and getting involved with stuff happening inside the ICU room. Maybe I caught him during one of the mandatory breaks all family members were REQUIRED to take, when the WOUND CARE team came in to care for the tender wounds on your body.

It was nice to meet your dad in this quiet atmosphere. After many hours at Desert Regional Hospital, some of the Q's began to feel tired. They dealt with this in various ways, including taking shifts, having hot tea, going for walks or taking catnaps.

elise

fierce and demanding

Someone said they couldn't handle the situation. That it was too hard to see Jenny in this illness state and that he wasn't sleeping - that he couldn't see her for who she was, he was getting lost in the vacancy in her eyes and having nightmares.

I told him, "you cannot do this. You MUST see her for who she is – in her whole health. This is the only option. You cannot project anything but beauty onto her."

I felt fierce and demanding, and certain and clear that there was no room for any distractions of our own fears – whether they were "realistic" or not. Even when we were told scientific "facts," I could not allow them to be true. I just kept running energy up and down her body, up and down her whole entire beautiful being.

I was thankful for her family, for the communication of her sister and brother, grateful for them being there in such a strong way, every moment of every day. The love was palpable. The circle of Jenny's family was closed and tight, but they were there for Jenny and that was all that mattered to me. Together they made a strong team and we, her Joshua Tree family, made another and both teams together filled the waiting room, day after day after day, week after week, month after month…

jenny

the state i was in

piper keeps asking me to write about where i was when i wasn't present.. she tells me she was always so worried about what state i was in..

see, my good friend knows me well enough to know that i am "sensitive".. i use this adjective because it is hard to describe myself in the short version any other way..

i guess i will try and elaborate..

when i was young, say in my late teens, i subconsciously decided that, to avoid feeling the pain that plagued me inside, i would utilize the substances that were all around me in such a way as to remove myself from the deep truths and memories that were lurking in my belly and in the depths of my mind..

and i used these substances voraciously..

i used enough hallucinogens to take me on journeys that were meant to be experienced by devoted monks who meditated for a living.. those scantily clothed monastics who sit crisscross applesauce in the snow..

i traveled to places not meant for a youth that had no concept of self-worth or the divine..

because i was so ardent in my means of escape, i ended up suffering too long through unsolicited journeys to the otherworlds, never as bright a place as i wanted them to be..

i worked for years to climb out of a deep hole that i had dug for myself..

this included therapy, meditation, spirituality and sobriety (mostly)..

if i did imbibe on more than a wee bit of drink, i would revisit these ominous places ..

i would call my friend piper and ask for reassurance that one day i would be okay again..

she promised that my steady world would return and the fear would subside..

she had to promise this to me more than once, even though i would swear each time that i would never take another drink..

the otherworlds were always too close .. i was too susceptible to fall .. piper knew these were places that i never wanted to visit .. if no more than a cocktail could throw me into this despair, how would i react to being heavily medicated?

so she asked to write about where i was.. she asked because she kept telling me how worried she had been for me..

...

i don't remember so much of those first days when i was in pain.. those days before and after the initial surgery are such a haze.. i have clips of memory of being in the kind of pain that is above a person's threshold to bear— the kind of state one where the hurt is more than you can handle.. i have pictures of myself writhing in pain, screaming out when mysh attempted to administer my medication or searching out anyone who could stop the ravages through my body..

i remember arriving at the joshua tree hospital and being helped into the ER as i couldn't walk by myself, and being escorted directly into the triage area, as it was obvious that i had no time to sit in a waiting room.. and then fainting in front of the triage nurse ..

did i faint?

or do the wisps of memory slip away into smoke at that exact moment?

i have no concrete recollections after that for a long time..

but what i do recall about my journey while in a coma is almost inexpressible with words, so far is it from our earthly, human experience.. if i could only download my heart and my mind..

dark, crisp, silent, serene..

bright pins of light everywhere..

stars. faces..eyes in those faces shining like those stars..

everlasting space that is all the quiet but brilliant with sound..

as if each cell is screaming out with song, yet there is absolute stillness..

clouds too.. wispy clouds of brilliant color.. purple, blue, pink..

there were no thoughts. no conversations.

eyes spoke, perhaps, but without words.

we were

all

being

in indescribable joy..

but without emotion.

absolute presence..

and we were

all

being.

my grandmother, my tete, became.

she sat with me.

there was no conversation, she just was..

with me..

being.

she did point,

i did look.

there was a bookshelf.

it just appeared in space before me.

it took my whole view and held my childhood treasures..

my stuffed winnie the pooh.. my wooden abacus.. a book or two..

my gaze slowly swept up the shelves and rested on the top one.

only to see yazzy's favorite book

and SNAP!

immediately i was in my body.

i know this was a choice i made but no one asked,

and no one told me i needed to choose.

i just knew i would be on earth for my yazzy.

i still couldn't see, still was unable to rouse myself, but now i was aware of my body.

there were loved ones all around me. i could sense them by their heat.

you know when you are sleeping and someone comes into your room?

you remain asleep, but you're aware of their presence?

a warm spot darker than the rest of space?

this is what it felt like to be in a coma once i returned to earth.

to my body.

i don't know how long i was in the otherworld..

apparently, i was in a coma for six days.

the time spent in space seems like centuries in my soul,

but what is time?

how is one to gauge the difference between a journey and a long silent sleep?

georganne

how long have i been here?

When I heard you were going to be in the hospital for such a long time, I was so disturbed that I didn't know what to do except try to raise some money to help out. Being in a hospital even for a few days is one of my greatest fears. I never asked anyone what had happened to you and refused to listen to rumors, but when I finally got the news from Isobel, the dam burst and I bawled my heart out. I asked Charlyn, "Why Is This Happening to Her?"

Char said, "She must have something powerful to teach us."

Someone told me that when you first came out of surgery you were asked if there was anything you wanted and that you'd replied,

"A Scotch."

This may not be true or even grossly distorted but I loved it!

So, I painted you a picture of a lady in a dream state asking,

"How Long Have I Been Here?"

It was sold to Danny Elfman, who loves it dearly.

One of these days, I'll tell him the rest of the story.

karen

darkest hour

I built an altar for you the night of your "darkest hour," when we thought we might lose you. At dusk that evening, beside myself with worry and love, I walked outside to watch the sun as it set, and when I looked up, I SAW YOU in the trees, in the pink and yellow light coming through their branches, literally in the particles of air all around me. It was a holy night.

I understood, I KNEW right then that this night would be pivotal.

Oh, the despair! I could not abide any longer the feeling of helplessness that plagued me. I went inside and started lighting candles, pulling Tarot cards. I pulled the Six of Water, the Faith card. I lit resin. "Jenny, Jenny, Jenny". The room filled with one word.

After many hours, I went to bed, candles still burning, frankincense and the prayer, "We love you, do what you need to do" heavy in the air. That night, the prayers from my apartment, and that of thousands of other homes, held the space for you, with what I experienced as the quiet and stillness of winter's first snowfall.

Lïsa

lit the fire

I lit a candle and kept the flame glowing for four or five days. I said prayers and let them go into the light. I saw you in my mind's eye. I sat and watched the fire in darkness. I sat with you and the fire. I saw you begin to rise and walk towards a door. You looked back at the fire and then you walked through the door.

joyce q
something amazing

Wanting to protect Yazzy, we did not allow her in the ICU. We used the excuse that no one under twelve was allowed in the hospital room. Someone had the idea to record Yazzy's voice on an iPhone to talk to her mom. Between Yazzy's voice, her family constantly at her side giving gentle touch and words of encouragement and the hundreds of prayers from friends and relatives, something amazing happened and Jenny fluttered her eyes open after six days of near death.

kṛipa

altar building

In the days that followed our trip to the hospital, Paula and I felt that there wasn't much we could give by being at the hospital, yet we deeply felt the need to stay connected in whatever way we could. Fortunately, Elise, young 'wise old-soul' sister of our tribe, who was intimately woven into and dedicated to Jenny's healing journey, began to provide regular updates. Succinct and clear, she would share important information with precise instructions as to how we should focus our attention. "Jenny's kidneys need love. Send light to her liver. Visualize Jenny's blood circulating to all parts of her body, including her fingers and toes." She was virtually camping out at the hospital and would prove to be an amazing communications ally in the weeks and months that followed. We were deeply indebted to her, and to Piper, for delivering to us what we needed to know and keeping thoughts of Jenny in her whole perfectness uppermost in our mind's eye.

Jenny is a being who beautifully embodies the passion of fire, the forgiving nature of water, and the refined discrimination of air. It is perhaps in her feminine earthiness though, that I can most easily see her elemental qualities expressed. Friend to the flowers and wise woman with knowledge of their healing ways, she has shared her wisdom in the form of tinctures and balms, salves and infusions with those looking for natural healing. In order to keep the feeling of connection to Jenny's rite of passage alive, Paula and I decided that we would meet together in her garden, since we felt that to be an extension of her very essence. One early afternoon, we let ourselves into her walled sanctuary. It was silent and sad, a rather forlorn energy hung in the air and we were struck by the feeling of 'absence' - not one normally experienced in Jenny's environment. For a while we just sat in silence, reaching out inwardly, praying for grace. Eventually, in order to make ourselves feel useful, we started to pick up odds and ends, move furniture, sweep the porch, rake up some of the sun dried vegetation and build an organic altar to Jenny's health. Soon enough, we were fully absorbed in these tasks, as though through our actions we could, in a small way, contribute to the 'cleaning up' of Jenny's body. At some point, I opened the gate leading out of the garden to the small casita in the back, which Jenny rented out to tourists and vacationers. The experience was striking, the quality of light outside of the garden was somehow so much more vibrant! The contrast was intensely visceral, so much so that I called Paula over to see if she noticed the same thing. We both stood there in awe, wondering at the difference. It felt somehow symbolic of a certain aspect of Jenny's nature - she who was so good at nurturing and welcoming others, perhaps did not expect from others, or even from herself, that same quality of acceptance and love. Now it was our turn, the community's turn in fact, to give to and embrace Jenny in all of the ways of love that we could imagine. Paula and I stood at the threshold of Jenny's garden and ushered in this vibrant light to bless and uplift - hopefully Jenny would feel it somewhere, somehow in her vast, perfect being. As the day drew to a close, as we sat before the altar, Paula played her didge and together we sang and prayed for Grace on behalf of our sister.

A few years back, Jenny had offered the space in her apothecary, Grateful Desert, to be used for a fundraiser to raise money for a local charity. It was a beautiful event and the gathering was well attended by many people from our community. I remember leaving there with the feeling that Jenny was the perfect hostess for all of those individual threads of light. Together, the people of this village were becoming tightly knitted together to create a grand tapestry and I felt blessed to be part of it. Now, with this situation, the tapestry seemed to grow exponentially. Even people from out of state, who had never met Jenny in person, seemed to tune into her unique 'brand' of special. One friend from the East Coast messaged me, " I am reading your posts about your friend Jenny and just wanted you to know that I am holding you all in light...... Just looking at her pics, I can see that she is all of what you mention. I will keep her in my prayers as well as your community." So many were holding her as their focus and reaching out to strengthen that invisible blanket of light that we would wrap her in during this process.

Again the following day, Paula and I arranged to meet at Jenny's garden to finish off the altar that we had started the day before. Arriving there a few minutes early, I opened the gate and was so happy to see and feel with all of my being that the light that seemed to have been absent during our first visit, now was fully present. Everything had an inner glow and the 'mood' was one of ease. I sat and soaked it in for a couple of minutes and then returned to my car to retrieve my cell phone, just in case a message should come. Sure enough, as I re-entered the garden, a text landed. The news was that Jenny had opened her eyes - she was back. Her hold on life still was not exactly secure and remained tenuous, not to be taken for granted, but for now it was the best news ever. When Paula arrived at the garden, we hugged and danced and laughed and cried for the return of Jenny.

michelle q

what the f$%&

With my new passport in hand, I was on the next flight out. I finally arrived at LAX where my brother Jimmy was waiting and drove me directly to the hospital. Jenny had just had major surgery and I got there just as the surgeons were briefing the family in a private room. The teams of surgeons were awesome. They explained everything to a packed room of desperate immediate family, answered all of our questions and made it obvious that they were technically very qualified to be taking care of Jenny.

Everyone in the family was a wreck. No one had slept in a week and I could see the emotional rollercoaster in all of their eyes. It was touch and go for so long and they had lived through every instant of it. I was overwhelmed by the fierce determination that united my family: this intense love between us that brought us together when one of us was hurt. My mom refused to leave Jenny at all, but my siblings needed rest and I insisted that I was fresh and ready to be present.

I just wanted to see Jenny. I had to lay my eyes on her and I was jealous of every post-op recovery minute. It was not alright that this could have happened and there was nothing I could do about it, not even witness its passing. And then finally I could see her. I drank up as much of Jenny as that week of needing to be by her side demanded. I sat next to her and watched her, took assessment of her energy, her body, her monitors. I mourned her legs, already obvious that they would not make it, with deep tears. I gave thanks that she impossibly made it this far, and prayed that her mind and her spirit would make it with her. She finally started to wake up and looked up at me, a bit shocked, as if to say "what the f$%& are you doing here from Italy?!" And I smiled.

myshkin
journal

On Monday January twenty-second, eight days after driving her to Orange County to see Dr. Gregory, I wrote this in my journal:

"Today you came back to us and we are not letting you go. Hear this my Jenny my love. We are not letting you go. We are holding you, your family on Joshua Trail, your birth family, your Joshua Tree family, your giant extended family of interconnected love filled souls all sending love to you. We've got you. We are going to take care of you. Thank you for coming back to us. I did not want to picture a life without you my love my Jenny my heart my one my brightest dearest love of my life my Jenny."

karen

jenny's altar(ations)

no visitors allowed!
while heart and soul hear
c'mon down
and make their ethereal
way
to her bedside as
this body
stays put
panting pacing spilling
dusk arrives
worry and love walk me outside
i look up
and see jenny
jenny
in the tall stand
of eucalyptus
in the pink
and yellow
light
in the particles
of air
surrounding
jenny was leaving
but not yet

gone.

i'm going inside

jenny!

i say aloud to

my

friend

and fly up the stairs

fierce

with single

pointedness

to

light candles burn

resin

place symbols:

earth wind water wood fire

pull cards: six of water "faith"

surfaces

dining room

table becomes

altar

the room fills with that

one

word

light continues

its flicker

frankincense suspends

heavy

delivering

the one

prayer:

we love you we love you we love you

do
what
you need to do
the sacred
seeped from my
walls
and
countless other homes
that
night
it
overflowed
and
met in
One Great Field of Grace
with all the stillness
and
deep quiet
of winter's first
snowfall
by morning
jenny
had awoken
it haunts me still
the possibility
of what
other
miracles took place
that
night as
love

Jenny Q

from around the world
became one
with jenny's
spirit
when she blessed us all
and was everywhere
we
looked

ted

a village comes together

The days that followed the tragic news coming out saw the town of Joshua Tree become truly united in its shared concern for Jenny. The outpouring was genuine and deep, as we watched for Jenny's brother's posts on a website called Caring Bridge, looking for any hopeful signs.

"Jenny woke up today...but we still have a long ways to go before we can relax."

Kripa posted this message: "For today, can you all send focused light and prayers for J's circulation - all the way through her fingers and toes." Poet/artist Elise Kost announced a 'gofundme' site to help with costs, the momentum of love for Jenny was building.

Then there would be sad reports, of surgeries and many months of recovery: "Not yet out of the woods."

Elizabeth began making tinctures for Jenny's shop. Barnett made tickets to Joshua Tree Music Festival available as a fund-raiser for Jenny. I wrote to my friend Adriene Jenik, in Phoenix, where she teaches art at ASU. She replied, "My prayers are definitely out there for Jenny. I have benefited immensely from her gifts as a healer, her teas and tinctures are in my cupboard and have been real medicine for me. How very scary and horrible for her and her family." Her words reflected the thoughts of many in the community, who had gone to her for healing. It was strange to think of our town healer as being in such a dire health emergency.

joyce q

coma

The risks of the treatments were starting to outweigh the benefits. The more blood transfusions she received, the more proteins were degrading, clogging her vessels further. The higher dose of pressors to raise her blood pressure was constricting the vessels to her extremities. The line to survival was thin. But amazingly, the process of DIC subsided, her vitals normalized and Jenny awoke.

Unfortunately for me this was day six and I finally had to go home for one day to see my own family and sort out work issues. I was amazed to here the ventilator was removed and Jenny was sitting up talking. Later I learned everyone was laughing because she asked for a Scotch on the rocks.

I wish I could say that Jenny walked out of the hospital soon after. Unfortunately, day six was the eye of the storm. It was obvious she suffered severe ischemia to her extremities and she had a large area of soft tissue necrosis to her lower back. My dad had done extensive research finding the best hospital to handle her injuries. That day, she was transferred to the UC Irvine burn unit/critical care via helicopter.

boūloس

across the way

My daughter's fate was out of my hands. I was devastated. The Desert Regional hospital had a place where we could rent a room across the way. We took some rooms, where the family stayed, but I stayed in the hospital until she was stable.

Two hours after she arrived at UC Irvine, she went into surgery.

Once she was at UCI, I moved back home, which was close enough to the hospital to head home for the occasional shower and to sleep. I have been on the staff at UCI for decades, so while I was not directly involved with her care, I kept in close contact with her care team, which was led by Dr. Victor Joe.

myshkin

transferred

UCI. Dr. Q said: We are taking you closer to home. We are taking you to UCI. I bless his knowledge and instinct. Jenny remembers the flight, was flown only half way, landed in Riverside because of fog, ambulanced to Orange. I drove alone, arrived to a room full of her family and a smiling Jenny who turned to me and sang out "My fiancé!" and then apologized to her folks for not having told them yet.

She had two nurses sitting by her side and some amount of peace and quiet all the first night. Veronica and Robin. It was so calming compared to the open, wagon-wheel shaped ICU in Palm Springs. We met with Dr. Joe, a calming presence himself, but still everything was very heightened and on edge. There was no way Jenny was out of danger yet and indeed the next day she took a turn for the worse and was taken immediately to surgery. Jenny had pulled herself out of her coma, and rallied enough strength to reassure Yazzy, and us, and to survive the travel to Orange County. She had used it up, and then the infection dragged her down again.

jenny
who fed her?

who fed her while i was gone,

while mysh was visiting me?

who made her school lunches?

thoughts like this descend upon me as i exercise in the morning,

while i am on my eliptical, since i can't run anymore,

looking out of the window at the desert instead of being in it,

thinking about if she had enough protein for the school days when i was unable to fuss about what went in each lunch..

barnett. selah. myshkin.

she stayed with friends often enough to be like one of their kids.

friends who took her in held her during the most traumatic time in her life.

how does one even comprehend a way to thank someone for such deeds?

it seems impossible.

out of the range of my imagination.

michelle q

allah kareem!

Jenny is pretty articulate with her eyes, but at one point we finally started to use a letter board. Miraculously, she didn't strangle me as I slowly understood which letters she was indicating. At this point, she was still unable to move any part of her body on her own, so without using either hand we had to go through each row of letters each time. "First row, second row--OK, third row. Is it K? L? M? N?"

The first phrase that she spelled out was "Allah kareem!" --"God is generous!"

Indeed.

myshkin
staying

The first time I retuned to Joshua Tree, it was with my mother. I bawled coming down the driveway. I cried so many damn tears that year, mine and Jenny's and Yazzy's too I think, neither of them cried much at all for six months or more. The moment I'm thinking of, I just couldn't understand why I was coming home to Jenny's house, Jenny's life, still driving Jenny's car from the initial trip to the ER, without my Jenny. It made no sense. There was no way to make sense of it. I was here, walking and talking and everything normal-ing in this amazing home she created, in one of the most beautiful places anywhere, her world. And she was lying in a bed a few hours away, unable to move her body enough to roll over by herself. Unable to lift her arms a few inches, barely able to communicate. And even in that state, she was still giving whatever smiles would come to her, away for free to everyone, and had everyone on the unit swiftly falling in love with her. The feeling lingered, as I worked into my weekly schedule of home and away. Every day I was in Joshua Tree was a day living her life, a life I had no right to, no history in, and yet every responsibility to hold. To keep. To grow. For her and Yazzy.

michelle g

without tripping

The next two weeks were spent at Jenny's side with short breaks for sleep. As I was already on Italian time, I took the night shift. In the beginning, my eyes never left her. The medication for her pain was making her delirious and every time her eyes opened, mine had to be right there to meet hers, orient her and let her know that everything was OK. We wrote goals on a white board to discuss with the docs at morning rounds. The first was pain control without "tripping." One by one, goals were identified, met and crossed off. The team of docs got used to me, the Naturopathic Doc with years of hospital experience. They were open to ideas, incorporated nutrients into her IV and even took my treatise on Homeopathy to their Pharmacy and Therapeutics Committee to try to approve homeopathic remedies on their formulary.

jenny
icu psychosis

icu psychosis.. this we studied in nursing school.. it all made sense academically..

constant lights, the never-ending beeping of IV machines, strapped down to the bed with plastic tubing, being woken every two hours for meds, turnings, bathings, feedings, doctors' visits, nurses, residents, visitors... one rarely sleeps deeply and can't tell if it's day or night.. one is most often on medications that can alter thought processes.. one is in extraordinary pain..

but i never would have imagined that i would get to experience so much of this stuff first-hand. PICC lines. nasogastric tubes. G-tubes and J-tubes. catheters.

i remember learning about NG tube insertion in nursing school.. i was so nervous.. i studied hard and froze as i witnessed a classmate trying for the first time.. the patient was gasping and clutching at her face.. even our clinical professor got nervous and took over..

i remember inserting my first urinary catheter.. so many of those.. i always told my patients to take a deep breath.. there would be a bit of pressure instead of pain. but really? what did i know?

from the hospital bed, i came to understand the depth and importance of bedside manner. we are taught this in the classroom; we learn it and are given exams..

but this was no classroom..

even my family, so many of whom are doctors, have since reflected on what it is to be on the other side of the examination table. my sister joyce even told me her practice had changed. softened. she knows what it is like to be waiting for hours to get five minutes of the doctor's time, waiting for days to get test results or a week to hear back from the surgeon.. while the system may not change, she had a deeper empathy for her patients.

sometimes i daydream about going into nursing classrooms to give the students and professors the real deal—what it is to be the patient.. what the world looks like from a bed.. what it feels like to always be looking up..

liesl

of all people

they all introduced me to her

the whole town felt compelled to say

hey

have you met jenny q

have you seen her beauty

she's the goddess of grateful desert

sorceress of tonic and oil

lady of health with

listening ears

i did but didn't remember meeting her before it all went down,

but

i'd never seen barney's face so solemn

pale and as if his soul had been flipped

up into the atmosphere and

suspended in that temporary place

like when you're on a trampoline

and your body reaches an apex and floats for a moment

sure to come back down to the ground and get it back together

but

in those few days

i think folks call it shock

his wan perplexity relayed the depths of this magnificent woman

whom i barely remembered meeting yet suddenly grasped in my soul

it was barney's boyish, emotional turmoil

circulating the suffering

that tenderly ignited my connection to this lady

jenny, jenny, jenny q

yazzy's mom

the one who's with myshkin,

that soul-stirring artist whose longevity in love

gracefully presents itself in her hauntingly harmonious music performance art

jenny, jenny, jenny q

that moment when the stomach is abruptly lifted

from plummeting down the roller coaster's first drop,

but this was in silence

no rickety tumbling of wheels

or squeals of joyous thrills

the whole body is flipped around

but

there's an emptiness in sound

and time forces the brain into a secluded awareness of

just how fucked up

and unfair life can be

of all people for this to happen

tania

a fashion analysis of the emergency

the bad colors we had to wear to see you

The wristband-aqua and isolation gown-yellow were the two colors that no one wanted to wear, but had to, Jenny Q, while you were driving your body's highway back to us. Aqua was the color of the "VISITOR" handbands that a visitor received as part of the sign-in process, required each time we entered the UCI Medical Center Hospital doors. For me, getting the aqua wristband was a ritual that marked time at UCI. We would say who we were visiting (you, Q), then wait for them to find your room number, even though we might already know it. However, it was polite to wait. At Desert Regional, it was possible to bypass the whole waiting-in-line step, but in Irvine it was not possible at all. I put the wristband in the glove compartment of my car when I left the hospital grounds, sometimes begrudgingly.

The yellow ICU gowns never grew on any one of us, is my guess. Nor did the masks or gloves. Yes, the outfits fit better at Desert Regional versus UCI, but who cares – the distributers of the yellow gowns, masks, and gloves are all corporate bozos, so why waste the word count to complement a corporation on the style of its plastic? The yellow gowns never messed with my personal daily style, which I wanted to mention, since I know this will make you happy. I felt quite at home as a radical queer Arab-American butch boi in the hospital gowns that we had to be in. That was a good thing – the gowns democratized us into one lump category. No one could fluff their own feathers by flashing brand names or related class-based snobbery.

myshkin
letter board

It's all a bit dreamy now, the memories of the week after the coma. Constant surgeries, meetings with doctors, Jenny remained intubated for way too long, after that short day or two without a breathing tube. She was in much pain, and on a constant drip of fentanyl, the strongest narcotic made. Her tissue continued to deteriorate. Her youngest sister Michelle arrived from Italy and was a great comfort to all of us with her doctor-like calm detachment yet big affection.

Michelle made Jenny a letter and phrase board so she could communicate with us while intubated. Jenny occasionally pointed to things like "pain" or "nausea". The first time she was with it enough to spell anything out, it was this: Allah Kareem. God is Generous.

The doctors at UCI told us in the first day or two what their expectations for Jenny's recovery were. They were fairly certain she would lose both legs below the knee and much of her right hand. They always followed up with reassurances: she will get prosthetics, she will walk. None of us could really accept it at first I think, though we were watching as her tissue turned deeper shades of purple. We watched as the nurses dopplered her legs every few hours, seeking pulses in her ankles, behind her knees. Jenny watched too, I knew she knew what was happening, she is a nurse. I prayed that she did not, in her state, make sense of it. Or would remember. For a few days, after her first surgeries dealing with the dead tissue at the original infection site, her feet began to pink up, and we got excited that somehow all those shut down blood vessels would reopen, circulation would resume, dead tissue would heal. I wrote to my group of closest friends: the doctors are amazed at her resilience! Pray for circulation! And this actually happened in a few places, her nose went from purple back to pink, and remained whole.

jenny
regaining

i watched the world unfold around me, observed my life happening through a fog.. i would come in and out of awareness, sometimes floating on a cloud, sometimes being snapped into focus..

i remember one day finally feeling some bashfulness as six or maybe ten people were in the room examining me, picking up my limbs, spreading them, studying my most intimate parts..

all peering down at me, not noticing that i was awake..

no one was speaking to me. they were busy, taking notes..

i realized at that moment that this had been happening all along.. that i had many hazy memories of people looking at me.. eager groups of people poring over me with concern and interest, this anomaly..

and me being too sick or out of it to care..

but at this moment, i cared. i was finally well enough to feel some semblance of modesty. as uncomfortable as this moment was, surrounded by scores of student doctors and their specialist teachers, it was also a significant sign that i was regaining a sense of myself..

tania

bee in a bonnet

I asked Mrs. Q if I could sit with her. The inquiry was timely, because in a way we were becoming acquainted. It seemed she really didn't want to, but then she said yes. I credit this to my winning personality.

Your mom made the best of the salad bar, I observed. My cafeteria meal provided needed sustenance, though bland. I enjoyed your mother's company, as I stared down at my plate. We talked a little bit about I'm not sure what.

She asked, "So, how did you get into this mess?"

I looked at her curiously. "Which mess?"

She kind of motioned towards my dapper demeanor and said, "Looking like a boy."

I received her overture gently, wondering how to skip over butch identity theory, and arrive at the doorstep of her question. I told her I looked better masculine, and that even my mom thought so.

Mrs. Q suggested that I was a beautiful young woman, too. Which is true, because my good looks go both ways. I thanked her for the compliment. As she nodded her head, she added another observation, "You look lost to me." Mrs. Qaqundah lets her opinions be known. The force of Mrs. Q's words hit my chest like a bullet. They hurt my feelings, which then weakened my strength. The illusion of our friendship sort of fell to the ground like a soft waterfall, tears in my heart.

Yes, I was lost – but not for the reasons she was thinking. Holding up half the sky is not easy, I wanted to say to her. With some lettuce on my fork, I gazed up from my hallucination and looked her in the eye. With an air of conclusion in my tone, I said to her, "Well, even though you do not approve of me, I like you very much. I sincerely enjoy your company!" Mrs. Q was stunning in the afternoon light, and seemed to receive the compliment out of the distant corner of her eye. There remained food to eat, so we conversed onward. Did I "want a man?" and so on to which I answered yes (trans-men). We had a nice ending. It was brief. Like many creative people, I sat at the table with a hat on, lingering in the stirred feelings and fiery energy left in the wake of Mrs. Q's return to her daughter's bedside.

jenny
jerks and jumps

i lie in a bed.. i lay in a bed without the ability to move.. time creeps eerily, jerks and jumps..

days get bumped about..

crowds of people peer down at me, moving my body..

lifting a leg..

spreading them apart to look and show..

me, without the frame of mind to care that ten people are staring at my naked body and inspecting all parts of me, and that they seem curious and alarmed..

groups of people craning forward to stare at my yoni; me too afraid to wonder what they are seeing..

what is so interesting that all the clinical professors want to show their colleagues and students?

i am a nurse.. i know what it is to be curious..

i too wanted to check out all the weirdest and most intense illnesses..

i know what it is like to want to learn from those who are the anomaly..

now, that anomaly is me..

lying there without the ability to move.. without the memory of even how to move my body.. without the ability to shout out THAT HURTS!

i know something is very wrong with my yoni..

i watch the nurses check for pedal pulses and not find them.. i see the consternation on their faces as they search and feel..

even the doppler can't find pulsing on my feet or legs..

i watch as the doctors check my skin and my lack of blood flow to my fingers and toes..

i am a nurse.. i know what that means..

but my yoni.. when they look down there, i don't inquire.. i don't even dare to wonder.

i know i cannot handle what they will have to say..

elise

understanding soup

I held her feet, which were cold and turning slightly blue. I talked to her and visioned energy moving.. moving down, down, down into her feet. I felt like she could understand me more without words, but I felt her mother needed me to say things, to be "normal" – and of course, everything was extremely not normal. Jenny was on a journey beyond my comprehension. I tried to reach her. I heard "keep holding me" and so I did. One day at a time, I checked in and I heard "keep holding me", and so I did....day after day, for six months and beyond.

At home, I did long-distance reiki and chakra work – I cleansed and illuminated, and with all certainty, saw her alive and vibrant and joyous.

I sat on the lawn of the hospital and played music. I prayed. I don't remember crying or feeling anything but certainty that she would pull through – I felt like I couldn't allow any doubt or even any emotion to waver my stronghold. The situation was so fragile...it felt like even a moment of doubt could alter the outcome of whether or not she lived.

One day after much praying, after seeing her, after not eating for a long time, feeling weak and tired and allowing sorrow to crawl in for the first time, I went into town to get some soup and felt like I was a dark shadow walking between the worlds. I was dressed in disguise so no one would see me, feeling like a conversation of any kind was impossible. I was bundled up with a hood and unlike myself. But someone did see me and took my darkness as a sign that things weren't well with Jenny.

It was a shocking reminder that every moment needed to be impeccable – absolutely no option but optimism.

I ate the soup, but even more so, ate the understanding that being strong and stable was necessary in every moment until Jenny woke up, not only for her and myself but for the whole community who loved her and needed optimism from someone "on the inside."

myshkin

intuition and support

I marveled a lot about how intuition worked in both Jenny and I, to meet and fall together just in time. Jenny found me when she and Yazzy were about to need me the most. She showed the same kind of psychic forethought with her business. Her first long-term clinical student, Isobel, had just completed her internship in the lab. Kristen, our sweet mutual friend who had introduced us, had just begun working in the shoppe. And six months prior, Amanda had begun helping Jenny with accounting and bookkeeping. The second day Jenny was in the hospital, I called each of them and asked them to help me hold all this during the time ahead. They were amazing and we all held the businesses together. We met weekly, they gave generously of their time and energy, the community supported the shoppe like never before, and we managed to keep the whole thing afloat.

And my family's voices on the phone were a constant lifeline. My mother went home after three weeks of helping to hold down the fort. Sailor and Felicia arrived just before she left. They changed their plans, arrived earlier, and stayed for four months to help me take care of Yazzy, the house, and the casita. Another example of Jenny's (not so) accidental good planning. Sailor and Felicia were my most profound daily emotional support. They knew how to keep the house physically stable and emotionally buoyant—how to keep Yazzy's mind occupied and to be ears for my sorrows. How to keep the music alive in me when I was too depleted to even think of playing on my own.

anita

ceremony

I walked into Jenny's Grateful Desert Herb Shoppe in J.T. and fell in love. Then I met her and it made perfect sense. I had an instant feeling of connection to a soul sister. The store is a reflection of her. I feel at home there. It delights my senses. Just visit the store if you never have. You will understand.

Not long after, I had heard that Jenny had a hospital procedure done and that complications had developed. I felt concern for her wellbeing but didn't realize the seriousness of her situation. Then I heard that she was in critical condition. I grasped the seriousness and felt deeply concerned.

I saw a social media post that Paula was hosting a healing circle on Jenny's behalf, so I showed up. I believe that the power of love is a healing force. I believe that love is an action. You need to show up and take action.

I arrived and found myself in a group of powerful, loving humans. The mood was set for the calling upon divine intervention. I was in the midst of so much love. Jenny was in the midst of this love. The middle of the circle was filled with offerings, candles, sage, flowers... adornments to please the gods and goddesses. How could this fail? The intention to call her back to health was the goal.

The ceremony began, we prayed, we sang, we chanted and called out. We laughed and cried. We worked organic magic. I am aware of how fragile the veil is between this world and the other, and I felt that Jenny had a foot in both worlds. I had been walking closely with the goddess Kali for a while so I called to her. Kali, Goddess of time, change, power, preservation and destruction.. will you destroy the disease stealing Jenny's life-force? Or, Kali Ma will you take her into death? Jenny is in the hands of the Goddess, as we all are. Be merciful Kali Ma.

What is there to do for each other but to love and serve? I know that love is strong magic. I felt that the Mother's love was especially strong in this circle. We called out on behalf of Jenny's daughter.

ted

i love jenny day

Around this time, Joshua Tree lost JR, who owned and operated Windwalkers, a pottery and Native American art shop with his partner, and word was around that Jenny would be in the hospital for six months!

Our friend Tee wrote to say that Jenny would need multiple procedures over the coming several months and she asked for music to be sent to her.

Throughout, Jenny's partner and fiancée, the singer/songwriter, Myshkin, kept vigil, silently, while sharing the responsibility of caring for Yazzy, with Yazzy's papa Todd and the rest of Jenny's family, blood-related and otherwise.

Around Valentine's Day, Jordan organized an 'I Love Jenny Day' at the Beatnik, where people could make cards or play a song in Jenny's honor. We heard that Jenny was grateful for the many cards and letters she was receiving, and only opening one when she had the energy to really appreciate it.

Christa spread word of a way to help Jenny by bringing meals to Myshkin and Yazzy, at home, on a planned schedule. Sage and I took Yazzy out for dinner once a week after school, to our favorite sushi place.

marilyn

prayer circles

After the shock had worn off a little, I immediately started alerting all the prayer warriors that I knew. And yes, I am a firm believer in the creator of this beautiful universe. And yes, the bible promises us that God always hears the cry of our hearts. I could not go to her bedside but I could gather all those who would stay steady and loyal in praying for Jenny around the clock.

We soon had several hundred men and women, some offering all night prayers for our Jenny. Most did not even know her, but still they prayed. Day after day, week after week, month after month. They never gave up.

During that time, I was especially thankful for Jenny's mom and sister who would text me with updates. The online website with Jimmy giving updates on Jenny's health became a daily check... then I would share those words with family and all the different prayer groups.

As time passed slowly, some weeks good news, some not so good, family and friends would share what we all knew: Jenny would someday share her journey with others. She would use that beautiful smile and the love flowing from her heart to bring hope to others.

Hope. What a powerful word. All the love shared and all the prayers sent gave Jenny the added boost she needed to hang on to hope.

eva

women's circle

I received a call to convene quickly at Paula's house for a women's healing gathering.

We ten women sat in her circular room and chanted to the low soothing tones of her didgeridoo. We meditated and sent as much loving energy Jenny's way as we could muster. Feeling scared and nervous, we didn't know what else to do.

News of her condition was not very hopeful at that moment. One at a time we went around our circle and reached out to our sisters' ebullient soul and spoke about what we saw and felt.

I recall the pictures were mostly shadowy and grey of Jenny reaching out to her daughter and struggling to stay in this world. Nearing the end of the circle when it came to be my turn, without pre-thought I was overcome with warmth as the scene of a joyful wedding with bright colors, music and laughter animating the air came to me. It was a celebration of the love I had witnessed between Myshkin and Jenny from the moment I was introduced to them together. Jenny was too vibrant a person, full of life and love of a daughter who needed her and a budding romance, she couldn't possibly be ready to leave us.

That's my story and I'm sticking to it!

Lena

wept and prayed

When our mutual friend Amber contacted me to pray for you, because you were in critical condition, I fell apart crying. I wept for days. How can my Jenny Q, my Habibti, not be other than jubilantly singing and dancing with joy? It affected me deeply. I followed the fundraising. I cried and meditated. For days, weeks, perhaps months, you were my primary thought. I prayed for you every morning and every night. I visualized you getting better. I hoped for a bright future. My way of coping was to tell people about you, you who were in my life, my experience of you. I showed you off from Facebook and I still do sometimes.

boulos

accepting otherwise

They told me she had a ten percent chance of survival, but I never accepted that.

I knew she would live. I wouldn't accept anything otherwise.

lynne

yazzy was strong

Weeks and months passed and we received bits of information about what was happening with Jenny. Yazzy continued to come and have sleepovers and play dates. We made every effort to make our house a comfortable, fun and safe environment for her. Yazzy was so strong. She was so resilient during this time. I felt blessed to have been able to spend so much time with her.

myshkin

yazzy

My sister Sunny brought Yazzy to the hospital to see her Mama, once Jenny had woken from the coma. Jenny's hands were turning blue already, we tried to keep them covered, but the sheet fell off. Yazzy was of course in shock at the sight of her vivacious Mama so still and sick, Jenny pulled all her reserves to the surface to be as present and strong as she could for Yazzy, her voice almost steady. Yazzy stayed very calm, and said when she had had enough and wanted to leave. As I remember it, the second time Yazzy visited was the day Jenny was transferred to UCI. It was the first day they gave her food— jello— and she who would never have touched the stuff was excited! Yazzy was too. Jenny was bright and a bit more herself again, though she was so incredibly sick, a real testament to her strength throughout this process that on that day she could smile and laugh.

I didn't see much of Yazzy those first couple weeks. Todd took her on the weekends, and my sisters, then my mother, took care of her during the weeks. I stayed with Jenny while she was so close to the edge, and as she got more stable I made plans for a schedule. I would be at home with Yazzy from Sunday night through Thursday morning, then drive to be with Jenny at UCI. Yazzy would go home with Barnett and Lynne and Lola on Thursday, and get picked up by Todd after school on Friday, who would bring her to visit her mom in Orange County on Sunday, then we would drive home together. Once we settled into the schedule it worked well, and stayed the same until the end of school. I think it was a comforting routine for her, and good to see her dad every week during this time instead of the usual every other. Yazzy and I were so new to each other, I had only been a part of the family for a couple of months before Jenny got sick. She was on her best - terrified - behavior for a long time. Things only got hard for me towards the end of the school year, when she grew to trust me enough to let her fears and angers out. I knew it was a compliment of her sense of security, but as someone who had never really even been around kids, much less parented, much less while everyone was in trauma, it was scary and confusing. I was appalled at how badly my buttons could get pushed, and utterly without tools. But that was later. We had a lot a sweetness and bonding during those hard months, both thrown in the deep end as we were, and holding on to each other for breath and comfort.

jenny
of yazzy

i wanted to share the experience of having a baby with the right person, and barring that, i wanted to be stable enough to do it on my own.

when it was finally time to try, fifteen years after the desire took hold of me, it took me three long and painful years to conceive.. each month drinking too much wine when my moon blood flowed..

my desire was so well known that wherever i went in our small town of joshua tree, people would ask if i was pregnant in casual conversation..

ashraf, a friend and local doctor, talked about writing a play about life in our little town, and wanted me to walk across the stage, full and pregnant, as the epic end of the performance..

i wanted yazzy for so long that in my late teens and early twenties, i watched my close friends with their kids and observed how they parented. i took notes.

i compared what parents did and decided then that i wanted to utilize the attachment parenting concept.. i bought books and planned and took my temperature.. i dreamed and desired.. i knew i would have a girl and i asked her to wait for me and told her how much i wanted her..

opening an old dream journal randomly the other day, i came to a page that described a birthing dream..

"they put my daughter on my belly and i was thinking 'i am so exquisitely happy!! this is perfect joy!! oh.. wait.. is this is a dream?? no, this can't be!!' when i awoke, it took me several minutes to realize that i didn't yet have my daughter.."

the journal entry ended with:

"please, be patient, my little girl! please know i am readying for you!! please goddess, bring my little girl to me!!"

this dream was ten years before i was finally blessed with her conception..

attachment parenting is a concept that is anything but new.. it is based on the idea that indigenous cultures carried their babies wherever they went and throughout their workday.. what would happen to the baby that was set down while the mama went to gather berries and herbs? what animal wouldn't be delighted to find her? no, mamas did their work with their child strapped to them, and children grew that first year listening to the beating of their mama's heart and learning the rhythm of the adult life..

what child would survive sleeping separately from the protection of the parents.. we were evolved growing closely to our parents.. and in cultures where the connection to the land is still strong, these ways are still practiced..

..these practices always resonated with me..

i did indeed strap yazzy to me and went about my days.. if i wasn't breastfeeding her or reading to her or playing with her or just staring at her, she was in a sling while i cooked, cleaned, ground herbs to make tinctures and salves.. and i was blessed enough to cuddle with her all my nights.. i was enamored with the precious gift that is my daughter and never took one moment for granted..

piper still giggles at the time i called her weeping because my daughter's placental cord fell off her belly, which happens after the first week of life.. i was devastated that the symbol of our connection was gone and that i had already lost a whole week of her life, never to be savored again.. already, i was floored by the speed of the passage of time and of the fleeting nature of my time with her..

every milestone that yazzy came to, every rite of passage, was celebrated and ritualized.. for each passage, we had matching jewelry pieces made and blessed in ritual..

when her baba and i split up, i went into nursing school .. an apothecary was my dream but i needed a backup plan, as i was becoming a single mama.. those years were what i thought would be our hardest..

without my close community, we never would have made it..

i often had to drop yazzy off, my child who never even wanted me to leave her at a play date, at different friends' houses while i ran to nursing classes and clinicals..

barnett and kris and selah and katie.. what would i have done without them?

barnett would wake up early and hang out with yazzy for two hours before lola even woke..

i remember one morning carrying her through a long, dark, dirt path, praying i wouldn't trip with her in my arms..

and her waking, crying and asking, "where are we now, mama?"

yes, those were heartbreaking times.. and later, i would congratulate us and remind her of our strength and our ability to rise to any occasion..

about halfway through nursing school, i secured the building in which i had been dreaming of opening my apothecary..

nursing school was such a struggle for yazzy and i and to make it through on particularly arduous days, we would drive by the building and blow kisses, calling out,

"Sweet Little Shoppe! Sweet Little Shoppe!!"

that was our mantra.. it got us through many a month..

because of our close relationship, people assumed that she was shy because of my parenting style.. too often, folks mistook my daughter's personality for a defect in the way i was raising her.. i don't believe in that theory.. too many kids in our community, raised in the same fashion, are extroverts and are happy to have slumber parties and go away to camp..

but not my yazzy.. when she was young, people called her 'velcro'.. there were few kids in our circle as quiet as her.. and i was happy to allow her to be who she was..

a few of us started a school in our community..

at first, it was yazzy, lola and emmett..

three precocious kids whose parents all lived creative lifestyles..

half a year later, more kids and families joined us— sage, anu, forest, then many more— to form what we called the Living School..

during a parent/teacher conference, when the school was up to twelve kids, the teachers told me they had never met a kid like yazzy.. that she rose to meet the personality of each kid she encountered.. an empath..

i think about this kid, this gift, this sensitive beloved of mine, and what it must have felt like when i left.. she was only eight years old when i got sick, when i was gone for six months and so close to death, surrounded by amazing, but in truth, barely known people,

people brand new to her life..

so many people told me she was courageous and strong.. that she always answered questions of her well being with, "i am ok.."

and that breaks my heart the most..

that i wasn't there for her to later whisper in my ear that she was terrified,

so scared, and that she just wanted to sleep with me in my bed..

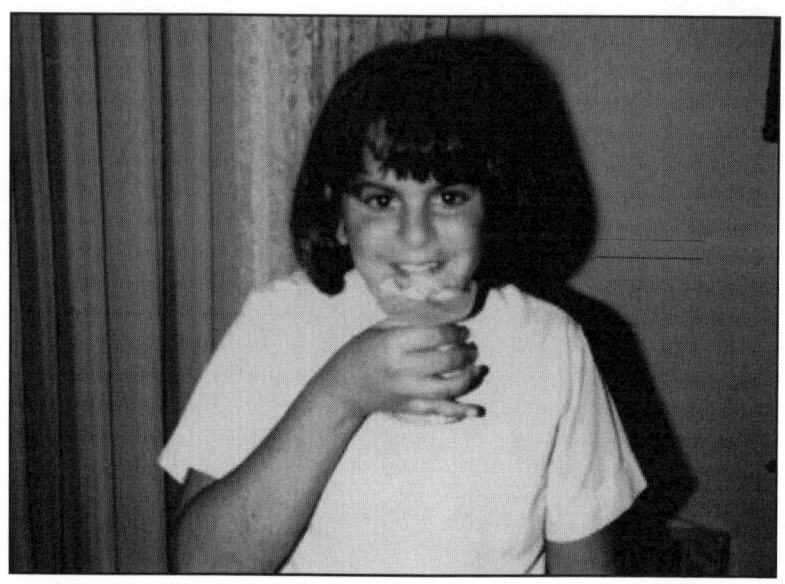

Arabs love to celebrate. We grew up in a household full of parties-food, drink and of course, dancing.

My mama, baba and tete (grandma). They were incredibly strong protectors and influence.. full of love.

High school

My siblings and I are all very close.. and silly.

Actually, one can say we revere each other.

I must say, I believe I have the greatest family in the world.

My tete (my grandmother) was with me in my coma/cosmic journey, and is with me always.

She was my greatest teacher while alive and has never left me.

My parents give us everything. They taught us that we could have anything we desire in life; of course, as long as we put the work in.

They gave us courage and confidence.

Again, Arabs love to dance.

The seven of us.

This may be the only picture I have of my time on Grateful Dead tour.

I went to herb school in Sonoma County and began studying herbs in earnest with David Hoffman, master herbalist from England.

I started Jenny Q's Herbals while finishing my bachelor's degree from Sonoma State University.

I belonged to a drum circle for a couple of years- led by Onye Onyemake, a brilliant man from Senegal. All of us who were in the class (which was more spiritual guidance than a class) became very close. This is the time I recognized my spiritual practice; my life was led by ritual and the sacred.

Dancing has always brought me to Presence and my deep joy.

Working at Rosemary's Garden helped me find the certainty of my path- my heart and professional path as an herbalist.

Two of my loves.

Tasha and Jackson

My first herb faire, in Sonoma County

I was proud and exhausted- after hand-making all of my labels late into the night.

Dreads, gone

Jackson and I, right after I moved
to Joshua Tree.

Feeling the love in Joshua
Tree.. with my beloved Ronnie.

Getting serious about Jenny Q's Herbals, but still tincturing in my kitchen.

I was also starting to develop the Joshua Tree Climbing Salve. This started in my kitchen, in a Le Creuset pot.

Todd and I moved to Joshua Tree to climb these rocks.

We were only supposed to stay for one year- so Todd could climb everyday- but after that year, we bought our first house.

When pregnancy hit, a joy came over me deeper than I had ever known.

That joy only expands every day.

Me and my girl

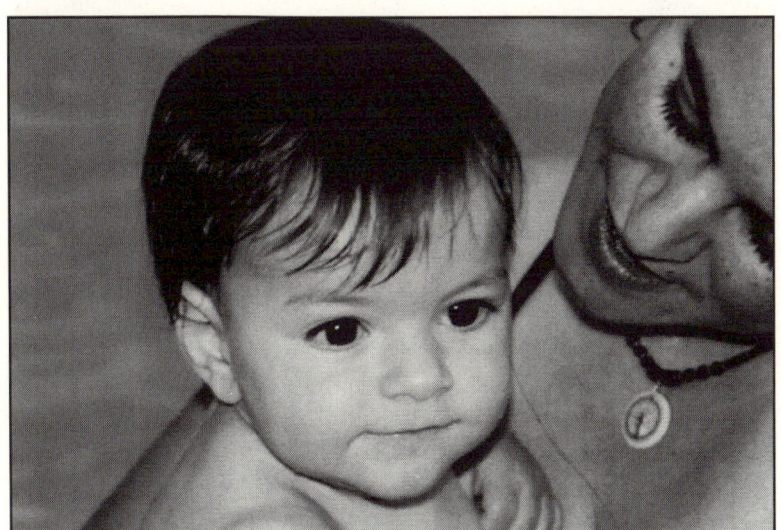

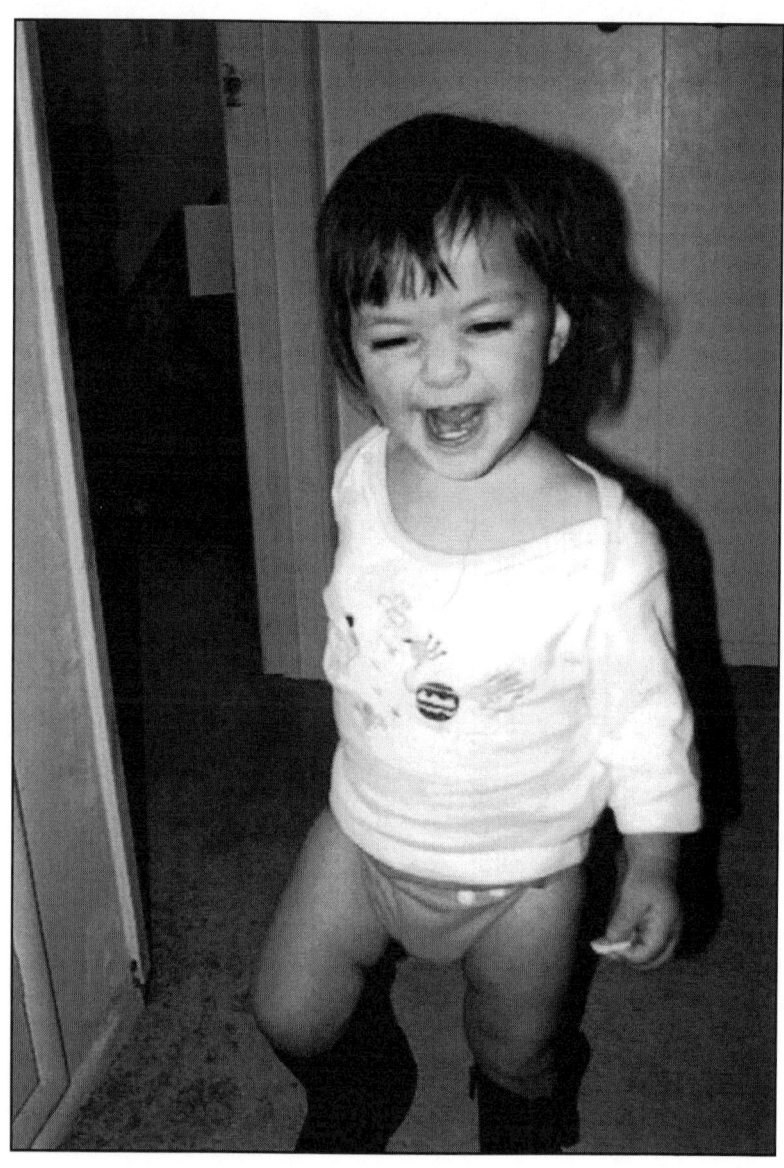

part two

metamorphosis

jïmmy 9
an arab thing

Here's the thing. Arabs don't talk about things.

We're not allowed to talk about good things in our lives. For example, if you like your child, you better call her ugly and stupid. And for good measure, you should probably spit on her a little bit, just to really show how little you would care if something happened to her. That way, hopefully you won't instigate the evil eye to cause harm to you and your family.

On the other hand, we're not allowed to talk about bad things going on in our lives either. You have to make sure everyone knows things are great. I guess if the evil eye catches wind of your family's hardship, it will feed off of it and become even stronger. Perhaps just enough vanity in play keeps the evil eye away.

In other words, you must at all costs portray that everything is going perfectly fine – to the point of bragging at times; but not too well – to the point of insulting yourself and others at times. And, just to keep things fun, each of those rules goes out the window at the drop of a hat, subject to countless unspoken exceptions and social cues.

Within an insulated Arab community, this social framework works fine (if perhaps somewhat problematic by Western standards of emotionalism). But crash it into American culture, and it can become cumbersome to the point of being hurtful. The circumstances of Jenny's sudden illness was one of those times.

I got the call that my sister was in the hospital at some time during the night. Before I was fully awake and comprehending what was going on, I had booked the first flight south and hatched a plan to meet my brother in Palm Springs. He was to arrive about half hour later from another city. I made it as planned, but my brother couldn't get to the airport in time, so he had to wait for the next flight. At the time, we did not know how important minutes were, but I left without my brother, who was to rent a separate car about an hour after me.

When I arrived, one thing that stuck out to me was the amount of people there for my sister. The waiting room was over-full, and there were people in the courtyards around the hospital. In large part, there were two groups: our large Arab family and Jenny's large Joshua Tree family.

For the benefit of white people, I will explain that I use Arab family in the more tribal sense often seen in indigenous and other communities of color. Family is not about blood; it's about community. Everyone you grow up with is an auntie, an uncle, or a cousin. We don't so much inquire into the blood ties or degrees of relationship. While blood is all-important in Arab culture, it's often not relevant. So there was our immediate family, and there were aunties, uncles, and cousins from all over.

The Joshua Tree community was also local and from all over. One would describe Jenny's JT family as hippies. None, or very few, are related in any familial sense, but – similar to my family - they are a family, deeply connected through shared values and experience.

Normally, the Arabs and the hippies keep their distance. It's not that they have a problem with each other; there is just a disconnect between the two worlds that keeps them apart. In the waiting room of the Palm Springs hospital with Jenny inside the ICU, however, the two families were together in a way I'd never seen. They were sitting together, speaking together, and praying together.

Even in their differences, there was striking similarity. For example, the doctors could not keep the Arab family out of Jenny's ICU room. I believe only two people were supposed to be in the room at once. By the time I arrived, whatever limit existed was long forgotten as a crowd of Arabs constantly spilled out of Jenny's room. The only time I can remember there being less than five people in her room was during overnight shifts, where one of our immediate family stayed with Jenny while others slept. At the same time, even though they were not actual family, the hospital could not keep members of the Joshua Tree family from sitting outside the halls of the ICU, praying, singing, and just holding space for Jenny to heal. When they were run out of the hall for a time, there would be people gathered right outside in a little green space.

Jenny always had that way; she travelled between worlds with an ease that seemed effortless. Somehow, she was drawn to every community, and open to every aspect of the people within it. At the same time, people have always seemed drawn to her and her openness.

Openness is not a typical Arab quality. As mentioned before, communication in the Arab community often takes place through a series of veiled exchanges adhering to a complex, seemingly ever-changing yet somehow concrete set of rules.

Confront this with other communities where the communication is different, and it gets pretty confusing, pretty fast. Jenny easily navigated those cultural differences, but with her unconscious in the ICU, we did not have her to navigate for us. And yet, people around the world – in both our Arab family and Jenny's external family – were looking to us for information. We were all getting inundated with messages asking for updates. It was up to Jenny's immediate family to update the world, and as the youngest sibling, the task largely fell to me because it required the use of technology.

The family settled on a website/app that creates a hub where we could post updates and receive messages from visitors to the site. After settling on the forum, we began discussing the initial update. People all over were beginning to learn that something was going on with Jenny, but nobody knew what. At the time, the doctors were still figuring things out.

Immediately, it became clear that it would be difficult to balance the need to put out information with the family's deeply-seeded resistance to sharing private family business with the public. The fact that the information was so painful to each of us did not help matters. In the end, the family settled on the following opening message for Jenny's website:

If you know Jenny Q, you love Jenny Q. If you don't already know, she had some complications from a minor procedure the other day, and is now in the ICU. She has her family and many friends around her, and we appreciate all of your support.

The first update was not much more helpful:

It's been up and down. Yesterday was good and we were celebrating. This morning we were down. We are hoping for a strong rally this afternoon. Will keep you all updated here. Thanks.

Over more than six months of Jenny in the ICU, the family posted less than ten messages, at least two were from Jenny herself. In short, we were not very helpful in the information department.

Of course, we immediately began getting messages pointing out that the updates were almost worse than posting nothing at all. People needed to know what was going on, and we were not providing it.

Several things prevented this. First, things were constantly chang-ing, and the doctors were moving more quickly than the available information at times. In addition, messages needed family approval, which was difficult to come by. We were all worried, stressed, and tired. In short, we were barely holding on to each other. In that time, we reverted to our default – keep information close to the vest. We also reverted to another default – debating. You probably would be surprised how much discussion went into a update that merely stated "things were up and down today." Looking back, the messages became more informative as time went on, and my recollection is that we did catch on, albeit slowly, to the prompts that everyone else needed more.

I understand and appreciate that Jenny never belonged to our family alone. I can admit I am prone to the awe a younger brother has for an older sister; but Jenny has always been a large personality who quickly becomes the heart of any community that she calls home. And when that heart was down, those communities needed information in her absence.

But ultimately, Jenny is ours. She is my sister, my parents' beloved daughter, and the heart of our small family first and foremost – and we could not and would not stand to lose her. I know our failure to com-municate more openly probably was hurtful and added to the stress of others, particularly those far away with little access to information. But during that terrible time, her immediate family needed to be selfish and keep Jenny for ourselves to some extent.

I hope people can understand that.

jenny
the meeting

foggy times.. not much of reality to grasp a hold of.. in and out.. people around me.. doctor after doctor after doctor..

confusion, pain, hallucinations, fear..

starting to recognize people around me.. the nurses, the doctors..

watching nurses do their jobs, taking vitals, administering meds, dressing wounds, looking for pulses..

there is to be a meeting.. it is talked about..

i remember it because it was mentioned over and over..

the meeting, everyone will be there, a big deal..

a party almost.. this is not correct, i know, but they are talking about it with such anticipation and preparing me for it as though there will be cake and candles..

everyone will come! all your doctors and nurses and family! let's clean you up and prepare you!

everyone is there.. they are all around me.. in a wide arch around the room, squeezed in because there are endless surgical teams.. colorectal, wound, infectious disease.. what else? social workers?

my sister joyce is there, and my brothers johnny and jimmy, mom, dad and myshkin..

as a matter of fact, it does feel like a party: doctors sitting on stools, people perched on my bed.. everyone talking and looking at me..

it is long and i drift in and out.. they are talking about my health, speaking of my progresses and declines.. i sleep a little, i think..

then sharp focus to doctor bernal.. she is talking about my legs.. they are not getting better..

they will need to be amputated..

everyone is looking at me.. holding their breath it seems, and staring..

i know i need to hold them up, let them know i can do this.. i somehow know that this is my job...

so i let out a deep breath and say confidently, "let's do it!" and start to cry..

everyone in the room is crying..

elise

prayer requests

Jenny's siblings were our lifeline. They gave us just enough information to have something to hold onto. I had no fear of approaching Johnny and asking for updates.

One day, he told the three of us who were there every day that Jenny was going to lose half of both of her legs and the fingers from one hand.

Oh....

deepest heart ache....

and, an uplift that she was going to LIVE..

Very strange, powerful, potent sensations of both vast grief and gratitude.

He told us not to tell anyone. Of course that was understandable since it hadn't happened yet. All our closest friends, all of Jenny's closest friends wanted to know and we couldn't say anything.

So, I sent out prayer requests: pray for kidneys, pray for blood circulation, pray for energy moving all the way through her beautiful body into her fingers and toes....and on....I sent prayer visions to a few loved ones and they sent out from there to more — and so it fanned into the community what to pray for and how to hold our beloved Q without knowing any specifics......

and we prayed, and prayed and prayed.

tɛd

despair

We were told that Jenny's condition had required doctors to remove fingers - and both of her legs from the knee down.

katie

family

Jenny, I understood your family's desire to be protective of you.

I have a sister who has many friends as well, and as a family member I feel like, "Who the f— are all these people."

I get so sick of friends being too big in my sister's life.

She's MY big sister.

So, you know, I understood your family.

kali

prayers

Details emerged about the septic shock, the induced coma, the extremely high chance of Jenny not making it. Jenny was a pillar and the whole community felt her absence. I put a picture of her on my shrine. Lit a candle whenever I could. I discovered praying in a way I had never known, tapping and harnessing energies, literally sending them to her. I gave coordinates to healer friends of mine from all over, so that they could do the same. I was not the only one to do this. For months, many people directed healing her way.

Amazingly, doctors were keeping her alive. But it wasn't getting better.

I heard she had to have both legs and a hand amputated. I cried.

jenny

sensitivity

i am psychically sensitive.. this is what i call the condition i find myself in after years of navigating my personality.. i am sensitive of going anywhere near the "other worlds"..

experiences in my life have led me to be extremely careful about stepping too close to the Edge.. i even have to be careful being in the same room with people smoking pot or doing hallucinogens..

but here i was going through crazy surgeries, my skin deteriorating and my limbs slowly dying.. they needed to give me heavy-duty pain killers..

so they had to experiment, because my family knew enough to let the doctors know that i am sensitive..

coming out of a particular surgery, i was certain that all of the nurses around me were involved in some long and complicated conspiracy.. that everything they told me was a lie, part of the web they were weaving to fool me..

i was terrified.. i didn't know who to believe.. i didn't know how to respond.. they kept sending different nurses in to try and talk to me, but i was certain it was all part of the trick..

so certain that i was frozen in terror..

so much so that i couldn't move a muscle..

i just stared out at everyone.. eyes feeling like orbs taking it all in..

the story in my head, my reality..

at some point, i saw my mama come to me.. they were doing anything they could to get me to respond, to move.. i watched as my mama started crying and then becoming hysterical that i was not moving, not answering her, unresponsive..

later, myshkin told me that my catatonic episode happened during the time they decided to try a drug called ketamine, one of the most powerful psychotropic substances in existence.. too much of which can produce a psychic paralysis so profound it's known as the "k hole."

this experience happened as i was being wheeled out of surgery..

the surgery where they cut off my legs..

what an unfortunate time to have a bad trip..

robbï

godammit jenny

There started the strange slow creeping through swamps of uncertainty, through waiting, through worrying, through praying, though texting, we knew Jenny's nurse, Elise just heard this, Paula and Kripa cleaned Jenny's garden, the goddesses gathered at the Casa Dari, the news came in more terrible than the last each time, the septic blood, the failing organs, Elise found out this, Piper thinks this, someone said that, Jenny's parents did that, Patricia came for tea, Myshkin came for dinner, Ted wrote a song, slow and cold the thought took hold, Godammit Jenny might die. This cannot be happening! I can't watch! The emotional coward that I am I withdrew to the edges of our community in silence and fear- I chanted for Jenny, slow meaning-filled chants. The news rushed through our community like an ice cold wind, Godammit, pray for Jenny. ICU, surgery, more in the legs, ICU, surgery, Godammit, please! For fuck sake, give the girl a break – it's too much!!!! Send light to her extremities, ICU, surgery, ICU, surgery, fuck me! There go her legs! Godammit I screamed out at the sky Godammit! I punched my steering wheel. Godammit. There it went like a roller coaster on and on for a year or more. And every time I drove past her house, I shook my head and muttered "Godammit Jenny."

myshkin

thirty or forty

Jenny had somewhere between thirty and forty surgeries during her time in the burn unit. The surgeons were conservative, preferring to keep taking her back to the operating room, take only little amounts of tissue each time, and see what might recover and be saved. They worked on stabilizing her big wounds, and waited for her hand and legs to reach some point of stasis.

Today, the 2nd of September 2015, I am sitting in a waiting room at UCI, while the surgeon who saved as much as he could of Jenny's right hand is working on it again, trying to release some scar tissue and keep it as functional as possible. It's a crazy, and sometimes kind phenomenon, how time can make extreme things feel so normal. The night she lost her fingers it all felt like such horror. She was wheeled back into the room with a giant foam box on her hand, cushioning her from the world. I wanted to put a big foam box around her heart. Her giant, sweet heart. How would it take all of this, once she was off the steady drip of Fentanyl, once she could feel her losses?

jenny
shame

there is this idea that our bodies need to look a certain way for us to be considered beautiful in this culture. to be considered worthy. to be considered.

there is such body shame put upon women. and while i have known what bullshit this concept is for most of my life, i have still been so affected by it.

i have had to work hard throughout my life to see my beauty. so damn hard.

how crazy it is that when i am finally in a place in my life where i feel strong and worthy and beautiful, it all changes.

my body changes so profoundly that i have to work incredibly hard to see myself as normal.

as human, let alone beautiful.

i have to struggle to find my sexiness. to stave off shame.

and i think..

thank goddess for all the practice that i have had in digging deep to find my desirability.

it gave me a robust toolbox that i am wholeheartedly utilizing.

myshkin

why do we love?

From my journal, February 21, 2014

"my love how many times did the tears come today. as they took your sweet feet your legs your sweet ah goddess. they are carving you up with such skill and care and i am grateful for that and yet goddess. and i promised i would be your legs if you lived and i will, but your eyes trying to understand your new body break my heart into more pieces than i can let myself feel. especially in that room with my guard all up because anything i say or feel too loud gets denied, pushed aside, drowned out. ah goddess. so i escape to this little cell down the hall not so bad just fine but i can't see your face and that sucks. but i need a space i don't feel my walls up around my ears in. but i can't see your beauty and i'm not there if you wake. goddess dammit. ok. breathe. you will sleep, i will outlast this too. we will be autonomous free beings once again, in each others company, alone. and i will be your legs when you need me to love. as you are my heart. your shining face tonight was every passion painting, every master's stroking of suffering, holy, dammit. why do we believe? is it because we need it? random microbes yeasts bacterium ok ok ok but why you, love? in such a way? that mirrors all we had been dealing with?

at home you said, what is it with doorways? they are all sticking and i said maybe it's time to emotionally leave your parents house. did that push you over the edge? was there way too much dissonance, their house or ours? too much of a line in the sand? my jenny. our jenny. no one's jenny. holy. shining with some crazy brilliance in your hurt. please no more hurt for you jenny. please don't remember any of this, please let the pain subside and never ever come back. and you healed and holy and laughing my jenny. please."

christa

story

I knew our kids in the community were scared. They were nervous about the stories they were hearing about Yazzy's mom, Jenny. I also knew that their parent's were worried about how the kids would react to someone so close to them becoming so disabled.

So I wrote them a story.

christa

the willow tree

Willow was a strong, beautiful, thriving tree living in the wilderness amongst her friends. She was the type of tree who, in the heat of the day, would make a shady spot beneath her for those friends that needed it. Or, when someone looked sad or lonely, she would wrap her strong branch arms around her in a loving hug. It was also known that in the dead of winter, if you ever ran out of food, Willow would peel the bark from her own solid trunk to feed you.

On most days, when you walked by the Willow tree, it wasn't unusual to see every one of her strong branch arms full of friends just wanting to be close to her... to feel her strong limbs beneath them, or just sitting in her shade below while taking in the beautiful colors of her vibrant green leaves.

Then one day, Willow felt sick and called on the healers for help. The healers came and found that some destructive beetles had gotten under Willow's trunk and were making her very, very sick. Poor Willow was too weak to grow leaves now, and her once strong and healthy branch arms felt old and tired.

Her illness quickly spread throughout her body and Willow went dormant for some time. The healers decided that in order to keep Willow alive, they had to cut off a few of her branch arms. Otherwise, they would surely lose her forever....

It was a quiet day in the forest when Willow's branch arms fell back to Mother Earth.

The news of Willow spread far, her friends gathered and prayed for her wellbeing, and they lit candles envisioning her strength. They hoped for her fast recovery.

Word got around that Willow was getting new branch arms to replace those that were removed. Many of her friends wondered if Willow would be the same because of this. Would she still want them to come and visit her? Then, some wondered if they came to visit her, would they get sick too? Or maybe they did something to cause Willow to lose her strong branch arms?

So the day came when Willow came out of her dormancy. Spring was in the air and the other trees in the forest were sprouting fresh, new buds. Willow saw that her forest friends were slowly gathering around her, unsure of what to say or do, when the youngest of the bunch walked right over to Willow's strong sturdy trunk and touched her. She sure felt like the same Willow, he thought. He then slowly climbed high on her trunk to one of his favorite spots and saw that his usual branch was replaced with one of the new branch arms. It sure looked a little different, he thought as he slowly climbed onto it. He felt the smooth limb and lay down. It sure felt a little different too...

But as he lay there, he felt the same familiar loving energy of Willow flowing through him. He closed his eyes while he took hold of the new solid branch and hugged it with all his might.

As Father Sun shone down on Earth that day, he smiled as the friends made their home yet again around Willow tree. They were relaxing in her shade, hugging her new arms, sitting in her powerful silence... and mostly appreciating the differences between them.

cheryl

yazzy

I thought about Yazzy, and how scary seeing her mom ill in the hospital must be for a little girl. But kids, they are so resilient and this little girl so full of good things, well, she seemed to handle her mother's journey with a simple trusting grace.

felicia

routines

At the house in Joshua Tree, we watered the plants, kept the house clean, gave Myshkin and Yazzy lots of hugs and did our best to help keep Yazzy on as regular a schedule as we could. Yazzy suddenly had her mom missing and in her place came an entire community of "aunts, uncles" and family and friends, new and old, doing their best to hold Jenny's space. Yazzy is an amazing person. Just like her Mama. Even at eight years old, she was so powerful and strong in who she was, and she maintained that will and strength through it all.

Mornings getting ready for school and getting ready for bed were the hardest. But between Myshkin, Sailor and I, we got through it! We made sure her hair was done and her teeth were brushed and we got her fed, made her lunch and got her to school. We made sure she did her homework and had a good dinner before getting her pajamas on and getting her to bed. We even made sure that, like her mama always did, one of us sang to her every night as she fell asleep.

Each week included a sleepover at Lola's house, two nights with her dad on the weekends and pizza night with us on Sundays. Her tutor Tony continued to come over twice a week, which helped the continuity of her schedule immensely. Sweet old Tobin defied the odds and slowly healed from his fall and Yazzy would often enthusiastically accompany Tobin and I on our evening run.

jenny
coming out

i have been going back and forth about this.

the first time i thought of it, i was swimming ..

i burst into tears.

who knew one could cry with their face under water?

should i? how vulnerable am i willing to make myself?

so much of me was damaged.

so much emotion erupts when being dis-abled in society.

you are stared at or feel the discomfort of the people around you. you hold your pee for hours rather than ask for help through an inaccessible bathroom. you are constantly reminded of your dependency or deformity in public.

but there is more. there are disabilities that one can hide but that carry such a heavy weight. and so much more emotion than having a couple of missing legs or some missing fingers.

it is my bag. yes. a colostomy bag. there i said it. and somehow i can't believe that it will live in any book. it carries so much shame. as though i have a scar burned across my forehead that says untouchable. filthy. an object of ridicule.

my colorectal surgeon says that among all the disabilities that people have to live with— even those that are life-threatening— the hardest emotionally for most people is a colostomy or an ileostomy bag.

i told him i believe this, because it is harder for me to deal with than my legs.

the shame is unbelievable. have i hurt someone? stolen from someone?

am i a pariah? perhaps not.

but it sure feels like it.

elise

divinity and suffering

Slowly, the statistical chances of her survival crawled up after several months in the ICU and we were finally allowed to see her and touch her (with gloves and gowns) and communicate with her more freely.

She looked, sounded, and felt like both a childhood and elderly version of herself. I couldn't find her in present time. Her innocence and confusion bounced back and forth as the various digital signals of the machines and liquids her body was hooked up to moved up and down.

I have never been one to pretend anything, but upon seeing her and knowing that, like a stumbling baby recognizes her own condition based on your expression, my emergency instinct kicked in and I found the smile deep from within my heart that was certain of her journey being a beautiful one.

I wanted to weep at her lost feet, I wanted to weep into her hands and scream at the world, God, or whatever Source designed this situation. I wanted her to know how devastated I was for her, that I felt her pain and confusion as thoroughly as I could.

But that was not my role. My role was to be certain and clear and look her straight in the eyes and tell her that her journey had meaning, that it - that SHE - was divine and beautiful and on the perfect path. That I would stand by her side with a sword until all worries passed.

And I believed it.

I truly believed that all was blessed – anything else felt pointless.

Behind the awareness, the duality of this truth combined with the obvious suffering of her situation was vastly deconstructing everything within me, as I moved through life one moment at a time, trying not to try.

The grief was so great that I couldn't digest it, I couldn't grasp it – I could only feel it growing in the shadows of me, building until I had to weep and scream and pray and plead for her peace, slowly growing exhausted from hope and from holding the heavy certainty up so high.....

selah

my story

"Selah, the news is not good." Amputations? What? This was not the phone call I was expecting. I knew Jenny was very sick. I knew she had fallen into septic shock and was alive at Irvine Medical Center... that she was in a burn unit there, but nothing else. How does a better than healthy human, blazing with life, end up defying death within twelve hours of a "minor outpatient procedure?" I was shaking, scared...what does this mean for Jenny...for Yazzy?

This may sound selfish, but I was mad. It had been months, maybe five, that she had been fighting for her life in the hospital. I know there was mostly nothing I could do: no way to save the circulation to her extremities, no way to even hold her hand and tell her stories to keep her company. I couldn't stand the idea that she had endured so much alone. I felt I could have shouldered some of this burden if I had just known. I know it sounds silly, but I still believe this. I just know I could have helped.

She visited me one night in a dream. We were vending, (because if you can make it, Jenny can sell it) sitting behind a table at a booth and I asked her, "Are you okay?" She replied simply, "No, but I will be."

The next day I drove to Irvine to visit her. I didn't ask or tell anyone for fear that I would be advised not to go, even though I had been told I could. The secrecy surrounding her illness had been stifling and intentionally exclusionary. For three hours in the car, I prepared myself to lay eyes on Jenny. A weekend, seemingly not long before all this, I had served Jenny at the J.T. Saloon while enjoying a beautiful "child-free" evening of dancing, flirting...living. I entered the burn unit and donned the multiple garments necessary for safety. Jenny's safety, not mine.

There was nothing in this world that could have prepared me for what I saw. Jenny's mother, Susie, greeted me casually. She had been living there, steadfast by her bedside. Jenny was a corpse. There was not a single part of her body that had been unaffected by this illness.

Her head was shaved with skin graph "patches" and countless tubes running from all parts.. less parts...no legs. The skin she had left was purple with scarring from having been rearranged. I couldn't imagine the pain. Jenny turned in painful slow motion and lit up in her usual fashion. It was then that I realized in horror that she was fully aware, seeing...knowing... that this girl was very much alive.

I cried even though I tried not to. There was no hiding feeling sorry for her. My mind reeled; your poor body, where did you go? There is so little of you left. Has Yazzy seen you? Of course she has, poor baby. This is your improved condition? Will you survive, because, oh man, this is bad.

Trying desperately to talk about things normally, I updated Jenny on my dental implants. I had recently had my front two teeth pulled and was wearing a partial. I comically removed it and was quickly urged to replace it by Susie. Jenny's heartfelt sincerity was crushing. "Oh honey, you were so worried about having them pulled!" That she could muster any empathy for me seemed impossible. Jenny has always given generously to the people she loves, even at this moment with seemingly nothing left to give.

jenny
infantilized

i felt infantilized.. there i was, struggling with all my mind and coordi-
nation and strength to feed myself bits of cereal.. it wasn't so long ago
that i was helping yazzy to learn to feed herself.. the nurses would
come into my room to change my colostomy bag because i couldn't
even look at it, i was so ashamed.. how many years ago did i change
yazzy's diapers?

i love to care for people.. it is my passion, it is what i love to do, it is
my job as a mother and an herbalist.. but me being cared for? that is
not my specialty..

ronda

meeting jenny

"I am not afraid of storms for I am learning how to sail my ship"

– *Louisa May Alcott*

I don't know about you, but the sound of the didgeridoo hits me deep in the core, in a healing sort of way. I can't explain it; it just does. Much like the story of my dear friend Jenny Q, who I first met at one of the first JT Didgeridoo Festivals in Joshua Tree, CA. Some fellow local artists/friends and I, had a collaborative art booth and Jenny Q had the herb booth next to us. We ended up hanging out the whole weekend. That was the beginning of our amazing fifteen year friendship. A friendship that has taught me about healing and sailing ships! She has always impressed me with her wealth of knowledge about plants and medicine and also with her love and care for people and family. Over the years we have bonded through dancing, having and educating our children, wine dates, dinners, the Grateful Dead, continuing education in the medical world, long talks about herbs, health, relationships, and much more. Heck, we almost homesteaded land together when she considered, for a moment, buying land next door to me in Pitown. She is a beautiful, kind, loving, badass, brilliant woman whom I consider an honor to know and call friend. She has healed me, inspired me, and impressed me.

She heals me.

Over the years, my career had brought me to spend a fair amount of time in Asia on business and travel. On one of my trips there, I developed an infection. Treating it there wasn't working, so I came home early to seek medical attention as my condition was worsening. After many visits to my local health care provider and antibiotic prescriptions that caused dramatic adverse reactions, my local nurse practitioner recommended that I go see Jenny Q. "Great idea!" I said. "I happen to know her very well and don't know why I hadn't thought of that". My doctor explained to me that she thought my immune system was compromised and not responding well to the antibiotics and proceeded to pull a bottle of Jenny Q's Immune Power out of her lab coat and told me that she was using it on her kids and thinks I should give it a try. Off to see my friend I went! Jenny formulated a custom herbal blend and gave me a regimen that included that bottle of Immune Power. I strictly adhered to her recommendations with amazing results. I now consult with Jenny first before going to the doctor and she usually has the answers I need. She had healed me; just like so many others in our community, including my doctor's kids.

She inspires me.

At one point, I had decided to further my own education in the medical field. I wanted to be knowledgeable about my own family's health, but also to be of assistance in the developing world, particularly with women and children. I trained and certified as an Emergency Medical Technician. In 2013, I registered for an intensive hands-on course in the Philippines to train in International Midwifery and Disaster Preparedness with an organization called Mercy in Action, which provides free women's and children healthcare in northern Philippines. "Hands-on" is just what I got when Typhoon Haiyan, one of the strongest tropical cyclones ever recorded, devastated portions of the Philippines in early-November 2013, a few months before I was due to arrive. The seas rose thirteen feet with winds over one hundred and ninety miles per hour, decimating the city of Tacloban and surrounding areas. What I thought was training in a small village birthing center in the north of Philippines transformed into going to the disaster zone to administer help in Tacloban, the hardest hit region. I landed in Manila in January 2014 for a few days of training before heading south for relief efforts. Upon doing a thorough scan of my email the night before leaving because I was not going to have any connection for three weeks, I discovered that something had happened and Jenny was in a coma. No!!! No way! My healer! This can't be happening! Gulp. Pause. After taking a deep breath, I said prayers for her, Yazzy, and her family and trusted in the universe that all would be okay. I was sure that this badass friend of mine would put up the biggest fight of anyone I knew. She has put herself through nursing school, worked diligently at being an amazing single mom, and had opened her own apothecary, the Grateful Desert Herb Shoppe & EcoMarket. She is disciplined, strong, and committed. For God's sake, this woman gets up at four-thirty A.M. every morning to run without fail. This is the woman who has healed so many in her community. She can get through this!

And then off I went into one of the most intense and amazing things I have experienced in my life. We birthed over one hundred babies and saw around two hundred people per day in our general health-care clinic. It was a case of "cowboy medicine". We had to make do with what we had. Sterilizing suture kits in our pressure cooker, birthing babies in tents, making splints or breathing devices with what we could find lying around, generating power, and purifying our water by hand. We had our work cut out for us. We were all learning to sail in real rough weather. I prayed and cried with so many patients but Jenny was still on my mind. I must say that I often channeled my healer during this time. Her care and knowledge came rushing back to me. I knew she must be okay...because here she was, answering my questions when I needed her most. One day, I shared her story with an herbalist/midwife from Idaho who was working with our team in the Philippines. To my surprise, she knew Jenny and her Joshua Tree Climbing Salve. Serendipitously, her name was Jenny, and she made the Joshua Tree Climbing Salve with her friend who bought the formula from Jenny Q. What? There was no doubt that her presence was real and it was strong; keeping me inspired!

She impresses me.

Needless to say, when I got back into signal, I was quick to check in on Jenny. I was not all that surprised, but relieved to hear she was awake and talking. I read her first words, "Allah Kareem"! So right she is! After crying with parents who lost their babies, and children who lost their parents, I found myself crying for life. Her life! It was when I arrived home a few months later that I learned more about Jenny's condition and results. With a heavy heart, I found out she had lost her legs and some fingers, but still knew if anyone can get through this, it's Jenny. When the seas got rough, she fought and fought hard. We all fought and learned to better sail our ships. Jenny turned hers from a near capsize.

jenny

profound empathy

i love people.. that's what i do.. it's easy for me..

i have many a time said that i was put on this planet to love..

i often feel that becoming an herbalist gave me a vehicle to love people, with herbs as my tools.. the plant spirits love so simply and fully, and together we work with the souls and physiology of people to bring about change..

so in the past, seeing clients was never hard because i could see people and intuit their pain: could love them and hold them and use my senses to understand what was going on with them..

they may not have noticed that i had no personal experience with their issues..

or maybe they did, but i got away with it..

now it is so different.. i have experienced so much..

someone comes to me with pain and i understand the trauma of that..

they come to me with insomnia and i can relate to the agony of that..

they sit and talk about loss and i can hold them and know what they mean..

the herbs might be the same herbs i used before, but a depth of feeling and capacity for empathy have expanded to reside within the deepest part of me..

selah

our people

Jenny was the second person I met in Joshua Tree. My boyfriend and I decided to look for a room to rent for our second winter in the desert. I figured, like any college town I'd ever lived in, we'd find the bulletin board and see what was available. The closest we found was Sue's Health Foods in Yucca. Jenny was at the counter. There was no bulletin board, she informed me and after a quick bit of conversation, she gave me her phone number. It was clear we had each found "our people."

That evening, I called Jenny from the hallway entry phone at the Joshua Tree Saloon, right after happy hour. We were invited to her and Todd's new rental home of only two weeks, beautifully placed on Tortuga Ave, one mile from the National Park kiosk. After brief introductions and a tour, we reclined in camping chairs and cracked open our half rack of Natty Lights. We rented the extra bedroom for Jenny's price of seventy-five dollars per month. The following climbing season, after much disagreement, I raised our rent to one hundred and fifty dollars.

Having a child was not part of my life plan but ten months after Jenny gave birth to Yazzy, I gave birth to Olive. We joked that there was something in the water because, well, we weren't the only ones having babies. New families were popping up everywhere, so many in our tight-knit community procreating at the same time. Like most of us here in Joshua Tree, Jenny and I practiced attachment parenting. It wasn't until we each became single parents that we realized how fortunate this was.

The need for childcare was the scariest concern I would have faced. How do you leave a breastfeeding three year old- one that has never slept alone- with someone in order to make a living: working night shifts at the bar or fulfilling work criteria for your R.N. degree? Of the many challenges that faced me as a newly single parent, it turned out that this was not one I would have to deal with. Two days a week,

I would bring Olive to Jenny's in the evening, then gently scoop her out of bed, Jenny's bed, at three A.M. to take her home after work. In return, Jenny would gently ease Yazzy into my bed in the wee, dark hours of morning and then travel the two or so hours for her R.N. clinicals. For a while, this was life, and it worked.

One night while closing the bar, I made a very bad decision to stand on a swivel top stool to turn off the outside lights. I fell hard on that concrete floor and broke my front tooth. With nothing left to do but feel sorry for myself, I drove to Jenny's to pick up my sleeping little girl.

I snuck in the back door, shouldered Olive's overnight bag and tiptoed into the bedroom. There lay Olive, Jenny and Yazzy, peacefully asleep in that order. I leaned over and began to scoop Olive into my arms, as I had done countless times before. All of a sudden Jenny sat bolt upright and grabbed my arm, "Selah, are you all right?! I had a dream that you were hurt!"

I sat on her bed and sobbed, letting out my worst fears about a broken front tooth. She held space for me as I wept many tears. I left after that catharsis, feeling amazed that Jenny's psychic ability had woken her from a deep sleep at the moment I so desperately needed her.

myshkin

privacy and prettiest mama

Jenny's birth family was very protective of her privacy, and her Joshua Tree family was going out of their skins trying to get information. I was the conduit and I walked the line carefully. I had a group of about seven close friends in town that I sent updates to constantly, letting them know about each event and surgery so they could send their energy her way. We all agreed that the specifics of Jenny's illness and recovery should not be public until Jenny herself could be aware enough to permit the info to go out. It's a very small town, people love each other and talk, and I had special concerns about Yazzy hearing anything about her mama's health on the playground or at a friend's house. I will not forget the heartbreak moment I had to tell Yazzy about the upcoming amputations. How could she take it in, really? But she said, "She will still be the prettiest Mama." And she was absolutely right.

melissa

said sustenance

Seeing you for the first time when finally visitors were allowed was shocking. There you were, tiny and emaciated. Shaved head. Legs gone at the knees, hands bandaged. So little and delicate looking. I was told things were still touch and go. But when I left, I told Wendy I knew you were going to make it. There was no question in my mind. And I was reservedly, hopefully, faithfully encouraged. On subsequent visits, while you might drift in and out of medical-induced haze, sometimes confused about exactly what was occurring around you, YOU were there. Your essence, your unmistakable personality and spirit shined through. And we laughed. I was able to remain for some extended time periods, which gave me a chance to be with you and see just a snapshot of what you were going through on a daily basis. Trying to get sustenance into you. Surgeries. Procedures. The fragility of flesh and body.

Your mother was always there- with various forms of said sustenance from home and Mother's Market. She thanked me profusely for driving up, coming to visit you and spending the time. That was so reverse/ contradictory of how I actually felt. I was honored and humbled to spend that time with you, to experience you in your grace amidst the unfathomable suffering and the reality of your ordeal. Those visits were precious to me and I could not have been more grateful to have the opportunity to be in your presence during that time.

jenny

bite in the ass

the other day, i was giggling about a grateful dead song and how archaic it was… it seemed so simplistic! it was so degrading to women!

then it suddenly hit me that when you create art and put it down on paper or canvas or recording, it's set in stone… galvanized for the ages… there for everybody to see and judge through the ages.

the boys were probably twenty when they started singing that song…

of course they were still singing about clichéd love and had not yet evolved.

is that what i'm doing here?

when i look back at these words twenty years from now, will i chuckle at myself for the musings that i set down in stone and put out there for my loved ones to read?

oh, the joys of even a moment's judgment…

it always comes back to bite you right in the ass.

kali

community pulls together

There were fundraisers. There were 'Jenny Q Days' down at Teddy's Listening Lounge, with snacks and crafts, where you could make a card or send a video message. There were so many prayer circles and moments in time and space dedicated to her. Though many of us still cried about it when alone, on the communal level we pushed on, not leaving any room for doubt that she would come home to us. I would watch Yazzy when I could. I would try to not let negative thoughts get me down or fill me with questions like, "Why does the universe always seems to be so harsh to those that are the best?" At the Joshua Tree Music Festival that May, which is, first and foremost for all of us, a celebration of our community, her absence was a hole that made us all love each other more than usual.

At home, on my quiet nights of candlelit vigil, I would imagine dancing with Jenny again. Regardless if she didn't have legs anymore, she was my sister in dancing especially, and I would watch the earth gravitate to move us, rhythmically and melodically, to the tune of life's bittersweet song. How I hoped I would see her again...

mary rose

prayer in the shape of a circle

It had been a very long time since I had said a prayer. I went into my studio and turned on the light, then turned it off. In the end, I lit a candle and sat down on the floor, looking out of the window into the dark. I closed my eyes and thought of Jenny; instantly there was some kind of connection. It was the strangest thing: I felt like I was somehow not alone. I realize many people feel this connection whenever they pray, but at other times when I have closed my eyes and tried to ask for help, I had never felt it quite like this. I didn't really think about who or what was connecting with me, but it was a good feeling in spite of the fear in my heart for my friend.

After that first time, the prayer became a ritual. Every evening, I would sit down and send my love and any specific messages that had come to me in texts or emails from friends within the prayer circle. The messages would be something like 'pray for her kidneys to heal' and 'pray for her lungs to work of their own accord'. I passed these messages on to my husband Brian and also to Rosa and they also prayed. I found myself looking forward to these quiet times in the company of this connection, or presence, which seemed to form the shape of a circle, of which I was a part. I only saw one or two of the other people involved face to face during this time, but felt them always as loving energy, whenever I sat down to join them in prayer.

eva

cash mob

Vera sent us each a gorgeous photo of Jenny that she had taken so that

we could all remember her on a daily basis and continue our vigil.

As the days became weeks and the weeks turned into months, I would.

stop at the Grateful Desert for my "medicine/chocolate" and try to glean news of her condition. It was usually in hushed tones with a heavy heart that

brief and vague references to her operations would emerge. More often

than not, I would find Fox at the counter trying to keep the doors open

to her friend's shop and vision, that was there to help heal a community.

How ironic that we couldn't use Jenny's own medicines to heal her.

The summer months were approaching and it was clear that it would

be a struggle to keep enough business coming in to weather the

less populated scorching hot, summer months. I asked Fox how much money it takes a day to keep the doors open. I thought maybe I could help by organizing a Cash Mob.

After several weeks of coordinating dates through Fox and Myshkin,

we went for it. Martin designed a poster and we spread it on social media.

Kripa and Paula, the most dynamic duo, played music for the steady stream of shoppers. It was a fantastic expression of what community can do when people care for one another. The 'mob' turned out and bought enough to keep the doors of the Grateful Desert open though the tenuous summer months.

myshkin

the light, the light

The energy sent to Jenny during her time in the hospital, especially those first precarious weeks, was immense, palpable, and surely a giant factor in her survival. Dr. Joe, her lead surgeon said as much to us one day; her chances had been so slim, medicine alone would not have pulled her through. Jenny is such a uniquely giving soul, a fact that could likely be confirmed by every person she has ever spoken to. During her time near the edge, it seemed as if all the love she had poured out on everyone she had ever met was multiplying, squaring and cubing, and flowing back at her to keep her afloat. Friends and family spent time in prayer and healing work, their friends did the same, their friends' extended networks did the same. There were very many people who knew her, and many that did not, helping to hold her. At times I could tune into this wave breaking on our shore.

I saw and felt it as a net, built of light, glowing strands woven between uncountable hearts, holding us. Holding Jenny, Yazzy, her family, myself. I have never felt anything like it. Once while she was in surgery and I was waiting in the main lobby, a student cellist was donating their sweet low tones in the cavernous space. The music opened my spirit to the web of light and I felt it lift me like a dancer, a waking dream of dancing, gravity-less on the pulsing light, filled me as I focused on sending the light to Jenny in the operating room. I had many moments like this, filling with the light and channeling it into her body.

allison

stealth butterfly

Being somewhat intuitive, and upon hearing news of Jenny's sudden onslaught of challenges that invited prayers, I did a check-in with inner guidance, and, I didn't sense any ultimate alarm... My greatest feeling was that this period of unknown-ness was to serve as a blessing of some kind.!?!.

I pondered that a bit, and reflected that this could, for one, serve Jenny as a period of a very serious yin orientation. With our predominant orientation toward all things and expressions of yang, why wouldn't a unique sanctuary of yin yield at least some good? In any case, I knew that Jenny's spirit is formidably bright and loving, and also courageous. I could not help but envision goodness for her, through and through, (and unyielding tenacity) that this serve her in the supremest blessing way!

This was still in the beginning to middle stages, but during the time when Jenny was in ICU and couldn't receive visitors or access electronic correspondence. Her journey deeply away was quite intense, and I still felt that she would prevail. Her eventual physical losses saddened me that she must go through more, and muster yet more courage, yet I felt and "sensed" that she would be okay, and make it okay. I think my optimism was and is not exaggerated. I do believe, and know, that Jenny is a stealth butterfly. Jenny wills her spirit to prevail, because her inner flame must blaze in vivacious color and spark.

katie

horses and ritual

I needed to feel you and feel connected to you, but I knew I would have to wait.

So I would take a walk down to the horses and cry and go the place to where I knew you were.

And I'd just take a minute several times a day to pray. I would send my energy out that you were going to get better and that you were healing. And letting you know that I was here and I cared.

It became a ritual for me that I did all day long.

I tried to keep it together around the kids, because I didn't want them terrified that they were going to lose you.

Every night at dinner we would send out our love to you. Kay would always say that she sent you love and that she hoped they were feeding you well. She was very concerned that they weren't going to be feeding you good enough food because you always eat so well.

michelle q

family of docs

Between the two Medical Doctors (my dad and sister Joyce), the Doctor of Pharmacy (my brother John), the Naturopathic Doctor (myself), the ever-present reporter who missed NOTHING (my mom) and the Voice of Reason (my lawyer brother Jimmy), every detail of Jenny's case was discussed and dissected with new action plans discussed with Jenny's physicians constantly. If her physicians had been closed to our expertise, this could have been a nightmare. But this great group of docs listened, appreciated and responded. Between all of us, Jenny had the dream team on her side. No team could have been more motivated to move mountains and fight for miracles. And Jenny was always a miracle of spirit, and a miracle she proved to be again.

jenny
hymns

i have some foggy memories of being in the hospital bed in terrible pain..

maybe my throat was being suctioned while i was intubated.. maybe they were cauterizing my skin as i was bleeding..

foggy, painful memories..

but what is significant about those flashes in my mind is the sharp picture of my mom's face close to mine..

my mama and my sisters so close, singing to me..

singing religious hymns that i hadn't heard since i was a child..

though the only church songs i have surrounded myself with in the last twenty-five years are chants to the goddess, these old, christian hymns worked their magic: they calmed my spirit and took away some of the fear and trauma of was happening.

what beautiful things the recesses of our minds and hearts can hold..

tania

your mom

From when you arrived to Desert Regional Medical Center in Palm Springs, Q, to time immemorial, your mom did not leave the hospital. Of course you know this better than I, since she was by your side most of the time. I caught glimpses of your mother in the first few hours, although I did not know who she was. I finally saw her walking with Joyce, and began to make the connection based on her intent listening and the focused look in her eyes. Her head was often to the ground; she talked while walking and received the transfer of information and emotions moving around the Q-hive.

jenny
family

i grew up in a family of seven. five kids. we have always been so close.

i didn't even realize how special our family unit was, our cultural dynamic of closeness, until i moved away and went to college.

there, people would call their parents names or tell me they hated their sister or brother. i was shocked. i hadn't really been exposed to that attitude before— and hadn't until then felt so grateful for the cohesiveness my family shared.

after spending time with my family, a close friend once laughed and said that she had never seen a family so intimate, where everyone is so devoted to each other and every sibling openly adores the other. "what a blessing," she told me. "but, when i make a decision, no one questions me. no one ever assumes i would need their advice! i am, after all, over 40," she said.

not so in my family. any life decision is a family affair. when i decided to quit nursing school, i got six very intense phone calls urging me to go back. my oldest brother alarmingly told me to contact the director of the program to say that i had made a huge mistake and to beg her to let me back in.

even the baby, my brother who is eight years younger, called to counsel me about the mistake i was making.

as horrible as it seemed at the time, i was ever so grateful on graduation day, walking down the aisle with yazzy in my arms.

in the end, it worked.

it's pretty amazing how close we are. i have never looked up to anyone the way i do my siblings.

and there was never a greater man than my dad. or a more devoted mother than my mom...

mᴸamᴸa

no mother

"Mom. Will you write for Jenny's book? She would love to have your voice in her account of what happened. You were there every day."

"No."

"But Mom..."

"I will not, Joyce. I do not want to think about that time. No mother should ever have to endure watching her daughter going through what she did."

joyce 9
mom

I recently asked my mom if she was going to write her memories of Jenny's medical calamity. There was silence on the phone. She said she could not relive the feelings of her daughter's brush with death.

Besides Jenny, my mom suffered the most. Now Myshkin might beg to differ and she may have a point.

Jenny was in-patient in the hospital for six months then in a rehab for another month, and my mom slept in her room by her side almost every night. I think two months after it all started, in March, my dad finally forced her home a few nights but she only agreed to this if one of her children or Myshkin promised to be by her side, monitoring her closely.

My mom would have made an amazing nurse. She anticipated Jenny's every need. Jenny probably never had a dry mouth her entire hospital stay. My mom meticulously flossed and brushed Jenny's teeth twice a day, applied lip balm, spooned ice in her mouth and when allowed, fed her patiently. Jenny got a facial every morning with amazing products. When Jenny could finally have food by mouth, my mom would go to Whole Foods everyday and get Jenny pressed juices, yoghurt and smoothies. My mom insisted that the hospital allow a small fridge in the ICU room. At the staff's amazed refusal of such a request, my parents loudly protested and the refrigerator was installed. My mom constantly stocked that fridge, but most of it wasted as Jenny barely had an appetite. When my sister Michelle, who is a naturopathic doctor, suggested that gum might help stimulate Jenny's sluggish bowels, I noticed about twenty packs of gum of every brand and flavor in her room. My mom was a task-master three times a day when physical therapy was finally prescribed.

Over time, the nurses started to understand my mom. At first they found her a nuisance. She would panic and call the nurse if Jenny felt hot or looked pale. My mom would monitor her vitals and report to the nurse any deviance from the norm. She monitored her urine output and oral intake. She would ask to speak to the doctor if anything was out of order. Soon the nurses knew to communicate and include my mom in Jenny's care. She would help with dressing changes, bathing and pretty much anything that did not include the IV pole. Giving my mom a purpose that was more than just giving comfort care was actually treating my mom's feelings of hopelessness and anxiety.

But what was really amazing was watching her patience and devotion, and the fact that she completely relinquished her busy life to be with Jenny for however long it took until she was safe.

Jenny underwent general anesthesia for over forty surgeries during her time in UCI. Many of these were skin grafts as the skin of her extremities became ischemic and sloughed off. She also had a few orthopedic surgeries to remove her ischemic legs just below the knees and four fingers from her right hand. Thankfully Jenny is a lefty. She also had abdominal surgery to remove the ischemic portions of her bowel and small intestine, her gallbladder and had reconstructive surgery to her backside as well.

Each surgery required waiting in a cold pre-op room for two hours and then waiting anxiously during surgery. Post-op was no party as Jenny usually was nauseated and in pain. My mom was right there holding the basin and wiping her clean or asking the nurse for pain medication.

jenny
sisters and mama

my sister michelle came from italy to be there for me..

nights were hard.. filled with dark and terrible visions.. i would wake every fifteen minutes, wide-eyed and searching.

each time i awoke, my eyes would find my little sister's.. solid, calm, reassuring..

she would be rocking in a chair beside my bed and gazing down at me.. not once did my eyes fly open that i did not find michelle's eyes holding me..

how did i continue this journey once she had to fly home to her son?

what would i have done during those early weeks if her eyes had not my steady ground?

i find myself laying in a bed without the ability to move any muscle.. every two hours, the lift team comes to turn me to stave off decubitus ulcers.. one day, i find the strength to reach out toward the bar to try and help.. to try and pull myself onto my side..

just the mere movement of me reaching out makes people start yelling out and cheering..

joyce comes by early on her days off to help with my morning routine.. it was her joy to brush my teeth and wash my face.. even to do a facial on me!

if she came and my mom had already cleaned me up, she would be so disappointed..

my mama was there every day.. i don't think she left the hospital for the first three months that i was living in the hospital.. she slept on the tiny couch in the back of the room..

she awoke every two hours when the lift team came to turn me..

she awoke every time the nurses came in to administer more meds..

any moan or groan from me was met with my mama's concerned face..

"what, ya mama? what do you need?"

it was not until two months after i was admitted that the nurses finally convinced her to go home for a night's sleep..

myshkin
diamond moments

Laughing. I keep thinking, this week, that I need to be writing this down for you, to read later, when you have hopefully forgotten all this goddesforsaken trauma. But you will also have forgotten all the goddessblessed sweetness, the moments our eyes arc and shine, lazerlove, the way you make everyone smile, proud of you, happier with themselves, even from your hospital bed. The way you are healing ancient family wounds from your most vulnerable place. You warrior, Jenny. I keep thinking I need to write it down and then I realize I already am. I don't write to anyone else. About anyone else. It's all you and what is happening in this crazy moment out of time, this bright room. The African music I play you to see you through hydro therapy, the legal-pad gowns we are always in, a world of white and yellow, a world you make even brighter with your beauty. My beauty girl. I crave time alone together so much I can taste it. And when it comes I don't mind what we do. Talk or not. More often than not you sleep. I just want to share sweet space with you, sweet rare intimate precious diamond moments. Jasper moments. Today they repositioned your feeding tube that has been giving you so much trouble and I watched in awe: the videoxray live movie of your insides. Your heart beating, lungs expanding, ribs moving, dancing around them. Your gorgeous architecture, your beautiful spine. You tower you. My towering love.

ritŭal

the seven palaces

Robbi:

Hidden forces of the Limitless Light who establishes the boundaries of the universe, we invoke you in your secret name (Stillness....) To seal in just orientation the inner limits our temple, may the secret virtues of the Radiant Truth be established on the thrones of our hearts.

Oh secret flame that burns in every human heart, thou art life and the giver of life. Behold the seven lamps before thy throne, the seven centers burning bright… the Limitless Light within.

Venus

I represent Venus

I Am the Door of Life

The passage from the world of ideas

Into the world of form

I Am the fruitful womb

Whence all creatures have their birth

I Am the Mother of mothers.

Oh my sweet sister Jenny unto whom I send this kiss, May the Eternal Victory of the One Truth be established on the throne of your heart.

(Blow a kiss from heart and mouth)

Saturn

I represent Saturn

I Am the summation of all things

The end which is without end

Even as the beginning

Through all shifting changes of existences

I remain my Self

And the self which I AM

Is your own True Self.

Sweet sister Jenny unto whom I send this kiss, May the understanding of the One Truth be established on the throne of your heart.

(Blow a kiss from heart and mouth)

The Sun

I represent the sun

I Am the face that shines eternally

and before which the darkness rolls away

I AM the Profuse Giver of Abundance.

Oh my sweet sister Jenny unto whom I send this kiss, may you behold in all things great and small the Eternal Beauty of the One Truth.

(Blow a kiss from heart and mouth)

Moon

I represent the Moon

What ever exists

Is as a ripple on the surface of the stream

But all are of One Substance

Thus all share in the quality

Of the stream itself

Which is the mirror of myself to myself

The root of all remembrance.

Oh my sweet sister Jenny unto whom I send this kiss, may all your actions be established on the sure foundation of the One Truth

(Blow a kiss from heart and mouth)

Mars

I represent Mars

I Am the mouth breathing forth the Breath of Life

I Am the all Devouring One

Where unto all things return

Destruction is the foundation of existence

And the tearing down is merely

The assembling of material

For a grander structure.

Oh my sweet sister Jenny, unto whom I send this kiss, may all your thoughts words and deeds be established in the strength and justice of the one truth.

(Blow a kiss from heart and mouth)

Mercury

I represent Mercury

I Am life itself

And without mind there is no life

I Am the essence of mind

And the essence of mind Is Will

All created will are reflections of my Will

And the essence of that Will

What is it but Desire.

Oh my sweet sister Jenny, unto whom I send this kiss may all that you do radiate the Eternal Splendor of the One Truth.

(Blow a kiss from heart and mouth)

Jupiter

I represent Jupiter

Forms are as vases into which I pour

The precious perfume of mine inmost essence

And where I Am

There must truth abide

For every vessel is an aspect of me… the Most High.

Oh my sweet sister Jenny, unto whom I send this kiss, may you find in all things The mercy and benevolence of the One Truth.

(Blow a kiss from heart and mouth)

Robbi, "Repeat after me,"

Jenny Jenny Jenny

love love love

laugh laugh laugh

dance dance dance

bump bump bump

grind grind grind

jump jump jump

run run run

Shake Shake Shake

Jenny Q we love you. Jenny Q we love you. Jenny Q we love you.

(everybody ululate and blow kisses)

Sweet sister Jenny unto whom we blow these kisses, by these blessings may you attain Enlightenment, having attained Enlightenment, may you defeat all evil, through the endless storms of birth, illness, old age and death, may you help all beings, to cross the ocean of the suffering of the world.

Pray of Compassion

AUM.

karin

golden net

I held a piece of a golden net that supported your physical body while your soul wrestled with its challenges. I was massaging our friend Alexis when he said, "Oh, by the way," and let fall the news that you were losing limbs to the fight.

What was it all about, Jenny? I'm sure you must wonder. It's a hideous experience to have to go through, your journey, but I know you to be a serious, gifted and determined healer. This is how true healers are made, I believe. We are shaped by the Creator and are forged in the furnace of enormous adversity. The heat of the furnace, my dear, has a tremendous amount to do with how capable a sword we will become in service to the forces of light.

michelle q

mom missed nothing

We had a million setbacks. Her labs were constantly reviewed and every drop in hematocrit or platelets was lamented and worried over. Every new wound culture had us going crazy. She had surgery after surgery and endless nighttime hours were spent putting all of our energy into that next part of the body that had to heal or start to work on its own again. One night Jenny almost bled out in the middle of the night from a fresh surgical wound and the only indicator that it was happening between blood draws was that my mom noticed that Jenny started to "look pale." My mom missed nothing. While she was still intubated, my mom and I held her and sang each time they suctioned her throat. "May the Lord bless and keep you..." For Jenny the suction was torture and the nurse knew exactly when in the song to do it as quickly as possible. I contacted colleagues who are Reiki Masters and asked them to perform remote Reiki. They did graciously and let me know that my sister's energy is spunky.

We had a million small triumphs. Little things like the glorious joy of a wet mouth sponge on a dry tongue. When Jenny was finally allowed to suck on ice cubes, we guiltily kept sneaking her more than she was allowed...there is no arguing with Jenny's raised eyebrow! Jamming out to the Go-Go's while we did the Physical Therapy exercises that we were instructed to do. Gentle morning "facials" with damp cloths, eye drops, mouth rinse and lip salve. And we had big triumphs. Having the ventilation tube removed! The continual dialysis stopped! The bowels started to move!!! I was actually in the cafeteria when I heard that it happened and ran up to the room to do a crazy 'poopoo in the potty' dance while the residents were still in the room. Jenny laughed and told the residents "she is actually a doctor!" as they stared at me in amazement.

jenny
popcorn

there was a new nurse on staff one night.. i hadn't met him before, and he told me he was a traveling nurse. a floater.

i don't think he got the memo that i was on an ice restriction, whatever that means.

i could have ice, but only a very small amount. they wanted me to only have a cube every so often. but it was the only solid food i ate, so i craved it and often tried to manipulate whoever was with me to give me more than i was supposed to have..

my siblings, or whoever was sitting with me at the moment, would sneak extra pieces of ice, which i would greedily devour.

this night was a lonely one. my mom had someplace to go, myshkin wasn't there and i was alone in the room. this didn't happen very often, so i had nothing to complain about. but it was quiet, and i was restless and in pain.

this new nurse was sympathetic.. he stuck around and asked if i needed anything, probably more times than was necessary. he checked in on me often..

he propped me up in bed and turned on a movie..

i had been in this hospital room for months already- hazy, foggy, spacey.. months of staring at the television screen with pictures of streams and fish and birds, with a quiet classical-music soundtrack.. i couldn't have anything else on that screen.. anything else stressed me out.. i couldn't really focus, and everything seemed to move too fast..

pictures could be traumatic..

one day, my dad was so tired of those damn birds that he switched the channel to the local news.. there was a fire.. casualties.. was it close to where we were?

i stared at the screen in panic.. my eyes must have had a frantic look, because my mom yelled at my dad and turned it back to my birds..

you see, i would stare so hard at those nature scenes in order to force myself into them.. into the water.. allowing it to cool me, flow over me.. especially in times of extreme pain.. it was a respite.. a sanctuary..

well, this night, the nurse put on a movie.. it was the first time i had the clarity of thought to follow a story line..

what i didn't know was that my little brother was worried about me..

concerned that i might not regain my full cognition.. maybe i wasn't following any conversation to an end.. he asked my folks to buy me an ipad so that i could watch shows on netflix, just to train myself to be able to concentrate for a good twenty-five minutes..

but this night, the nurse turned on a harry potter movie.. and he brought me

a whole cupful of ice.. it was really hard for me to feed myself, so he turned me in such a way that i could hold the cup up to my mouth and shimmy a cube into it with a spoon and a movement of my head..

i got pretty of good at it, actually.

there i lay, all by myself, crunching away on this who-needs-pop-corn-when-you-can-have-ice, watching a movie and feeling like a queen..

and that nurse, he kept bringing me those cups full of ice.. i am pretty sure he never saw someone so pleased with a feast of fro-zen water.. perhaps he was enjoying how happy he was making somebody..

i knew that if any of the usual staff saw me in my room, three in the morning, crunching away on cup after cup of ice, there would be a stop put to it immediately..

i was on a serious fluid restriction due to kidney insufficiency..

so as i happily crunched, i kept sneaking glances at the door, won-dering how long this heaven was going to last..

elise

fire and chaos

Patricia and I were visiting her in the ICU, gloves on and hopeful, so happy to see her and have the opportunity to share love.

I decided to offer some energy work while Patricia talked with her and comforted her with her sweet nature of ease. I began a very gentle session as she drifted in and out of consciousness.

During the session, my hands were getting hotter than they ever had, and I thought perhaps because of the rubber gloves. Then she began getting hot. I lightened my intentions and gentled the session, and she still grew hotter, and hotter, and my own heat was so high that Patricia made a comment about how red I was getting.

I closed the session and almost simultaneously her temperature made one of the machines go into alert and another part of one of the machines break. The worry in the room was as loud as the fire that was running through her body...

And I felt responsible.

Doctors rushed in and fiddled with her machines and tubes and looked at her with concern, whispering edgily while trying to understand what happened to the machines- unsure of how to repair them.

Jenny's mom looked at me seriously with strained compassion.

They gave me ice to put on her forehead and I talked her through visions of glaciers as she moved in and out of consciousness, and Patricia spoke to her about her daughter and all good things in a relaxed and reassuring way.

Slowly, slowly she moved back and forth between fire and stabilization, and slowly it was clear that it was time for us to go, and slowly we went home and hoped she would stay stable and that the fire would stay tamed.

robbi

penny for your thoughts

One day after the usual Godammit, a new thought came to me as I turned onto Star Lane. I thought, I am going to nickname Jenny. She will from now on be called Penny. You see, she wasn't very tall before anyway, she was if one could say a quarter height before, but now she has been short changed, and is just a penny. Get it? "Short changed." I amuse myself, I blow my own mind and laugh out loud. But a penny is the best thing. A lucky penny, penny for your thoughts, penny for a kiss, take care of the pennies and the dollars take care of themselves, pennies from heaven. Yes, I will call her Penny, Penny Lane. But no, seriously now, how will I deal with her? Will I look into her eyes – oh yes remember those eyes, dark black listening pools? God forbid, what am I gonna do, or say to her? Make jokes ?? Tease her? Hey shorty, come here! Or will I be all solemn and serious? Hmm, what will she say when I see her? She's not going to be the same person I knew before. They must have therapists for us, her friends and family, Psychological Adaptation to Amputation. Google it, Robbi. Oh don't worry, Jenny will teach you a thing or two. And BOOM! When that thought hit, I transformed.

elise

conundrum

It is perhaps easier to trust in the life process when it is out of our hands, but when our hands may have played a part in the turn of the wheel, everything changes.

If she had died that day, the day I laid my hands on her, I would have felt responsible.

If she'd had a healing flash, then it was the doing of Spirit-Source-Mystery.

What a conundrum I was in now...a choice began to form..

Stay on the path as a healing facilitator and risk accidentally being a part of tipping someone over into the beyond, or withdraw from the path and play it safe?

Is there is such a thing?

I imagine every practitioner runs across this question at some point in their life– but this was the first time it had occurred to me that what I'd been doing all of my life (and what my mother has done all of her life, and my grandfather before her), may actually not be appropriate after all.

Who was I to get involved in someone's possible fate?

Who was I to think I could guide the path to someone's healing?

How arrogant of me to lay my hands on someone and think that it would help them?

jessie mae

in threes

Some superstitions you never want to come true. But as I have grown, I learned that they carry their own weight in validity. Things do come in threes. In the months leading up to Jenny's dangerous sickness, I had learned that my father was going into an assisted living facility and hospice. I realized he would never see me married or with children. I learned what it meant to be present with all forms of family, biological or chosen. I learned that my sweetheart's dog, Phoenix, who I loved as my own, would be passing shortly as well. So I embraced the swelling grief that was about to come, the initiation into the stench of death that is inevitable to us all and makes you nauseated and fall to your knees. Phoenix's death was a ceremony of the highest kind, my love and I held him sandwiched between our hearts and sobs as he whispered his last breaths into the salted sunset of Moonstone Beach. From there, we drove to sit with my father's rapidly declining body and mind. For the next few weeks, I would glean what I could from the little I knew from him. I would feed his frailness, hoping he would get better. But he didn't. He would die a day before the new year, and I would hold his hand one last time desperately seeking the similarities and differences between us, before my sweetheart and I would lift his body into a bag and say goodbye to a part of my existence.

After what I thought was the dust beginning to settle, I visited my beloved in Portland and her roommate came home to tell us in a frantic upset that Myshkin's girlfriend, Jenny, was in the hospital and dying. In a rush of panic and confusion of how this roommate could know some intimate details of one of my dearest long-time friends, I somehow managed to find out the hospital she was at and called to demand some answers. I spoke to Joyce, who, rightly so, was dubious of my call. Someone she had only met a handful of times over the course of fifteen years. She herself was obviously trying to understand the mystery of her little sister's dying life. In that moment I felt helpless to the situation. I had just assisted two souls into death two weeks prior. But this one was out of my hands. This body was too young to die. I couldn't move. I was frozen in fear and grief. This COULD NOT be the third death. I needed to know what I could do with the little I had. Elise became my interpreter. Almost daily I would receive updates on her condition and instructions on what to visualize for Jenny's health and healing. Elise would tell me that she was drifting away. That she was talking. That she was in a coma. That she was being transferred to another hospital. That her body was dying. That they were amputating her legs, her fingers. Her body was necrotizing but they were somehow keeping her alive. Or rather, she was keeping herself alive. And then...

she lived.

After endless surgeries, skin grafts, tubes, drugs, and constant monitoring, the greatest person in the world lived. Whether on her own terms or the hundreds if not thousands of people, praying for her life to keep living, she did.

jessie mae
whatever it takes

My courage and strength to see her came four months later. I arrived in Joshua Tree to see Elise to thank her for holding me in the container of healing for Jenny and understand what I was about to see in our strong and fragile friend. I went to see Myshkin to share with her very recognizable far off stares of exhaustion, trauma, and the need for ice cream. And then I drove west.

Jenny was still in critical care, in and out of consciousness from the cocktail of painkillers. I arrived in the allotted window of allowed visitors. I made sure to thoroughly wash my hands, make sure my clothes were clean, and if I needed to sneeze, blow into the crook of my arm, as per Yazzy's instructions. I found an unrecognizable being in the bed. Her hair shaved and silver white. Wires and tubes hovered over, under and into her. Her skin was ashen. Her legs were missing from the knees down. But my friend did NOT participate in the superstitious folk tale of death coming in threes.

Jenny's mother sat me down to explain how it all worked around there. She was solid, calm, and confident with a vigilant eye that only mothers carry. I brought my tuning forks to offer a small treatment for her healing. Jenny greeted me with that same enthusiasm that she always had in the past for everyone she loves. And then I began. Jenny fell asleep and I sat with her mother.

Her mom pulled out a huge crochet needle with the letter Q on it. She said she needed to teach herself how to crochet, so she could teach Jenny when she got out. I asked her how often she came to the hospital, and she told me every day. All day. She told me she slept there. I saw her notice the subtle sounds and shifts of Jenny's movements and witnessed her alerting the nurses of changes. She said, "You do whatever it takes to make sure your children are safe."

Jenny was so cared for by the hospital, her family and her community, that she was being willed to live. That's what you do for a friend who shows you your worth. That's one of the things that makes Jenny precious.

Jenny did die. But She returned as a saint, a goddess, living to tell us how to shine bright.

I left the hospital and drove north for ten hours sobbing for my dear friend's life, the near loss of it and the incredible miracle of its return.

robbï

there will be dancing

The thought thrilled me, Godammit! Jenny is going teach us all a lesson! A day or so later, I stumbled upon a Youtube video of a woman amputee, I don't recall her name, she had won skiing championships, and was now in a dance competition, doing this complex thrilling dance, it was amazing! I screamed in Joy. Godammit Jenny is gonna dance!! I sent the video to close Facebook brothers and simply wrote, "there will be dancing!"

Slowly without much thinking, I became excited about the future, I sent a message with Myshkin to Jenny and all it said was "silly girl!" You see, that's a thing a brother would say to a sister who might be worrying or scared of something – "silly girl!" It's a brother's way of saying, I love you sister, don't worry about a thing. I don't know how that all happened inside me really, but I was no longer afraid. Something snapped. And every now and again I was imagining Jenny standing in front of me. You see? My mind makes shit up and I talk to people in my head, long conversations, and in my mind I was like, "okay Penny – what's next?" It reminded me of the movie Jonathan Livingstone Seagull. The scene where Jonathan the seagull perfects flying at the speed of a hawk but accidently smashes into a rock and is killed. There is a moment of silence, as Jonathan lies on the rock, dead as a door nail, and then the voice of the Master says, "Okay get up, next lesson." I was living this now. This was actualizing within me, I was like "Okay Penny, what's next!?" I felt healed.

willow

day after day

I was so grateful for Facebook and your friends, especially Kripa and Maya, and the created websites, as they kept me in touch with you and your long, challenging healing journey. I knew I was not alone in lighting your candle day after day during waking hours in my home, nor was I alone in visualizing your healing. Although nearly fourteen hundred miles away from Joshua Tree, here in Vancouver, I felt part of the community around you and all its reaches, literally all over the world. To be part of that is one of the most sacred blessings I have in my life—and there have been many.

myshkin

let the healing begin

It was such a long slow ride, that hospital time. So many days of sitting on that bench, so many nights sleeping on it, getting up to check on her with every murmur, every change in tone from the monitor, those nerve-wracked companions. And so precarious, so many times we almost lost her again. First there were more infections, so we had to change rooms and take down the wall of pictures and letters we had taped up to keep her connected to her life. In the new room nothing was allowed on the walls. She was in isolation the entire stay, meaning gowns, gloves and masks always on when in the room with her. In March or April, she began to throw everything up, couldn't hold anything down, became physically incapable of getting nutrition. She bottomed out at eighty pounds, almost starved right there in the middle of Orange County. She started to turn around with fresh juices her mom began bringing from the health food store. Her father brought a small fridge into the room, her mother packed it full, and she was able to start eating again. No more bags of corn syrup and vitamins tubed into her intestine. She moved on to fresh yogurt and organic foods, whatever sounded good to her we brought. What a joy to see her eat!

I tend to think I have a pretty well rounded social history. I've worked many kinds of jobs, and as a touring musician have met a lot of people, from varied circumstances and parts of the map. But I have never really known many medical people, and those months at UCI were revelatory. Some of the kindest and bravest people I have been lucky enough to know worked in that burn unit. The nurses were beyond amazing, pushing for things they knew would be good for Jenny. Robin and Dennis began taking her outside when she still couldn't sit up. They had something I believe they called a cardio chair that they shifted her on to, strapped her in to, and tilted up, so that she could see the outside world from a not-quite-horizontal position. Trees and sky, open space, the sweet air, after months in a room looking at a ceiling or wall. This too was a turning point. Jenny in contact with her spirit's food, the good earth. Let the healing begin now, and truly.

jenny

surrounded by greatness

i was so blessed in that hospital.. i was surrounded by greatness.. it wasn't only that my mama sat in my room by my bedside night after night after night.. or that my siblings were there again and again.. or that i had a fiancée and that she was by my side..

yes, all of this is true..

but i was also surrounded by the most amazing team of doctors and nurses..

those doctors— young, smart, eager— would come visit me, one after the other, sometimes as early as four in the morning on their rounds..

my two head surgeons were doctor joe and doctor bernal..

doc joe was the man who had gotten me a bed at uc irvine medical center.. my dad had sent him pictures of my initial wound, of the necrotizing flesh, and this compassionate, brilliant wound care surgeon secured me a place in their burn unit..

doctor bernal was a young, rock-star surgeon who treated me and my family with such compassion.. she was barely thirty plus and she was a deadhead, which somehow felt like home..

and the nurses.. how were we so blessed? they treated us so superbly that mysh and i often referred to them as our nurses..

so many wonderful ones that would come back, day after day, and treat us as if we were family..

dennis would come to my room with a new pack of gum for me, or a smile and a joke.. i got to know news of his partner, his dog..

candy, veronica, julie..

and robin was so close that i began to feel anxious if more than a couple of days went by and i didn't see her.. she was so competent and fought mercilessly to get me whatever she felt i needed.. she had a magical ability as a nurse, could find anything wrong and fix it..

she checked in with me even when i wasn't her patient..

amy was my hydro nurse.. this was a process that had to happen daily.. it was a burn unit, and though i wasn't a victim of fire or chemicals, my skin fell off as though i was.. so i had to have this treatment where they scrub and clean the old granulating tissue that was growing over the wounds..

what a terrible and dreaded time each day..

the hydro team would start setting up the special table full of the necessary gear about a half hour before, and fifteen minutes or so before the treatment, they came in to give me extra pain and anti-anxiety medication.. by then, you really needed the anti-anxiety meds.. then they would enter— confident, kind, determined..

the pain that was a part of this process is difficult to describe, even impossible to really recall.. only the dread..

i never really wanted to take pain meds, but amy wasn't having it.. they're not supposed to give you meds unless you ask for them, but amy would sternly order me to ask for them when she saw me struggle..

these special nurses are angels, able to withstand the fear and anxiety in their patients as they do their necessary work, even through the pain it is causing..

one day, after the treatment, they weighed me and i had reached eighty pounds.. everything was so hazy at this point and i didn't comprehend any details, but i somehow understood the gravity of the moment..

and then amy put her face an inch from my face and yelled, 'if i come in tomorrow and you have lost more weight— if you lose one more pound— YOU ARE GOING TO DIE!'

now, you have to realize that at this time in my ordeal, i was only half there, drifting in and out of consciousness, not able to hold a conversation without trailing off..

but i heard amy.. that cut through the fog..

and while i wasn't eating, full of stomach tubes and IV nutrition and had no control over my own body weight, i didn't lose one more pound after that day..

something shifted in me and i slowly started to thrive..

ted

a song for jenny q

I walked from the Beatnik to Grateful Desert and Natural Sisters and back. Along the way, near Gonzo's infamous, empty, blue building, I called Jenny on the cell phone, not expecting her to answer, in her hospital room. When she did, I was surprised. She sounded like a child but still, very clear. Definitely Jenny. She wanted to know how I was, how Sage was doing. We only spoke for a few minutes but for the first time, I could hear that she was going to make it.

The following day I went for my morning walk, barefoot, to try out this idea of 'earthing' that I'd been hearing about. It was springtime, and the ground was filled with tiny yellow flowers, and as I walked along, a song came to me.

Jenny Q

Walking barefoot In the Desert

Walking barefoot for you

On a lovely spring morning and I know if you could

You'd be out here walking too

Stopping to see all the flowers and pull out a thorn or two

Pulling it all out for you - putting it out ther.

And I know that you're going to pull through

I'm running my hand through your long brown hair

My fingers over your eyes

I know they've been crying - mine have been too

Every day they grow a little more wis.

and Childlike

Childlike

I could tell when you answered the phone

You're not used to having no choice

I know you're ready to come back home

I can hear the longing in your voice

So Childlike

That beautiful boy and that brave little girl

Were playing with the robots one day

The animatrons were dancing

You should hear the music they play

He was showing her all around the place

A gentle little man

I can see she's a strong little girl and she's growing up

As fast as she can

Childlike

Childlike

Playing my guitar for you

Thinking of those big brown eyes

Awakening to a brand new world

Every day a little more wise

and Childlike

tania

mrs q

I learned things. Such as Mrs. Qaqundah is a literary lady. She reads, writes, and does various things to keep her brain active. Like Mrs. Q, most of the Qs have good stamina. Mrs. Q is, like Jenny Q, a deeply spiritual woman. As Jenny Q, she is a source of powerful energy — which explains where Jenny Q gets her magnetism and strength, at least in part. Mrs. Q laughs and sings and dances about, she reads, writes, edits, has conversations, cooks and eats food with gusto. There is so much overwhelming love and shared joy between Mrs. Q and her daughter that it is confounding that the hardship that also therein also exists.

joyce q
mom mysh

Jenny met Myshkin about eight months before she got sick. Jenny was giddy in love from the start. Myshkin is a musician who travels a lot but from the few times we all spent time together, it was obvious they were a great couple.

November 2013, Jenny and Myshkin came to San Diego and a group of us went to see the band 'Beats Antique' at the House of Blues. It was packed but the music was great and Jenny was rocking out dancing in pure bliss. I remember my friend screaming out to me over the loud music that Myshkin had lucked out. Later on, I would think how Jenny had lucked out.

Jenny realized she was gay and started dated women in her early twenties. She wrote a letter to my mom explaining the way she felt but my mom pretended she never got the letter. She could never accept that Jenny was gay. The subject was dropped when, in her thirties, Jenny eventually fell in love and married Todd but after their divorce, she started dating women again.

Jenny did not push the subject with my mom until she met Myshkin and wanted to bring her into our family. My mom turned to ice whenever this subject came up.

When Jenny ended up in the hospital and the whole family was brought together, we thought this event would help my mom push aside her feelings regarding same-sex couples and support Jenny in her wishes to love Myshkin. Unfortunately, we were wrong.

Myshkin and my mom butted heads the entire hospital stay. Of course Myshkin wanted to also care for Jenny and be her support. They would be together in Jenny's room for hours at a time and my mom would not acknowledge her presence. If I was in the room, my mom would refer to Myshkin as 'her' and never call her by name. It was maddening but there was no reasoning with my mom on this subject. She even started blaming Jenny's illness on Myshkin. The behavior was cruel.

Myshkin is not a push-over and demanded her rights. Through my dad and myself, we were able to negotiate times that Myshkin could be alone with Jenny. Even when Jenny was strong enough to express her wishes that she wanted to be with Myshkin and that she wanted my mom to accept and get to know her partner, my mom refused.

One evening, early on in Jenny's illness, my parents and us four siblings were having dinner in the hospital cafeteria. My older brother John made the astute observation that we need to accept and welcome Myshkin into our family. Besides Yazzy, Jenny needed something beautiful like a budding relationship to look forward to. Driving Myshkin away might actually affect Jenny's health. My mom did not see it this way.

jenny

mama roses

love is often so complicated.

we say that love is not always a bed of roses,

but i disagree..

it is exactly like a bed of roses, full of beauty and sometimes you get pricked.

sometimes you bleed.

this is very much the case with my mama.

i will take the pain because of the beauty of love that i cannot live without.

myshkin

jenny's mom

Eventually I have to write about Jenny's mother. I am not excited about it. I am wary. I don't want to throw blame around, I don't want to make anyone suffer, I don't want to make anything worse for Jenny. We have decided, those of us working on this book, that we will write everything, and edit later. Anything that is too hot. Too raw. But we will write freely, because the writing itself shall be healing, we decided. So here I go. Jenny has a family full of amazing people. Super achievers, bright and kind and close to each other. And those five kids, they are the life's work of someone who is surely an amazing woman. Unfortunately, I will likely never get the chance to find out first hand, because she will not speak to me or acknowledge my existence, except on the very rare occasions she needs something from me. Jenny warned me from the beginning and I said, "Oh but she will know ME, she will learn to like me, I can be very charming, I respect people and and- well, just you wait."

Well . . . we're still waiting. At this point I've given up hope, which is something I don't do often. But I have never really met homophobia face to face before. Or someone quite so stubborn. The first time we met, Suad took a step away from me, as if scared. The second time she didn't say a word to me, and then the long silence ensued. I spoke to her often, those long months we shared so much time in a small, stress-filled room with Jenny. If she responded at all, it was with a sneer and a withering glance. She would talk to everyone around us lovingly. She would greet the sweet janitor like a long lost sister. Only thrice I remember her speaking to me directly. At the Palm Springs hospital, she told me I was not to say I was Jenny's partner when introducing myself to a doctor. On the first night at UCI, she turned to me and said, "When you see me speaking Arabic with someone, do not say you are her partner. We do not have such a thing." I said, " But you do" and she said "We have the decency to hide it." I said, " I think that's very sad". I knew I was treading on cultural ground I knew nothing of. But I also knew that I had dedicated myself to this woman between us, and really, I had no room for cultural sensitivity when it came to being beside my love as she lay so close to death. I was ever grateful that we live in the time and place we do, the hospital staff was unfailingly supportive of Jenny and I.

Jenny's mom would not leave her side for almost two months. I very rarely had even ten minutes alone with her during this time. I tried to sleep in Jenny's room a few of the early nights, but Suad would not lay down when I was there. She would sit up all night. And her mom was already putting herself under enough stress, we all feared she would get sick next. So I left at night, occasionally to the Qaqundah's next door neighbor's house, their family friends of decades. Most times I stayed at the hospital, I slept in a small room down the hall, where the staff was not supposed to let us sleep, but did. Eventually I drove to stay with Jenny's dear friend Laila, who contacted me one day and told me to come stay. She was such a perfect hostess, so kind and relaxed and such an old friend of the whole family, I felt I knew her right away, and she helped me steer through some of the harder family dynamics.

At some point, the social worker on the burn unit saw how I was being shut out and worked to get Jenny to create a kind of schedule of visitation, so Jenny herself could ask for some time alone with me. Then the the hospital could attempt to enforce that schedule. The first night we had together, Yazzy was there too, so Ashley the social worker called it family night, made a big plan around it, brought us a bag full of games and snacks.

Before our first family night, I tried to make some alone time happen myself. I decided I would have a talk with Suad. Joyce came in with me but left after a minute or two, fuming with frustration. I told Suad I wanted to talk to her about a schedule so that Jenny and I could have some time alone together and Jenny could get a break from the tension between us and she just kept repeating "There will be no schedule." Her husband left the room too, none of the family willing to argue my case lest her wrath spread. I kept saying I wanted some time alone with my fiancé and she kept shouting no, and eventually I said something cutting about wanting to control her powerless daughter, which I have forgotten now, but felt true at the time.

Sometime later on, in April maybe, Suad said to Jenny "Of course Yazzy will come stay with me when school lets out," and I freaked out. I suspected she wanted Yazzy as a first step to getting Jenny to come stay with her, as a first step to having her not come back to Joshua Tree, her life, or me. So I talked to Jenny about getting married while she was still in the hospital and she agreed. My family urged me to do so, to have some legal control in the situation. When Jenny told her father, HE freaked out. I started getting texts from her sisters urging me not to go through with it. I began to feel distrusted, like I was trying to take advantage of Jenny in her weak state. I was seeking to protect what I knew was important to her, the life she had built, her home. These were the darkest days between myself and Jenny's family. I had good and growing relationships with her siblings, but now I felt myself as the outsider with them as well. Everyone felt threatened and we all threw up our walls.

That storm passed, but the icewall lives on between Jenny's mom and I. I am not allowed in her house and I try not to be in her presence. It's depressing, and terrible for Jenny. She does her best to navigate it, and I work hard to hold more compassion than anger or hurt.

jenny
ay'aab

ay'aab.

a word i've heard so many times in my life. it was yelled at me when i was wearing a skirt too short, lipstick too dark or used words not allowed in my vocabulary.

a word probably used most often by any arab bringing up children in the united states. this word has many meanings, but it is probably applied most to teenage girls here in america...

this is a word that is engrained in me and pops up every time i think of publishing this book. at the idea of telling my innermost secrets. of airing family laundry in public.

ay'aab.

vulgar.

lynne
myshkin

Myskin was thrown into finding true and amazing love, then into chaos. She became an instant mother and caregiver. Where did she find the energy amongst all the grief? Myshkin held so much strength and, when she needed, confided in friends of her new community. Her strength and courage continue to be awe-inspiring.

jenny
the spell

"myshkin," i croak, "it's a new song..

i haven't heard this one.."

"myshkin, i am so happy you have a new song.."

i am panting now, with the exertion of speaking.

this was the time that was after the coma, but before my consciousness was stable, more in the clouds than on earth. i don't think i yet remembered how to move, and my days were filled with bits and pieces of reality..

much of that being pain. and more of it being joy to see my loved ones around me.

"it's so beautiful.."

"honey, i've been playing it for you for weeks now."

it was the first time i remember hearing it.

she calls it harmless.

i call it the spell.

myshkin

the spell

Every step I step I'm gonna pull off all your hurt

Gonna put it in the earth where it's harmless

Gonna put it in the earth

With every step I step

Every step I step I'm gonna pull off all your hurt

Plant it in the dirt where it's harmless

Plant it in the dirt

With every step I step

Every breath I breath I'm gonna gather all the light

Streaming in all day and night from every corner of the sky

And all the wild hearts we know that know us

In this world so wide

Every breath I breath I'm gonna gather all the light

I'm gonna gift it to your flesh cause it's holy, it's holy

Gonna gift it to your holy flesh

And your holy mind

Every beat you beat you're gonna open all your cells

You're gonna feed them on that sweet light

They're flowers they're flowers

Gonna feed them on your sweet dignity

They're flowers

Every blink you blink you're gonna see a whole new world

Cause you're a powerhouse my girl

You are power

The spell I'm spelling in your ear

The spell I spell to keep you here

You almost flew right out the door

I want more

I want more

I want more I want more

And every move I move I'm gonna make that move with you

Cause you are ten tenths of my view

You fill my sky, you do

You fill my sky

With your big eyes

And every step I step I'm gonna pull off all your hurt

Put it in the earth where it's harmless

It's harmless, it's harmless

jenny
angels

there were the most amazing angels that led me through that dark and strange tunnel.. we know all the main characters.. yazzy, my mama, myshkin, my siblings, my community, my nurses and doctors..

oh, but there was this one man.. i dream of him sometimes.. his name is moses.. he was one of the lift team members.. they would come around every two hours to turn me so that i didn't develop decubitus ulcers from not being able to move.. a painful and dreaded time.. every two hours, night and day..

but moses.. he would light up the room whenever he came in, yelling my name as though encountering an old friend by surprise.. each and every time he stepped into my room.. every two hours..

after some weeks, we started talking about sunrises and sunsets and how inspiring these times were to us.. i told him that taking photographs of the magnificent sunrises that i encountered had been a hobby of mine.. on my morning runs five times a week.. every week..

he started coming in with pictures of sunrises and sunsets from when he was off work just to bring them to me.. to show me the world was still beautiful out there..

i looked forward to moses coming to see me.. even to move my broken body, because he brought sunshine to my life..

myshkin

lion heart crazy ride

My Jenny, lion heart. Smile like a supernova, new world every time, my Jenny. My Jenny, canine eyes. Trust and giving the only thing I see in them. But sometimes it's fear. I hope I never see fear living in your eyes again—my Jenny.

Your mama calls you that too, and someone I never met confessed in a letter taped to the wall here that she does too, though her grasp is surely more tenuous.

So our Jenny. Nobody gets all of you. And this is now obvious. Apparently not even yourself, our Jenny. Wounded and sacrificed and please Goddess, don't let the pain last. Please Goddess, let her ride out the pain and not be revisited. Amen. No, Awomen.

Ah wow. Jenny on the crazy ride. Let's keep it fun she says, as the cart reaches the top of the track and tips. Down. And she's gone, taken by the pain and the killers of it, down and around the corner and into the tunnel and occasionally, as we run along above ground, there is a window, she opens both eyes big. She connects, and then gone again rushing on her underground river, as we trudge along on top, in the sunshine, hoping it's helping her, this subterranean time, hoping the waters are healing, the sleep not too deep, as we crawl along on top, lazy, fed, anxious, tired, angry, loving, swimming on our bellies on the sand in the sun, waiting. Jenny. my Jenny I almost can't remember your old voice. Oh there, there it is. On the phone saying HI, HI BABE with a sweet little growl, and your laugh. And your kiss.

And I see the way you are. The way you make everybody feel: loved, seen, real.

ronda

music fest skype

In May 2014, while Jenny was still in the hospital, her lovely partner, Myshkin was performing at the Joshua Tree Music Festival. I had heard so much about Myshkin from Jenny, but hadn't met her. I asked if I could record the set for Jenny. Then we had an even better idea.

So, I first got acquainted with Myshkin while crawling my way through the dirt, like a sloth, getting all the best angles I could of her. What most people thought was a recording for Jenny was a Skype session, with her secretly on the other end. She was watching us live from her hospital room! Needless to say, when people found out she was actually with us, we were all in tears. I was already convinced that if Jenny was so giddy about this Myshkin woman, that she must be fantastic, but what I was most impressed with was her strength and commitment to Jenny and her daughter. In the midst of all this craziness, Myshkin was just getting acquainted with our community. So many people's demands for answers to questions regarding Jenny's health, taking care of Yazzy, navigating the countless friends and family, and doing it all with grace and love, all the while holding strong for the most important thing to us, Jenny. During the rough seas, Myshkin was an anchor for Jenny, and still is today.

joycey 9
rehab

Mid June, Jenny was finally being transferred to a rehabilitation facility. After a large party with the hospital staff at UCI, Jenny wheeled herself to her home for the next month. This was the place where she learned to sit up and was eventually transferred to her wheelchair. Her legs were still too tender for prosthesis. She was building up her strength and recovering from her skin grafts.

After three weeks of living in the rehab and in celebration of learning how to transfer from a wheelchair into a car, I came to rejoice with Jenny, Yazzy and Myshkin. I brought take out Mexican food and we ate on the patio. Her doctor paid us a social visit and gave Jenny the OK to take a short outing!

Still in her hospital gown with tubes coming from her back collecting urine and several hospital bracelets announcing FALL RISK and other such information on her arms, Jenny gingerly but successfully transferred into my car. We all joyously piled in after her. I blared the radio and zoomed off. Jenny promptly vomited all of the burrito she ate for lunch. Claiming she was fine, we drove to the botanical gardens for a stroll. I knew the area well as I went to college in this small town of Claremont near Los Angeles. We ended up at an outdoor pub drinking pints of local microbrew. Of course Jenny was only able to have a few sips. The looks from the other patrons were hilarious as we wheeled Jenny into that bar. Funny enough, we spotted a nurse from the rehab who recognized her patient. After ascertaining that we weren't in trouble for allowing the patient to drink, the party began.

myshkin
rehab

Jenny was everywhere in the desert, even when she wasn't, her spirit in the soft air, her name on all lips, even the rocks and sky seemed to be calling her home. When the docs started talking about her leaving the ICU and going to a rehab, I visited four of them, took notes and talked them over with her and Joyce. It was our hope to find her a place closer to home, and one of the hospitals down the hill was looking like a good bet. But the burn unit social worker took the reigns and signed her up for a month at a place I had visited in Pomona, over two hours away from home. It was very SoCal fancy, and had good staff and facilities for strengthening and transitioning. Before the month was over, she cooked her first meal — a gigantic tofu veggie stir fry! — in the tiny model kitchen off the gym. But she still had major open wounds, the skin graft donor sites on her back would not heal, and the place was not a hospital. The change in level of medical care was a shock.

It was such a major disappointment to have her still be so far away. I was gone the first time they had her transfer from the bed with a wooden transfer board, to a wheelchair, then from her wheelchair to a shower chair, but I was alone with her the next time, and I can't overstate how terrifying it was for both of us. Jenny was still so incredibly weak and in pain, floating above the ground, inching along a slick board on her torn up body, from one precipice to the next, going over a gaping canyon of bathroom floor two feet down.

By the time she learned how to scoot herself into a car and we took our first wild jaunt on the town, it was almost time to go home. I'm grateful for the time at rehab for the many ways they helped her start to regain control over her body again, but also for the weaning time from the amazing doctors and nurses at UCI. The shock of going home would have been even greater without it.

ted

robotic limbs

Sage and I went to see an exhibit by the French Canadian artist/ musician Maxime De La Rochefoucauld, in residence at the Harrison House, described as a "'magical kingdom of sound and stick figures with a mesmerizing sound art installation" featuring an analog robotic system, invented by De La Rochefoucauld." "A completely new kind of surround-sound robotic music theatre."

Maxime's kinetic animatrons were programmed to randomly 'play' Indian classical instruments, contributed by Amritakripa's partner Robbi Robb.

Sage liked the robots playing strange instruments in the straw bale temple of sound so well he got his mom to take him back the next day. We both thought Yazzy would like the show so we arranged to take her to Harrison House - thanks to its guardian spirit, Eva - on the final afternoon of Maxime's residency. Without wanting to say any-thing specific regarding Jenny or her new body, I wanted Yazzy to see these strange, beautiful, automated limbs Maxime had created, dancing and playing music.

felicia

footprints

The whole community in Joshua Tree has made such an impression on me. The level of love, care and kindness is something very special. The house never lacked in love or food or help or warmth or hugs. It was all genuine, full of the best of intentions. Everyone stepped in, as best as they could, into Jenny's giant footprints to keep it all going. It was a beautiful thing to witness and be a part of. All of it. The love, the community, Yazzy, Myshkin....

julia
rubber band bracelet

I was approached by three lovely young girls at the Springtime Joshua Tree Music Festival, one being Jenny's very own daughter Yazzy, along with Lola and another.

"Do you want to buy something?" the three said to me at once. I peered into the basket and gazed upon lovely rubber band bracelets of all different colors.

"Did you make these?" I asked.

"Yes", said Yazzy. "I am raising money for my mom's hospital bills."

"Oh how very beautiful, of course I'll buy one of these lovely bracelets," I said at once, my heart skipping a beat at the purity of what I was bearing witness to.

"I like this orange and blue one. How much is it?" I asked.

"It's two dollars," said Yazzy.

"No, it's five!" announced Lola.

"Oh yeah, it's five dollars," said Yazzy.

"Well, five dollars is well worth it because it's made with love." I said, handing the money over to Yazzy, who promptly stashed it safely into an envelope.

In the meantime, I donned the gorgeous, handmade, one-of-a-kind orange and blue rubber band bracelet.

"Thank you!" the three beauties exclaimed and skipped off to the next participant in this love story.

"Do you want to buy something?" I heard them say in unison.

And in unison this story continues to this very day, with Yazzy and her Mamas Jenny Q and Myshkin home together, safe and sound.

And they lived happily ever after.

paula

once upon a time

Once upon a time, the family and the village people sent out a great call to prayer. Knowing that in their physical presence the prayer would be all the more powerful, the women agreed on a ceremonial gathering. There was a "healing light" altar built in honor of their Sister. Everyone who entered brought an offering. They sat, and together they prayed. All took turns around the circle. Each person spoke of the vision they held. These visions were clear. Dancing, smiling.. healthy and happy Jenny. They felt joy in all these beautiful visions. They became uplifted and hopeful.

After that, there were many calls to gather again. The altar was left open for the people to come. And they did. Everyday. One by one. An unbreakable web of prayer and communication was spun. And soon, the news of progress began. The people rejoiced, and the cloud became lighter and lighter. The healing continued, the sun began to shine. And She danced again. So is the story of the Joshua Tree Miracle. The End.

or…The Beginning?

johnny q
herculean ordeal

When my cell phone rings at three a.m., I tend to ignore it and hope it's a wrong number, which is precisely what I did that one night in January, 2014. But when the cell call that night was followed by the house phone ringing seconds later, I knew I was about to receive unwelcome news. Stumbling to the phone in the dark, I expected to hear bad news about my elderly father, but in fact it was my dad himself on the other end of the call:

"Johnny, your sister Jennifer is in the hospital. She is in the ICU and is very, very sick… she probably will not survive. Come on the first plane so you can see her before it's too late. Joyce is here, Jimmy is already booking a flight from Sacramento and…"

What?? Jenny's in the hospital? What's wrong with her? How come I'm being told now when others are already there or on their way? I was still half asleep but could feel my guts tighten and my skin go numb with fear. My wife Regan had gone into the bathroom and I was vaguely aware of her asking what was wrong. I started to talk loudly into the phone.

"I don't think I can get a flight until six a.m., how much time does she have?"

My dad didn't hazard a guess, he just said something about sepsis and shock and told me to catch the first flight and rent a car at the airport. I agreed to be there as soon as possible and hung up the phone.

Regan walked up and hugged me while I sobbed.

A few minutes later I was on the internet booking the first flight out. After sending a quick email to work letting them know I would not be available, I threw a few clothes and a toothbrush into a bag and drove to the airport. I assumed I would be in Palm Springs for two or three days so drove my car to long-term parking and awaited the shuttle. Everything seemed to be moving too slow, a feeling accentuated by the forty minute security line at the terminal. By the time I wound through the line and sprinted to the gate, it was about about two minutes to departure, but the door to the plane was already shut. I begged the airline employee to let me on, explaining that my sister was in the hospital and may not make it long enough for the next flight out, but the unforgiving airline rules coupled with a lack of empathy from the austere clerk shut me down and I was forced to sit and wait for the next plane.

Maybe waiting was a good thing. It allowed to collect my thoughts and think about last words to Jenny, how I would help calm my mother, when I could fly my family out from the Bay Area for the funeral, what would be said at the sermon. Goddammit Jenny, what did you do? Jenny had gotten into medical predicaments before, having followed the Grateful Dead, travelled with Rainbow Gatherings, and gone by herself to Hawaii to live naked on a beach, where her health suffered from chronic neglect. And while it was never anything life-threatening, I couldn't help but think that Jenny had gotten caught back up in life and had forgotten to look after herself.

When I finally arrived to the hospital several hours later there was a crowd in the waiting room holding hands, singing and chanting. I knew they must be Jenny's friends and walked past them to the ICU clerk to ask about my sister. The old woman looked at me with sorrowful eyes and I became afraid I was too late. Then she told me to proceed to the ICU door.

A minute later, I was buzzed in where I found my dad sitting and chatting with the attending physician. My dad greeted me like it was just a normal day and introduced me to Jenny's doctor then gave me a hug. I ventured into Jenny's room where I found Myshkin singing at Jenny's feet and my mom sitting against the wall staring straight ahead. My mom's face was white and wet but she was not currently crying, she was just staring blankly across Jenny's bed, somewhat oblivious to my arrival.

And there was Jenny: unconscious, intubated, and connected to multiple IV lines. She was totally still except for her chest, forced up and down in regular rhythms by the mechanical respirator. Despite the missed flight, delayed rental car, and the one and a half hour drive from the airport, I had made it in time, she was still alive thank goodness. I said hello to my sister in what I hoped would be a steady, optimistic voice but it came out quiet and weak.

Finally my mom registered my presence, stood, threw her arms around my neck and yelled "Johnny! Look at your sister! Look at Jenny! Ya mamma! What is going on? What is wrong with her Johnny?!"

"I know. She's sick mom," was about all I could mutter.

I didn't know it then but this was the beginning of a very long, painful journey for my mother, one that would test her physically, mentally, emotionally and spiritually. It would bring out both the best and worst in a parent who had invested most of her adult life in her children.

Past experience had taught me that people react to crisis in very different ways. Some succumb immediately to helplessness and sorrow while others start to blame everyone from God to the afflicted. I usually look for an opportunity to mitigate the calamity, to find any hidden solution. Walking back to the nurses station to talk to the doctor, I began to understand that the fight was not over, that Jenny had a real, albeit slender chance of survival. She was on the brink of death but she wasn't yet dead. She had a dedicated team of specialists who were willing to try just about anything and so a treatment plan would be enacted and followed. I knew it would be a very long and complex recovery, with expectations and goals changing daily, but there was a chance.

Jenny had septic shock and the full cascade of complications that accompany that, including severe hypotension and disseminated intravascular coagulation (DIC). Jenny's blood was hyper-coagulating, cutting off circulation to her extremities and certain organs while the pressor medications, used to keep Jenny alive, also shunted blood from her extremities to her vital organs (heart, brain, lungs). What this basically meant was that in order to keep Jenny alive, we would have to sacrifice parts of her body, one at a time. This started with her toes and and tips of her fingers and progressed to parts of her bowel, skin, fingers, and eventually her legs.

The first day was very long, with lots of commotion in the waiting room while many of Jenny's friends arrived and cried. Many tried to enter her ICU room and some succeeded, but we quickly began to see that their presence was interfering with her care so we had to stop her friends from entering. Visitation would be restricted to immediate family and to Myshkin. My first night there was spent at Jenny's bedside reviewing her drug list, watching her vitals and double checking every medication given to her.

As a pharmacist I was focused on Jenny's medications. I had experience in ICU care while working at San Francisco General Hospital years back, but I was never emotionally bound to any patient like this and I quickly realized this was a disadvantage. I scoured the long list of drugs over and over again afraid to miss something and probably over-pestered Jenny's nurses. Thankfully my sister Joyce, a physician, was able to fill in certain deficiencies in my knowledge about Jenny's specific illness.

As the nights crept by, we all eventually became exhausted both mentally and emotionally. With so much crying and so little sleep, we tried to divide our presence in shifts to get some sleep, but our mom refused to leave Jenny's room except to go shower every other day. She wore down quickly and soon we were dividing our concern between Jenny and our mom.

About three days into the nightmare, one of the ICU attending physicians, seeing the desperate measures we were proposing, took us aside to explain that Jenny's chances were extremely slim. She reminded us that the difficulty in balancing the many aspects of Jenny's decline meant that every hour could mean an end to her struggle, and that at best Jenny had a ten percent chance of survival. This just made us more stubborn. I called my close friend Dr. William Miller, a hospitalist up in San Francisco, and asked for advice. I contacted work colleagues to help me sort out the complexities of Jenny's medication list, to look for potential drug interactions, duplications in therapy, and accuracy of dosing. My dad, Joyce and I took turns talking to the medical staff, corralling the specialists and asking for every potential intervention.

Keeping ourselves busy and exhausted helped us to ignore the fear and emotional pain. But about four days into Jenny's struggle, something happened which pierced through my optimism. Jenny's skin had been mottling since the beginning, demonstrating potential damage to other parts of her body. But standing there that afternoon, I reached down to take Jenny's hand and found three of her fingers on her right hand had turned black and had shriveled up into thin, dead twigs. Here was physical, undeniable proof that Jenny was dying and it cut through all my exhaustion and deliriousness and brought fresh hot tears to my eyes. The tears ran down my face and fell on Jenny's hand and the nurse rushed over with tissue to clean it up because any such exposure presented further infectious risk to my sister. I saw my sister Joyce and my brother Jimmy next to me and they too were distraught. It seemed we were losing Jenny after all.

It became clear that I would not be returning home any time soon so I had my wife ship my work computer down to me so that I could work and remain longer. I missed my kids terribly but managed to speak to them over the phone for a few minutes each day. My boss was immensely understanding and allowed me the flexibility to work from the hospital in Palm Springs.

We knew that Jenny was at risk of losing more than just her fingers. The DIC caused clots which blocked off peripheral blood vessels and capillaries. In addition, the pressor medication, used to maintain Jenny's blood pressure, was further shunting oxygen-rich blood away from the extremities toward more vital organs. This meant that Jenny was at risk of losing her kidneys, her bowel and other organs as well as her arms and legs. Our biggest fear was brain damage.

I think it was day five when I was standing by Jenny's bed while my sister Joyce was speaking to the nurse. My mom was at the ICU room entrance. Jenny had been in a coma for six days now and we weren't sure if her brain had already sustained irreversible damage. Some of her other extremities were showing signs of acute ischemia, including more fingers and her toes. I was staring at the screen where Jenny's vitals were scrolling by and looked down at Jenny's face just as she turned, opened her eyes, and looked right at me. This was different from the other times I could see her eyes, where dull, unfixed stares made clear a lack of consciousness. She was looking right at me, into my eyes. "Hi Jenny," came out of my mouth before I had a chance to think of something better to say. I turned to Joyce and my mom, "Guys, I think she's awake." The nurse came over and confirmed that Jenny was in fact conscious. Jenny had a look of concern and confusion on her face, like "What are you doing here?"

This was the first sign that Jenny might in fact survive. She still had a long, long way to go. She was transported by helicopter to the UCI Medical Center burn unit where a team of sub-specialists could better care for her. At UCI, she had the first of what would be over fifty surgeries to to relieve her kidneys, to remove fingers and bowel, to install a colostomy, to graft on cadaver skin and when that failed, graft her own autologous flesh, and to eventually remove both of her legs. We watched as Jenny was cut apart piece by piece, all with the goal of saving her life. The medical bill exceeded five million dollars.

At one point in the herculean ordeal, when she was more conscious and beginning to understand the extent of her situation, Jenny asked, "Isn't this too much for just one life?"

Not if it's your family.

Starting the Grateful Desert Herb Shoppe was a dream that I worked incredibly hard for, making myself finish an RN program before jumping into the risk of becoming a small business owner.

I was a single mom and needed to have something to fall back on.

Little did I know that becoming a registered nurse would make me so much more effective as an herbalist.

I was so proud of my little apothecary. Most of the shelves were filled with my personal altar items, as the bit of nest egg I had to buy inventory only filled a couple shelves. Thankfully, I had my own tincture line to help!

What a beautiful Grand Opening party we had!

Eva Soltes cut a big, red ribbon, Robbi Robb, Amritakripa and Clive Owen played;

Tasya and Eva danced; and we all ate chocolate and Arabic bits and drank wine.

The shoppe was blessed with community love.

Tasya Herskovits and
Eva Soltes

The Joshua Tree Music Festival is a place that beings our village together twice a year, every year.

Unless it is mad, passionate, extraordinary love,

it is a waste of time. There are too many mediocre things in life. Love shouldn't be one of them.

A copy of this poem, written by Tiffanie DeBartolo, hung in my bedroom for years, calling my love to me.

This kiss. In Long Beach the day of the initial surgery that preceded all the chaos..

This would be the last day that, without effort, I stood on my own two, booted feet.

*This girl is my greatest
inspiration and teacher.*

How blessed I am.

part three

coming home and love letters

jenny

wonder and joy

when i came home from the hospital, i felt the need to support my loved ones..

it seemed only fair.. they all held me while i was a patient.. so i felt it was my turn to hold my community..

every time i went to town, i would see multiple people who were so happy to see me and so relieved that i was alive and so horrified for me that i had lived through this experience..

that my legs were gone, my fingers..

i held so many people as they hugged me and cried..

i cried with each of them..

it was a catharsis for me each and every time i journeyed with a loved one down their road of grief for me. and it was a huge blessing, because i didn't have the opportunity to shove down my feelings of grief ..

i feel as though it helped me to cry all of my tears out early on..

ok, well, i still cry most days, but so many of them are tears of wonder and joy to be alive..

myshkin

she's coming home

She's coming home. getting closer

No more no more, Disneyland out the window

But real wonder

Each grain of sand's got her number, and wants her

And every wind that can sing

Singing for her, singing … soon

She's coming round the biggest mountain she ever did see

And we are cut out for so much more than we knew we could be

And time is a clown, times ten thousand all tumbling from one tiny seed

And it's all that we own, still we can't keep it captive, still we can't set it free

We just ride

Watch what the world does to our tender hide

And try

Try to stay tender inside

And she's coming home

That Scorpio moon caught me weeping in her spotlight between the trailers

And someone had sown something sad,

Strong and sacred in the center of the circus

And each way we turn, someone's holding up a corner of the circle

And the road goes on and on, ever longer, but that net is even stronger

When we dive

Shoot from those big guns up into the sky

Covered in ash and the sparks in our eyes

Trying to stay tender inside

And she's coming home

myshkin
shell shocked

I was so overjoyed to bring her back, such a highly anticipated moment. When I rolled Jenny into the house she had built nine years ago, she looked shell-shocked and climbed deep into herself, something that had not happened during all of the hospital and rehab time. The dream time had ended. She was home and the full impact of the incredible change and loss she had suffered hit her, and I could not reach her. She came out of that dark place of course, being Jenny, but returned to it often. After all that fighting for her life, now came her long battle for joy, for mental and spiritual health. With only her friends and myself for help and guidance, and what did we know? The next six months were in many ways the hardest time.

cheryl
grateful

Finally, Jenny came home. Everyone was so relieved that she was finally out of the hospital. When I received an email about cooking a dinner, I signed up immediately just to feel somehow helpful! Brian and I were so happy to contribute something.

It seems like months later that I ran into Jenny in her wheelchair in the parking lot of her shop, out for one of the first times and though she was not at full strength yet, she stopped to talk to me, ever loving and engaged. It was a blessing to see her.

And now, with even more surgeries behind her, I have found her behind her counter at the store, greeting people and sharing her lovely spirit, inspiring everyone, so humble and grateful... especially to be there to see her daughter grow.

We are all so grateful, too.

mary rose

putting us at our ease

It wasn't until a month after she got home that we got to see Jenny in person. We went around with Rosa to visit briefly so as not to tire her, and even though she is a dearly beloved friend, I was anxious about how I would manage to be present without falling apart. I had no idea how we would find her after such an unbelievable ordeal. I was also aware that the crisis was an ongoing thing, a morphing of her life. We went through into Jenny's bedroom and I was completely disarmed by seeing her, sitting on the bed with her legs tucked into little socks, working away on some Grateful Desert problem on the computer. She reached her arms up for a hug.

Life was going on, but there was no question, no denial of what those last few months had cost her. Yet, we were all stunned by the energy radiating from her! She was tackling a mundane task, and she admitted that she tired easily, but there was a sense of a true warrior sitting there, completely inhabiting her own being, thoroughly present with all of the minutiae of life.

We were all uplifted and amazed. Rosa said, "Jenny is supernatural," and I know what she means. Jenny is supernatural in terms of a force beyond the understanding of science, and beyond the laws of nature…

a force of nature, a goddess in full possession of her powers, a clear vessel full of nothing but light. And she, tapping away on a computer, talking quite calmly about the strangeness of being home, the feeling within her coma of being surrounded by a circle of love; alternating between the sublime and the humdrum with just a heart beat in between…putting us at our ease.

jenny

coming to joshua tree

it took me a while to get used to joshua tree..

i didn't instantly fall in love with the desert.. i would come out here on climbing trips, newly transplanted from the oaks and redwoods, and ask, "where are all the trees?!"

while i was immediately intrigued, i was also baffled by so much brown and open land..

i was coming from sonoma county, humboldt county, hawaii.. all green, most lush..

sonoma county, in particular, was goddess country.. land of womyn-centered women and men.. women seen as beauty in all shapes and sizes, all colors and dress.. i was blessed enough to be surrounded by such womyn-- juicy, honest, courageous.. goddesses all.. we met often and with meaning, setting intentions each month and holding space for each other's joys and sorrows, struggles and victories..

i had been living in sonoma county. i loved it there and only decided to move to southern california to enter a master's program in nutrition, since there was a vegetarian program at loma linda university.

i cried for months before leaving northern california..

driving through the hills of sebastopol, i would shed tears all the way to work at rosemary's garden, the area's apothecary. the roots coming from my heart tried to grasp the trunks of trees as i drove by, winding around the oaks, stretching and pulling my chest as i passed.

"but i don't want to go to southern california!" i moaned to a customer.

"they need herbalists down there," this man told me..

"don't sacrifice me!" was all i could answer.

when i think of that, i chuckle.. he was right.. an herbalist was indeed needed down here.. north, we're a dime a dozen, but down here, everyone seemed impressed, and as the years and then decades passed, they trusted me.. what a blessing and an honor, that trust..

i met todd while going to loma linda and moved to joshua tree with him, because no matter where else i suggested, he said no....

"ahh, but the beaches in hawai'i are miraculous.."

"the trees in humboldt majestic.."

"the hills in sonoma are endless.."

"but where is the rock climbing?" he would ask..

finally, frustrated and newly in love, i said, "ok! we'll move to joshua tree for one year, in which we will climb every day.. and after that, it's my choice! we will head for the water and the trees!"

those first months, that first year, i cried a lot.. i missed my womyn.. i missed my trees and woman-shaped hills, grass, water.. this land was hard, angular, masculine..

two years later, we bought our first house in joshua tree and a few years after that, i found myself raising our daughter alone in this high desert.. no redwoods, no beach, no green rolling hills, but i had found home..

those first years in the desert, i was surrounded by climbers.. i was smitten by the rocks as well, and though i would never have called myself a climber, i sure loved to climb.. i was more the hippy-herbalist mama that was a soft embrace for my many male friends and slow trickle of women that started to move to the area..

over the years, the open sky started to seep into my psyche.. the moon rising and setting in full view without the hide-and-seek game of the woods, the slow pace of all of the desert's creatures, the way in which we are forced to see ourselves, unable to hide in the vastness. these potent and magical gifts started to settle in and take hold of me.. the desert pulls in who she wants and pushes away those not meant to be here..

years later, in the anguish of the realization that my marriage of six years was falling apart, i took my three-year-old girl to a yurt nestled in a heart home of humboldt, protected by the trees and my old community, while i shuddered with the shock and reality of the demise of my relationship and becoming a single parent..

and though yazzy and i lived with christina, my oldest friend, who could move mountains with her protective power, i realized that my desert community was calling me home..

it started with long phone conversations with my close women, like patricia-- women who had held me for more than a decade in the desert..

then the frustration of seeing the moon for only fifteen minutes a night as she poked her head out between the tree tops..

i had become addicted to the wide desert sky..

but the final straw was watching christina's kids embraced by the humbodlt community in which they were raised, while my yasmin, my yazzy, was still a stranger..

in joshua tree, our community had watched me yearn for and manifest my pregnancy, witnessed yazzy come into this world and knew every growth and development.. the post office women would weigh her on the postage scales each time we stopped by! i wanted the village that was invested in her to watch my yazzy grow up..

i came back.

called by the people of this tiny desert town

who wanted to comfort me in the despair of losing what i so desperately wanted for my child.. a family..

kept by the moon, who i watched traverse the sky from rising until setting..

but what finally pieced me back together was a family different than the one i had lost.. the family that is nowhere to be found like the one we have created here..

the family that is joshua tree..

felicia

reality we share

It took a whole community to try and fill your amazing and beautiful bootprints and now you're back! You've got your new legs and are continuing to blaze your beautiful trail. Yours is a powerful and magical path that not many could traverse. You are an inspiration to me. I will be forever grateful for the amazing journey you have taken me on. This experience has made me to grow in ways I never could have expected. So saturated in love, humanity and perseverance within this painful, beautiful reality we all share.

joycey 9
coming home

Jenny probably went home prematurely. She still needed dressing changes and was wheelchair bound. Myshkin was amazing as she took on the job of primary caretaker. I imagine it was harder than caring for a newborn for the first time. I felt guilty as Joshua Tree was two and a half hours away so I could only come about once a month. Usually I did laundry and prepared meals. I was worried about Myshkin as she had no time for her own work or caring for herself. Jenny and I both worried about Myshkin's drinking during this time. But who could blame her? Bills were piling up and she was spending literally hours on the phone with insurance companies. Jenny's morning routine of shower, dressing changes, helping her with breakfast and medication took three to four hours alone. Then there was physical and occupational therapy, laundry, shopping, doctor appointments and ominous bills to deal with.

If Jenny was feeling good, these chores would have been barely manageable. Unfortunately, she was suffering with intense stomach pain and nerve pain to her limbs most days. She ended up hospitalized four separate times generally for kidney infections and bowel obstructions. Myshkin was at her wits' end with anxiety and exhaustion.

During one of these hospitalizations, Jenny and Myshkin made a difficult decision. It was decided that Jenny and Yazzy would live with my parents until she was stable. They estimated a six month stay, taking into account Yazzy's school schedule. Myshkin's main objection was the influence that my mom would have on Jenny and the fear that my mom would turn Jenny against her. Jenny's main goal was to relieve Myshkin of being her caretaker. She did not want this type of relationship with her partner and she worried about Myshkin's deteriorating health, failing energy, increasing anxiety and loss of joy as her job of caretaker was overwhelming her.

It ultimately worked out well. My mom essentially cleared her plate so that the only job she had was taking care of Jenny and Yazzy. With the constant attention that my mom was able to give, Jenny flourished and quickly became independent. I remember coming home to visit and finding the downstairs bedroom empty. Surprised, I found Jenny in her old bedroom upstairs. She was walking comfortably with her prosthetic legs. She started driving soon after. Somehow her bowels healed and her appetite flourished. She started to look like the Jenny I recognized.

jenny
coming home

i was asked to write about coming home today..

i grimaced when patricia asked me to..

this is so damn complicated..

i will start by saying it was weeks— no, months— that i dreamed of being back home while i was laying in a hospital bed..

my sister michelle led me through visualizations on a daily basis that were nothing more than the minutiae of life at home with my family.. i would close my eyes and she would lead me through cooking dinner, sitting with yazzy and myshkin at the table, being surrounded by my loved ones. the desert sky, the rocks and sand. it seemed at times that this would never come.. that my only life would be in a hospital bed.. that i had been there forever..

six months in a hospital bed is pretty much forever..

i would close my eyes and always see myself in my red hoodie.. but why always this one? it was so old and beaten up, worn from my years of running..

it wasn't until months later that i realized why i pictured myself in that red hoodie: it represented the me that was strong and physically able..

and the pictures that arrived.. how wonderful to be gifted with photos by friends and family..

captured moments of my favorite people's lives to let me know i wasn't forgotten, that life wasn't actually continuing as though i didn't exist.. thoughtful pictures and yet they plagued me..

while i was in the hospital, i received so many photos of my beloved people smiling and hugging and waving at the camera to say, "hello!" "we miss you!" sitting in a pool, or on a hike, or at a show..

it filled me with such joy to see my people, to remember that i was loved, to see my friends remembering me.. and yet it was so excruciatingly painful to see that life was indeed continuing on without me..

pool parties, when how could i ever swim again? hiking memories, when how could i ever walk? ever even conceive of seeing the outdoors again? the rocks, sunrises, sand..

pictures of people in my shoppe, the warmth and love pouring out..

though it felt as if my business was slipping away from me as i lay unproductive and wasting in a bed..

when i was still at uci, they threw me a going-away party. at this point, i had been there just over five months.. everyone participated and there was such excitement in the unit..

as i sat in my wheelchair at the front desk of the icu, as the nurses presented me with a poster with all the staff signatures and love notes, as everyone was digging into the cake, dr. joe came walking towards me with a look on his face that mirrored a teenager caught in a scandalous act.. he hung his head as he told me that plans had changed and i couldn't leave that afternoon after all.. it would be weeks, maybe months.. there were a few more surgeries that were needed before he felt safe discharging me..

everyone around was looking at me, fearful of my reaction..

but what could i do? i just laughed ..

i forced myself to see the humor in the situation.. the guilty look on doc's face, the cake bites poised in the air as everyone froze, the balloons and poster all now inappropriately bright and cheery.. i had to see the hilarity in that moment, because despair was not a place where i wanted to reside..

i finally ended up in the physical rehab unit three weeks later in order to learn how to live a life without legs.,. it was a hard time for me.. i was on less pain medication and the pain was relentless.. my back consisted mostly of open wounds and i had to lay on it for most of the day.. the skin refused to heal, and the doctors were left trying to manage a back that had been harvested of most its skin.. i had to learn to transfer from the bed to a wheelchair with open skin everywhere and nephrostomy tubes..

it was excruciating and terrifying.. i was certain i would never be able to do it!

my mom came less and less as the road was long from her home. and mysh needed to travel out of town..

the time seemed to crawl without them, but i had friends make the trip out to see me and keep my spirits up..

tania, my dear friend tania, traveled from the bay area three or four times a month and devotedly took tender care of me.. she would blast pop music to encourage me to join her in my PT and OT, and she would feed me and help me dress.. goddess, i am blessed..

and then, yes.. i finally got to come home..

if i thought my new body was a complete trip, it wasn't until i left the confines of the surreal hospital bed and entered the life that i once knew that i was faced with the reality of my new reality..

i couldn't reach for a cup to get a glass of water. i didn't have the strength to wheel my chair across the carpet of my bedroom. i couldn't go outside by myself, as the deep sand was impossible to navigate..

i wasn't alone once for a good three months after i got home.. every-one was kind enough to worry about the dangers of what could hap-pen if left to my own devices, but it wasn't until i was actually alone that i realized how strange it is to constantly be surrounded by people..

people lived in my home for me, they drove my car for me, they reor-ganized the house.. i was simultaneously filled with gratitude and an overwhelming sense of alarm that this may have been my house at one point, but i was coming home to someone else's..

i have tried to articulate in my mind and with words the many emo-tions that plagued me upon arriving home..

the first was amazement.. i was struck by the colors of the house, the grandeur.. after being in a hospital bed with white walls around me for close to seven months, the colors todd and i had chosen for our home shocked me.. mustard yellow, pumpkin orange, chocolate brown, sky blue, aubergine purple.. never had i second guessed the explosion of colors that we had surrounded ourselves with, but at the moment i was wheeled into my home, i was filled with a sense of incredulous decadence.. why so large? the rooms so cavernous? i felt embar-rassed by the splendor of my home, my previous life..

as i struggled to sink back into my place in this home, i was continu-ously hit with the feeling that i didn't belong.. that while this had once been mine, i was now entering a place that was no longer my own. i was constantly triggered into that emotion when i couldn't do anything for myself, or later when i couldn't find various things that used to have a permanent and familiar place.. where were my kitchen scis-sors? where had the tablecloths gone to? minor, mundane things that triggered me into panic and despair, or brought me over and again to the realization that i had been missing from my life for a century, while beautiful and well-meaning people went on about their lives..

was this the truth? of course not.. these beautiful and well-meaning people were only here to support my family and help with those things i needed to keep the household going.. but these situations kept arising, and the triggers kept sending me into fits of tears and frustration..

i tried to reclaim some bits of myself soon after i got home.. much too soon.. i tried to hold a business meeting with my trusted and stalwart partners a couple weeks after i got back.. it was pretty much a disaster.. i believe i hurt some feelings as i was still full with of opioid painkillers prescribed to me and my truths were brash and a bit too close to the surface.. i can picture the looks of love, patience and maybe some confusion as i spoke of gearing up for our whole foods account.. i was still in and out of the hospital, and more days than not, wracked with pain and not being able to stay awake for more than a few hours at a time..

i hadn't had any counselling since the whole ordeal began, and i was still thinking through the fog of medication.. my emotions were all over the place and i ended up having to go into the ER too many times in those early months.. yazzy would wake up with patricia or piper at the house telling her that it was all ok, but that mama had to go the hospital in the middle of the night.. a couple of times she awoke to find paramedics wheeling me out to an ambulance..

my birthday came a month after i returned home and it was a celebration of a life that had been hard-won, perhaps a bit of stolen time.. some friends came over to celebrate with me, but the honest truth is that i was in such pain and shock, i seemed to be looking down at myself from a hundred miles above..

is any of this honorable or rational? absolutely not.. i knew it then and i know it now.. i could never talk about it, could never confide in anyone, because who could hear me and still see my gratitude? how many feelings would i hurt by wailing and pounding on the very people who were holding me up and keeping me afloat while i lay useless in a bed?

i couldn't talk about these things because i didn't know how to express them with grace.. i was terrified that i would hurt the feelings of the amazing people that took care of my life while i was gone..

how can one person hold so many complicated emotions at the same time?

myshkin

ship's medicine

Ship's Medicine
Mouth full of lime
Ten times the courage
In one tenth of the time
Holding you close
Holding you high
Holding you inside
Teeth on the knife
To not cry out
To not deny
Two knots of ship's rope
Lie rescued side by side
Turn to me now
Turn to me here
Barefaced and busted
Curses and tears
Rise to my bow
Spying my stern
Cheerless concentration
My gaping yearning
Ship's medicine
It's what we've got
You top every desert island
List that i've listed and lost

Jenny Q

Listing and lost
And taken by the wind
Caught by the cactus
Lost to the sun
Ship's medicine
Mouth full of brine
Pickled and punctured
And cut to pieces
And just
Fine
Now you're riding the mast
You're dancing the plank
Numbers all called up
You're cut from the ranks
And with all of that storm
You'd think you'd just sink
But your swimming home
And just
Fine
And i'm pacing the beach
And tending the fire
Dreams all come real
They just may take a while
And with all of this traffic
You'd know that i'd crash
But i'm holding on
And just
Fine
Ship's Medicine
Mouth full of lime
Ten times the courage
In one tenth of the time

jenny
body herstory

i am thirteen years old all over again...

at that age, i despised myself. i loathed my body. i was terrified of my yoni. i would look in the mirror at it. at its mystery and darkness.

it had been a source of pain for me. i wished i didn't have one.

since that time, i have worked on myself. i fought hard against my negative body image, and against my lack of self-worth.. i worked hard on loving this body.

at forty-three, i had reached a hard-won sense of beauty, confidence and strength. i was running at sunrise most mornings and loving the ability my body held. i was raising my daughter as a single mom, running three businesses, keeping our beautiful home intact and savoring my exquisite community. i loved what i could do, my endless energy..

this experience of becoming disabled, changed, having my body disfigured.. this experience has brought me right back to being thirteen years old.

a new body. a new yoni. i look in the mirror and see myself in darkness all over again. i have half the energy i used to. i can't run. i get tired so easily..

but i'm not complaining. i am able to do so much more than i could when i first left the hospital.

i am musing on this time in my life, these lessons. it's so familiar to feel disassociation from my body, to feel uncomfortable in my skin.

and i am completely aware that my previous fight for self-love has given me the ability to get me through this again.

when i think of this, it reminds me that nothing is an accident..

ronda

should i write?

When Jenny asked me to write something for her book, I have to admit I was pretty intimidated. What the heck do I have to say? She is the warrior! But with some nudging by her, how could I refuse? She has taught me that no matter how difficult the seas get, I can still learn to better sail my ship. After her harrowing experience, she turned her ship right around, sailed it back into the harbor, and got right back to healing her community.

I hope that it's okay to share, but I feel it's relevant. During a recent chat with her, she admitted to me that she was sometimes self-conscious with clients about her condition(s). If she didn't have her legs on and was in her wheelchair for a client meeting, she felt like she may not be taken seriously. "What kind of medical advisor is a woman in a wheelchair with no legs," she was worried they would think. I say the best kind! Give them two minutes of your story and what is revealed is the beauty and gift that you are there, giving of yourself to help them. You can't ask for a better consultant than someone who has your skill set, experienced the roughest of seas, fought hard, lived, and is here to share your strength, wealth of knowledge, and care! Tell your story…tell it loud, and tell it proud, Captain Jenny! Keep healing, inspiring, and impressing. We are in awe and gratitude!

jenny
a thought

as i come to the end of this project, i feel excited and joyous and also full of trepidation..

there is so much of me in this book..

i have laid myself bare..

there are so many love letters; i am embarrassed by the outpouring of love.

but the love letters are not a reflection of me, really..

they show the beauty of those who wrote the words, felt the fullness of emotion..

this community of joshua tree and beyond is devoted to each other,

in love with each other..

i begin to realize that the intensity of love is more a reflection of those that do the loving..

ted

jenny comes home

Jenny's crew of friends prepared for her return home, including widening her doorways and installing ramps for her wheelchair.

In July, around Yazzy's ninth birthday, Jenny came home.

Sage and I paid a visit. We brought some lunch and Jenny joined us for a meal. It was the first time we'd seen her in seven months. She was open with us, about her wounds, her pain, her struggle and her long road to recovery.

I left Jenny to rest and Sage to play with Yazzy for a while. Later, when I picked up Sage, I asked him how it had been for him, seeing Jenny. He thought about it for just a second, then answered, "It's just Jenny." My wise teacher son had reminded me that Jenny's spirit is intact, unchanged and perfect.

anita

soul sister

My mind drifts to a current picture I saw of Jenny hugging her daughter with huge smiles. My mind drifts to the gratitude I have for being a part of this community so full of love in action. I am grateful for the people I am friends with because they are Jenny's friends. We are all family after all. I am deeply touched by Jenny's journey, a woman I hardly know, yet I KNOW she is my soul sister.

Lena

glorious

It was awakening in some way. How much time do we have here on Earth? How shall we live that time? Have I been who I want to be? How much pain can be tolerated? So much contemplating! So much sorrow and also so much joy. The joy to see you again when you came by to visit Sebastopol was absolutely like the perfect dream. You are still my Habibti, the glorious Jenny Q, with your husky laugh and glittering eyes! YES, you are!!!

mary rose

worth the love

There is a moment that comes to my mind that is a symbol of this otherworldly quality to Jenny Q. It is the day she walked into our house for Rosa's birthday, at the end of September, standing on her new legs. It was completely incredible...the best birthday present Rosa could have had, and we were all overjoyed to see her. As always, there was this intense look in her eyes- loving and also joyous...so happy to be bringing Yazzy over for Rosa's celebration and determined to walk in on her own feet.

Jenny always uplifts me. She extends her energy to everyone around her. In spite of the fact that she undoubtedly needs more energy herself now than ever before, each meeting with her, each interaction, is a gift of the energy of life and love. Somehow since this experience of being so close to death, she is giving even more, emanating more love and generosity, even though just to get up out of a chair is something she needs to consider in order to accomplish it smoothly. For me, the experience of being within her prayer circle has changed my life. I speak every night to this Being or Force, with which I became involved when I started praying for Jenny Q. I have a sense of continuity in these prayers, although the words change from night to night. They have given my life more of a rudder, and I've found my eyes being opened every day to more beauty, and to gratitude for this life, directly related to this experience.

It feels like I have taken part in a miracle. I feel honoured to have been on the edge of a huge story, invited into a circle of light which helped perform the miracle of saving the life of Jenny Q. There might have been a time when she could have slipped away, but I do believe that the prayers and love of the community played a huge role in helping to knit together her spirit and her body.

But I also keep thinking that the beautiful, loving, warm presence I felt whenever I prayed for her was the spirit of Jenny herself...welcoming me in, uniting with all of us each time we sat down to commune with her, coming close, touching us, telling us, as she does each time we meet, that we are loved, that we are ok, that we belong and are worth the love that she gives us.

robbi

these boots are walking

Jenny is going to get prosthetics- I don't call them that- can't spell or say the damn word- Jenny was going to get her legs, and she wanted me to be there. Me? Wow, I felt so honored. I felt as if she was the master calling me forth into the new lesson. I did a little dance and sang a funny little song- and that was when I got the idea. Desperately, I tried to find an old ghetto blaster, and I made a CD of the song I was singing. This all got done just in time- on the morning before we left to go meet her. Gene Evaro had a ghettoblaster, so we swung by his house and picked it up.

Then, as we approached the clinic, fear and uncertainty crept into me, Oh fuck- I was losing my nerve! More and more as we got closer, I was losing my shit, my positive groove undone. What the hell am I gonna say or do?? Just act 'normal', Rob! I thought to myself, what? What the fuck is normal now? Doesn't matter, just act normal. Oh mother!! Oh shit- this is fucked. Oh just... oh no, I don't feel well, I feel faint!

The next thing, I was walking into that waiting room and there she was, scraggly rat head, sitting in a wheelchair. She turned her head slowly and looked at me, and as our eyes met for the first time, I blurted out "Goddammit, Jenny," and gave her the look that said 'what the fuck have you done now' and then I said "you silly girl." Jenny never missed a beat, she simply replied, smiling and with bright black sparkling deep pools of her eyes, "right?! I just thought maybe we needed another adventure, Right?!" We embraced.

Ahh, little wounded humming bird, my sister so dear, let's go- let's do this! It was very magical. You see, I didn't have to do anything- our love guides us in sweet ways, we just have to let go.

We- Piper, Kripa, Bella, and Mysh- who I had by now nicknamed Padmasambava, the fearless Bodhisattva- excitedly stood around in the stark white room as 'the guy' explained to Jenny how this all works. He was so matter of fact, I was losing my breath with some of the things he was saying- things like "oh it's never gonna be the same as real legs." Ouch mother fucker, don't say that!! "You are going to fall." Mother fucker, shut up! Godammit man! I wanted to kick him out of the room. We got this, just put the damn things on, let Jenny walk! I prepared the CD. Then it was the moment we have all been waiting for. Jenny took the bars, slowly lifting her frail frame up, I hit play on the blaster. With Myshkin at her side, Jenny stood up and the voice on the ghettoblaster belted out as Piper, Kripa, Bella and myself all clapped and sang along.

These boots are made for walking.

Jenny took her first steps, crying in joy and in pain. We cheered and clapped and sang and wept. Jenny sat down and after awhile, I was watching her from the side, I saw a sad cloud come over her and she cried quietly to herself. So I pulled my chair up close to her, right in front of her, eye to eye, and told her a story of the first amputee I met. The guy had a wooden leg, I explained, and I didn't know him, but I said to him hey bro, I got a word for you, what? he asked, woody woodpecker I said, and he laughed and then we introduced ourselves. I asked him how he lost his leg. He smiled broadly and said– I never lost my leg, Robbi, I am just that much Immersed into the Goddess of infinite space whom we love and from whence we all came and to whom we all return. Nothing is lost. And as I finished my story there came a bright sparkle in Jenny's eyes, that familiar sparkle, that would flash from her dark beautiful eyes, but this time it flashed so much brighter, so much brighter and so much bigger; you see that sparkle was magnified by the tears in her eyes, yea! Magnified by her tears and her gratitude. And therein lies a great mystery concealed and a greater understanding of compassion.

Liesl

first walk

as my truck rumbled up and down, over the dirt bouldered joshua tree trail, a glimpse of goddess presented itself like a shooting star, via two desert women so moving, yet hardly movin' at all.

i recognized jenny and her rock, mysh, literally takin' it step by step. as i approached, i jovially hollered an encouraging hoot; but pulling up close to them, their plight revealed itself.

rivers of physical pain streamed along jenny's olive cheeks. myshkin's gentle arms steadied her beloved's body, and granite eyes rested on me with determination, pain, hope, sorrow and love, all at once. they were taking jenny's first walk around the block in her new prosthetic legs.

my vocal support naturally shifted to solemn, solid, serious belief in their healing.

"you can do this. i am so proud of you both. keep going," i asserted from my serious heart.

serious? what did i know about serious? these women were serious. seriously fierce.

serious as the time it takes to learn how to play cello.

serious as the battle of remaining true to love in the wake of familial and cultural disapproval.

serious as sex.

serious as goin' to church every sunday.

heh, heh, heh.

before long, jenny was rockin' those new legs so good that she developed her own fluid swagger. i marvelled at her swift progress, eager to hear how she maneuvered everything from walking the raw desert roads, to balancing tree pose in yoga class, to calculating the precision of pressure it took her gorgeous knee nub and metal leg combo to push the gas pedal and make her handicap-tagged vehicle GO.

i think she figured out the brakes, too, but we'll just have to take her word for it, because i've never seen her stop.

she didn't and doesn't have time to stop. she has a thriving business. she has a fully female family - a precious preteen and an ever-giving agape partner - who both need her presence. she has good friends; a garden and home to tend; she has a tiny town with a giant community in which she fully participates; no, jenny does not have time to stop.

ronda

against doctor's orders

That following October was the best gift. Jenny was out of the hospital and insisted on coming to the Joshua Tree Music Festival, I do believe against doctors' orders. It was there, with her anchor by her side, that she gave me a big hug and kiss and told me to "stand back" while she STOOD UP. She stood up on her (new) feet so steady and strong with her arms out like a warrior! Did I mention that she's a badass?

jenny
getting up

my new reality..

i am tossing and turning in bed.. i have to pee!

but do i really want to get up? to take the time to wake up enough to find and put on the liners and legs and waddle to the bathroom?

oh, i don't have to pee that bad.. go back to sleep..

...

oh, but i really do have to pee..

the idea of getting up and standing on these glorious, yet painful tools that people call legs.. it makes me think twice, nay twenty times, before standing up, before assessing how dire my need is ...

i think, "i really am thirsty!"

"oh jenny, you are not that thirsty.."

"not that hungry.."

"you can wait.."

i argue with myself every time i need to get up when i don't already have my legs on.. do i really need to grab the phone? your shower can wait a little longer, can't it? i'm sure the dog is just barking at a neighbor..

it is only after much deliberating that i finally convince myself to muster the strength to get up..

okay yes, i am indeed ready to get up and go through the routine of plastering the silicone liners on my body to clip into my new legs..

..

often, it takes me a good twenty minutes to convince myself to go through the motions.. it's like having to lace up your big combat boots when all you want to do is throw on your flip-flops to run next door..

ach, just let me jump up and grab my pen, pee real quick, jump up to turn on the light before i get into the work of putting on my legs..

oh, i remind myself, it doesn't work that way..

anita

that which is real

I found that I was having fearful thoughts that life could end at any time. Yes, I say it sure can.

I recently had an elective surgery. Something I had wanted for years. I considered not having it because of what happened to Jenny. Then I remembered.. I make decisions daily to live in joy not fear!

My ego kept asking the question, "If this were me in the hospital, would anyone do this for me? Am I loved this much?"

My heart whispers, "Do not be concerned with that. Pour your love upon others with generosity. What you give returns to you in abundance."

Love is all that is real.

marilyn
ripples

Once the time was set, all of us counted the days and hours until we could all see our Jenny Q. When she WALKED through that gate into the courtyard, I did not see anything but my Jenny. I did not even notice the colorfully attired prostheses. Our spirits joined moments before she walked into my arms and there we held each other and cried. For several hours she was surrounded by family, all eager to wait upon her, give her whatever she needed. But mostly we all just gathered together outside in the beauty of nature and sat spellbound as we all chatted. How blessed we all were! We had longed for the day when we could hold Jenny in our arms.

Nowadays, I have to try and catch Jenny to set up times to come visit as that gal is on the move! Yes, she has a story to tell but most of all, she has love to share to all who need HOPE.

And Yazzy? She always has had such a sweet spirit. And yes, she went through such tough, heartbreaking times, that she didn't even know how to put her feelings into words. Surrounded by love of family and friends and many a prayer, she too will be passing on that love and hope to others in need.

And so the little stone thrown into a big lake keeps expanding, rippling….moving on….moving on.

jenny

what do these legs feel like to put on

so many people ask me to describe what it's like to put on my new legs..

there is so much to say about that..

do you remember in the '80s when tight jeans were in and you had to paint them on? i mean, when you really had to work on getting each leg in?

and then you had to hop around to pull them up over your hips..

that's when you had to topple down on your bed to get them fastened.

hold your breath and... snap..

now try sitting up..

yes, the new-fangled vacuum legs are that exact feeling..

paint your custom silicone liner on each stump, if only you can flip the bastards inside out.. they're made from a cast of your leg in order to fit that tight.

now, fit your linered appendage into the socket of your new leg and then roll the rubber sleeve up your thigh, if you dare.. it may take you some time.

it's so tight that a girdle would feel like a hip-hop dancer's pants..

don't think about how much hotter you're about to feel with that thick black rubber hugging your leg to the top of your thigh..

once you stand up, don't mind the pain.. "walk through it," they say..

that initial pain is just part of it. march out that feeling until the vacuum action kicks in and sucks all the air out of the space between skin and liners and sleeves.

was there any space?

as the vacuum takes hold, the tissue of your thigh is pulled toward the liner so as to distribute the weight of the legs.. this gives the illusion of less weight.. or i am sure it will once i have put the time into getting used to them.. at this point, wearing them for more than an hour exhausts me because they're so damn heavy. after wearing them for a full day of work, i often whine and whimper by dinnertime out of sheer fatigue.

it's quite a daunting task to practice getting used to new legs... to persuade myself to put on these new appendages .. i know i have to and i know that if i put the time in to wear them, it gets easier.. i know this, and yet i have to convince myself to do the work most days..

i got used to these legs once before, but it has been so long since i've used them. when i have wounds on my stumps, these new vacuum legs hurt too much to wear. and as i have had endless wounds from blisters bursting, i haven't worn them for months ..

these legs have been rendered magical by the most brilliant painter. i am so honored to be able to wear georganne dean's art!

most days i marvel at the fact that i am cruising around on these metal things..

one thing i will never complain of is a boring life..

the pin legs are easier.. i find myself resorting to them often.. maybe too often..

"pin legs" are legs that fasten on your stump by rolling on a silicone liner that has a large screw attached to the bottom that snaps into the socket of the leg ..

they are easy on, easy off.. one press of a button and your stump comes out..

these are great for whipping on and off, for yoga classes.. my slippers, as my prosthetist calls them..

and they are great for some comedy, as at various times the side button gets depressed unexpectedly ..

one time, yazzy and i were at a farmer's market with my parents. i swung one leg into the car and then the other one but it was so light that it swung too fast and hit my dad, who was in the driver's seat.. there was much confusion..

then yazzy and i giggled endlessly as we saw passersby staring at the leg sitting outside the car, waiting patiently for its owner..

one of the reasons that my vacuum legs are so heavy is that they have a moving ankle. first off, when they say it moves, what they really mean is that it moves ever so slightly.. nothing like your real ankle.

leading up to getting my new legs, i was anticipating this new ankle movement, and was so excited to have that function again, expecting it to move like the one i used to have.

then i stood up for the first time with them on, and all i could think was, thank goddess they don't move so much! i would be like a weeble-wobble! how would i be able to keep from falling forward and backward without feet and calf muscles to balance me and hold me up?!

but my ankles move, and this makes a world of difference when you are walking on uneven ground, like the dirt roads that i live on.

i am told that each addition to your legs has weight and that each thing you choose adds more at the end. a moving ankle or pretty outer shell adds a pound here and a pound there. it doesn't seem like much, but you should feel my legs..

when i took anatomy at the university, we had preserved body parts in the lab that we could pick up and study: a head, reproductive organs, an arm, legs.. these things weighed more than you would imagine. you should pick up a head sometime.. they are so much heavier than you would think! the arms and legs are heavy too. but what i have realized is that much of the weight of living limbs is muscle, and muscle tissue helps lift and move those limbs around.

also, weight at the end of a limb is so much more to manage than on the actual appendage itself. i often think of those serving women in bavaria at oktoberfest, holding out those steins full of beer in front of them.. if they had to hold them at the end of a stick, it would be harder still.

one more thing that i have had to manage with regards to my new legs are the pros and cons of each set of prostheses..

if i wear my pin legs all day long, i have the ease and comfort of being able to whip them on and off easily if i have to change or lay down to rest. they're so light, so they don't fatigue me near as much. but when i wear them all day, the bottom of my legs get sore and i get open wounds. since all the weight of my body is sitting in those plastic sockets on the stumps of my legs.

when i wear my vacuum legs, the weight is distributed all along the area where the thick, rubber sleeve attaches, most of the way up my thigh. while these sleeves are hot and itchy, they take the weight off the bottom of my legs. i tend to be less sore and have fewer wounds. but by the end of the day— good night! i am ready to collapse!

my first prosthetist gave me a lecture right before i stood up on my first set of legs.. it went like this:

"these are not your legs.. there will never be legs that feel like your own, that work like your own.. god gave you the perfect pair of legs, and nothing we can do will ever feel like the ones you had.."

while everyone in the room wanted to punch him, i understand now why he wanted to warn me.

it was a while before the concept of prosthetic legs even sunk in.. everything was so dreamy then, when they first started talking about them.. so foggy, mystical even.. people spoke of illness, losing legs, wearing new ones. then i lost my legs and they were fitting me for the fake ones, and i just went along. the idea of ever walking again was not sinking in. i could not even imagine getting over to the wheelchair. i just watched the process with a detached curiosity.

but during the next several months, as i was trying different kinds of prostheses, somewhere deep within me, i was imaging that new legs would replace my own. that at some point, i would find a pair of legs that would not hurt or wound me, and would be comfortable and graceful. over the last year, i have lowered my expectations considerably, and am much more accepting of these tools i have to get me around.

matt perry

that smile

I wound up in Joshua Tree just like everyone else. I had a story.

After only four months in Los Angeles, I knew I no longer wanted to live in a city full of traffic and conversations with people whose attention was always somewhere else.

So one day on retreat, meditating at the Joshua Tree Retreat Center and contemplating my next move, it suddenly struck me. Joshua Tree? The desert was a wonderful place full of beauty and mystery. Within thirty seconds I'd made my decision.

Joshua Tree.

Not long after I moved there in early 2014, I heard rumblings from various people that there was something wrong with the local herbalist, Jenny Q. In my short time there, Jenny had become a legend, her tinctures known as miracle cures.

She was also one of the first people I spoke to, stopping by her store Grateful Desert Herb Shoppe to ask if she knew of any places to rent. She greeted me with her signature expansive smile that made even the desert sun a bit brighter.

Yet soon after, I heard bits and pieces of a troubling story. Jenny was really sick. It was really bad. And she was getting worse.

The fluctuating stories were all shrouded in mystery. And they went on for a very long time. Finally, I heard that she had suffered the extraordinary loss of both legs and some of her fingers.

A year later I happened to be at Joshua Tree Health Foods, right next door to Grateful Desert Herb Shoppe, where Jenny resurfaced for the first time. She was in a wheelchair. The staff greeted her with absolute joy, ooh'ing and ahh'ing over her like over a newborn baby.

And Jenny was smiling.

Soon after, I saw her a second time, during a performance at the local arts center Harrison House.

She was smiling then too.

Sixteen months after moving to Joshua Tree, I knew it was time for me to leave the Mojave Desert.

Two days before I left, though, I stopped by Grateful Desert Herbals to pick up some magical potions, and asked the cashier how Jenny Q was doing.

"I'm Jenny Q," smiled the cashier.

Astonishingly, I hadn't recognized her, disguised under a hat. It was so nice to see her. And it was the first time since her illness that I'd talked to her alone.

"I have something to ask you," I began.

Jenny just smiled that smile.

"Most people complain about all the stupid little details of their lives," I said. "That they didn't get a raise. Or that their neighbors got a new car and they didn't. We have good lives, but we still complain about everything. But when I look at you, who has everything to complain about, you're always so full of joy and happiness. How do you do it?"

She smiled that smile again!

And responded with four words.

"We have a choice."

All spiritual teachers describe our life experience as the result of our reactions to, and interpretations of, events. When we embrace life just as it is, we can be happy all the time.

This is good in theory. And much harder in practice.

Yet standing in front of me on two prosthetic legs was a living example of this profound philosophy.

We talked a while longer, Jenny constantly smiling, me listening in perpetual wonder at this woman of sublime wisdom. We hugged and as I left I felt blessed to know such an amazing human being.

"We have a choice."

I think of that phrase all the time. And when I do, I think of Jenny Q's smile.

jenny

self-confidence, intuition

it took me a while to trust myself and my knowledge again after this past year, even though so many people were telling me that i would be an even better herbalist than before because of all the experiences i had been through..

i understood this cognitively, but i wasn't feeling it.

instead, what i felt was utter humility and a total loss of self and confidence..

actually, i felt that i didn't know enough to be able to help anyone..

after a few months, i started to realize that this loss of self-confidence in my field was a gift.. an expansion of my wisdom..

i didn't know how or why yet, just that it was so..

some more time passed and i felt clearer, as i got off the dozen medications i came home with..

i also started taking herbs again.. i began to intuit what my body needed and realized that my intuition had grown..

the more i listened, the louder it got..

then i returned to my shoppe and proved to myself that i had the capacity to hold responsibility once more..

that i was finally ready to see clients again.

you know that feeling in your gut when something feels right for you?

that feeling of, oh! i need to swim three times a week,

or oh! i need to go back to school,

or this smoothie feels so good in my body that i'm going to have one every morning this summer to start my day!

i have had a potent intuition for what my body wants and needs for a good long while.. i had worked on honing that skill..

so now when i sit with someone, i have that feeling so strongly— a resounding YES! for the right herb.

when i am formulating for someone, the herbs scream so loudly to be included in the remedy that i often laugh and say, "okay! i hear you! i won't leave you out!"

i feel so much more emotionally connected to the herbs and the higher selves of the people i am working with..

this is what people must have been talking about.. the growing of my capacity as an herbalist..

what a gift..

patricia
six months later

The months that followed Jenny's return are a hazy dreamscape. The trauma I experienced came from my own deep fear that something horrible could happen to someone I treasured. There are pockets of recollection that are unavailable to me....hidden from me. This is most likely a gift.

And yet, after all of it...a coma, six months in ICU, amputations,

fifty-one surgeries, Jenny Q did what I always knew she would: She Rose.

She rose from the ashes of an event that would have killed most.

She grabbed the silver thread of love that she had magically woven through the tapestry of her life and used it to pull herself back to her family, her friends and the community who had held onto the other end desperately, awaiting her return.

liesl
la señora

la señora qaqundah awoke from the drool of
coma-induced temporary death
took a look around
and with the haste of moon lightning
evaluated the situation
she ripped out the iv's
secured a shitbag
(who needs a fucking bowel system anyway)
and ascended through skin-shedded rebirth
into a new goddess of deeper understanding
deeper appreciation
deeper pain and sorrow
so therefore
deeper joy and love
i crept into her lap
her naked knees and my wet eyes
following the cliché of fearful people who turn to those who suffer
in order to ease their own uneasiness
about what suffering is
what it means
why it happens
and how on earth we can all possibly deal with it

Jenny Q

she shone

she shines

..

jenny, jenny, jenny q

love, liesl

melissa

the dead on stilts

April, 2015. The Dead, the last shows.

We have tickets; WE ARE GOING. This is huge.

A shared love experience, this band.. they grew us up and their music blew our minds open, pierced our hearts and, I believe it's safe to say, shaped the trajectory of our life paths. This cannot be overstated, right? For twenty years we talked about this. We are going to gather together and dance with the boys one last time. Joy! You said, "Oh, Melissa. I am so sad. I will not be able to dance." And immediately and without pause I blurted, "But you will, though." And then something like, "You know, in your own way, however you can." After hanging up, I immediately felt some regret. Why did I gloss over your heartache?

You know how people do that when they are uncomfortable with anything they perceive as negative? "Oh, I'm sure everything's gonna be fine."

End of conversation.

Ugh.

Later, at the Joshua Tree Music Festival, you were a FORCE. There you were, on your new legs, in the RV, making herbal elixirs for everyone. Opening the jars, pouring, taking requests, using your knowing to create a potion perfect for each and everyone. Medicine. Alchemy. Festival. It was wonderful to be there with you. And so darn fun. I pulled you aside to apologize for the conversation. It was not right of me to minimize your experience, your grieving, your truth. I expressed that I wished I had just listened and been present for you in that moment. You said you didn't see it or feel that way. Issue over and done.

At the Dead show in Santa Clara. Yes! We made it. Us, on the floor. Nighttime rainbow in a dusty rose sky. Is this for real? Come on, this is some ridiculous hippie shit. Omen, Blessing, providence. We are all together.

I was rocking with you and seeing you dancing. Not spinning and twirling but again, on your legs, getting DOWN. All the way down, shaking it out. Sparkling, sure, but how would I describe it? Working for the bliss. Earth mama digging into the dark and sacred depths, moving through it and moving it. The elation and despair. Unafraid of the intensity of feeling everything now. Unbowed and fierce. Raw and pure. This is what I came here for.

Sunday night, it's the encore.

"Fare thee well, my honey."

With just a few notes, the stadium energy dropped like a hundred-ton weight. Note to selves: this is our last song, folks. I wept without restraint. I wept for the whole of it: the sorrow for the end of the era and all things, the joy of the music, the immense gratitude for a band that forever touched my heart, the collective experience of seventy thousand people and fifty years AND generally, the overall magnitude of all life's experience.....

It was overwhelming. I could have laid myself down on the ground I was so filled with emotion. Everyone that was there- not only the sparkly, beautiful people, but the gutter punks swinging dope, the dope addicts, whoever made it to the show- what are we doing here? Why do we come? To experience the release, some relief. An escape from pain, if only for a short time, the magic and joy. There will never be anything like it again. And to be there with you was divine. My sister, Lisa and Andy, too.

Listen to the river sing sweet songs to rock my soul.

Amen!

We wheeled you around the stupid stadium, chasing the illusory and elusive Shakedown Street that was just not meant to be. But we were alive and radiant, finishing strong to the end.

Before I bid you and Myshkin goodbye in the parking lot, I couldn't help but reference again our conversation back when we got our tickets.

"But you know what, Jenny?

"The funny thing is, I was right, after all."

HAHAHAHAHA!

You did dance.

HAHAHAHAHA!

Because, as I said, you are a badass. And that's how it's gonna be. I read this line somewhere. "These are but minor setbacks on the road to glory."

I think that is humorous and profound. And apropos.

Love is real, not fade away.

I adore you,

Melissa

barnett

joshua tree

To witness the number of friends rise up to help Jenny, Yaz and Mysh gave a whole new meaning to the phrase. The help came in all ways-spiritually, financially, shopkeepers, housecleaners, cooks and moms; loving surrogates for every task materialized with grace.

julie
quiet and righteous

This is a small thing, piece of writing, recollection I hope you don't mind that I want to share with you

It is me sharing with you during a time that I only imagine was surrounded as if in another world

World within worlds and connected to interconnected worlds of support and concern.

Yours was palpable, you existed very deeply with us as we moved through the world

We travelled the Middle East with you our minds and the feeling of impotence was side by side with a deep wish and hope towards your growing well, despite deep hardships and losses.

These are pasted together recollections, thin, wispy connectors

My writing is awkward at its best

Thank you for bearing with me

This is merely a letter to you to let you know that you spoke so eloquently to me in your quiet and righteous fight for life

jŭlïe

yemeni honey

the air shifted over time as news was shared through a dearest of your.

worry fea.

grasping everyone at the core

as friend, respondent, community member, patron of Grateful Desert, inspired by your pursuits

i am also a familiar through caregivin.

A comrade through the deep touch and witness to loved ones' bod.

the act of being in direct response and the wraths of illnesse.

what felt familiar: worry. overwhelm. protectiveness. fear.

then quickly too: the desire to jump quickly towards the healing, the other side, the on-the-side towards getting better, the out of the woods, the non-intensive troubling tensions

the love desire to soothe immediately through the difficulty

the wish that you would not have to bear any pain (at all)

the awareness of sudden-nes.

our vulnerable sensitive precarious impermanence and its sibling, the logics of the body's homeostasis, is challenging enough

in writing to you, i looked back and wanted to share that i could only feel you healing

your motions, commotions, your here and back and around, the distance, the spaces

the edge.

healing was a force.

happening within you

but more.

it was this recognizing you as the healing itself

you, the force, your own force, our force

the fight, awareness, discombobulation, the language and tone of needed privacy, secrecy and silences

the cornerstones of need in the ai.

the ways towards spaces for you and yours to crawl and pace slowly

the language for your daughter

the projected imaginings like floating in water as a relie.

the language of touch and spiri.

your town absence was unmistakable but your person was ever-present

the jenny here and another place and other places, beyond hospital and condition

i wondered, as a person in your circles of communing, if holding you close was letting you fl.

you spread through me as Yemeni honey and in our reach into arid lands, sister middle eastern deserts in early 2014

i discovered you in faces of strangers, voices too, connecting us outside mere proximit.

feeling your we.

in the

harbors of mutual friend.

your bottle: middle eastern hair oil mixed with fox voracity and care was a daily viscous touch from you to us and in return

you remain and are the boundary-less futur.

the kindest hardest working sensuous and spirited soul of the jt land

you conjured the spirit of discovery

remembering the last time i saw you before this time

in town

coming from a session, jaw released, stunned and fre.

in the center of our little tow.

this soft recollection of yo.

opening and floatin.

in your discovery, past, present and future excursions bared

nina mihranian

you will laugh forever

A young lady, a beautiful mama, our very close friends' daughter is teaching us all courage.

Her parents, Boulos and Suad, had such super human courage, strength, hope, optimism and persistent hard physical work for their daughter's survival, for her well being and happiness and her comfort. This could only have come from God.

We got scared for her, we cried and prayed for her, we love her..

We thought we would give her strength, that we would tell her words of wisdom, of persistence or resilience...but No!!

We learned from you, our little Jenny. We only taught you belly dancing when you were a teenager.. that's all.

We learned that you are Love, you are beauty and sunshine and a sister to young and old..

That's our Jenny.

You mourn your body and ask what you look like to a stranger's eye?

You look like the beautiful, gorgeous, strong, sweet, kind, loving self you always were.

And yes, you will laugh after you cry ... you will laugh forever, Inshallah.

We are still learning from you.

Love, Auntie Nina

elise

journey

Ancient child
innocent life
we pray :……….
for your eyes to re-ignite,
our hearts, holding you tight…..
time and body
here and beyond
what a journey you are on….
beloved soul star Mamma Q,
we call you
come back!
…so we can thank you
for bringing us into
Love
at a level we never knew….
…so much left for you to do,
to teach….
i reach
to find you -
hands hot
fever fire light
weaving Life with Life
We all must Trust.
and

see you

feel you

complete and in ease :.......

you are Free

free of

machines and glaciers and labcoats and pain

release

release

release

and breathe)))

ah,,, Great Mystery,

in humble awe,

i bow to you deeply...

Brave Woman,

Mother of All,

it is an honor

to see you

stand tall.

elise

vision

I saw us,

maybe ten of us,

women, sitting in a circle.

We were sitting in a divine circle, inhabiting our celestial bodies before being born, discussing what we'd like to learn when we incarnated into beautiful human bodies this time around.

We said to each other that this time, we would need some serious experiences to give our souls the growth and evolution we wanted – for both our individual selves and for the collective.

Someone was going to have to sign up for an incredibly challenging journey for the continued awakening of us all.

We learn the most from our sufferings, from unlocking the areas where we are bound.

Jenny Q Mama raised her hand. "I'm doin' that!" She moved her head side to side as she does, and she said, "You know it!"

I said, "No, no. No, you're not," and looked around the circle.

No one else was volunteering and I certainly didn't want to. We knew it would be a big job.

She insisted. "I'M DOING IT!!"

I remember feeling pride for her strength and embarrassed for my lack, but I knew she would have it no other way.

Now I see.

Now I am beginning to see how such an experience can expand us all. Certainly Jenny's journey is growing her own patience, strength, passion, love, and much more in many ways – but our entire community is learning from her courage and grace. She was the One for the job, the one who had enough strength and determination. She was the one who could show us the way up the mountain. And not just the way up the mountain, but how to climb the highest mountain, alone, without legs! Of course we are all cheering her on, but her journey is one we can only support, not experience as she is experiencing. She makes it look so easy, but it's undoubtedly a full spectrum experience.

My days have been filled with more gratitude for all the love in my life, for my life, for my body, these precious feet.........having a "bad" day feels ridiculous. Ah! The perspective! What a gift!

What a gift she has given us by surviving and showing us how to walk this life properly!

ted

yoga and dancing

It's been over a year since then and Jenny is out and about, around town, hearing music at Harrison House, dancing at the music festival with prosthetic legs, doing yoga, working in her laboratory, advising people in her shop, going to hear her lover play her beautiful songs at the Beatnik and elsewhere, going to pick up her child from school, having more surgeries, healing, healing others, radiating love, smiling beautifully and laughing. Her teaching is our teaching and her lesson, our awakening.

kali

it worked we danced

It worked. All of it. Against all odds, Jenny got better. She made it home. A pillar reconstructed. In community, empathy is a common thread that weaves us all together. Gratitude is the result. The more gratitude there is, the stronger the community... and it cycles on. Positive feedback. Uplifting music to move forward through all life's trials. Our moons merge, our hearts beat together. It could have been any one of us, but Jenny had the strength to make it through. I think the universe knew that.

Oh, and that fall, at the next music festival, Jenny and I danced.

joycey 9
twenty months later

It has been twenty months since the beginning of Jenny's battle. My kids and I are going to Joshua Tree this Friday to celebrate Jenny's forty-fifth birthday. I'm thinking about buying her a short skirt. Jenny refuses to hide her prosthetic legs. She doesn't mind the stares and encourages people to ask her what happened. She wants to demystify disability and make people comfortable with her body's changes.

Of course nothing will be as simple as before. No more jumping out of the car to grab a few groceries. Still, she danced for four hours at the recent Grateful Dead show. She paid the next day with intense pain and wounds to her legs, but that night, she went back for the second show and danced again. Jenny has always had great enthusiasm for life. Despite certain physical limitations, none of that enthusiasm was lost. More impressive was her resiliency and resolve to get better and back to living her full life. Best for me is that I get to see Jenny this weekend.

myshkin
birth day

We had a birthday party for Jenny last night. My sister Sunny talked to Jenny's sister Joyce for hours. Yazzy and her cousins were joined by several friends' kids, formed a pack, dressed as mad clowns, hid and sought, fell asleep on the trampoline. I invited people too late—a week before—but that was probably a good thing or we might have run out of room. It is August, and hotter than hell. I set the music room up for jams but folks were having too much sweetness talking. We finally got into some playing, late, and it turned quiet and full of promise. What joy in this house, to celebrate a life so nearly lost, and so fully recovered.

boūlos

toughie

Over fifty surgeries later, she survived. If it wasn't for her love of survival and the love of her daughter, she wouldn't have made it.

She's always been a toughie, a clever business woman, and she still supports her family and her daughter.

What a miracle.

robbi

what's next?

Last time I saw Jenny?

Well, I hijacked her wheelchair, didn't I? And made her push me in it all the way up the steep driveway to her car. Howzat?

So anyhow Penny, what's next?

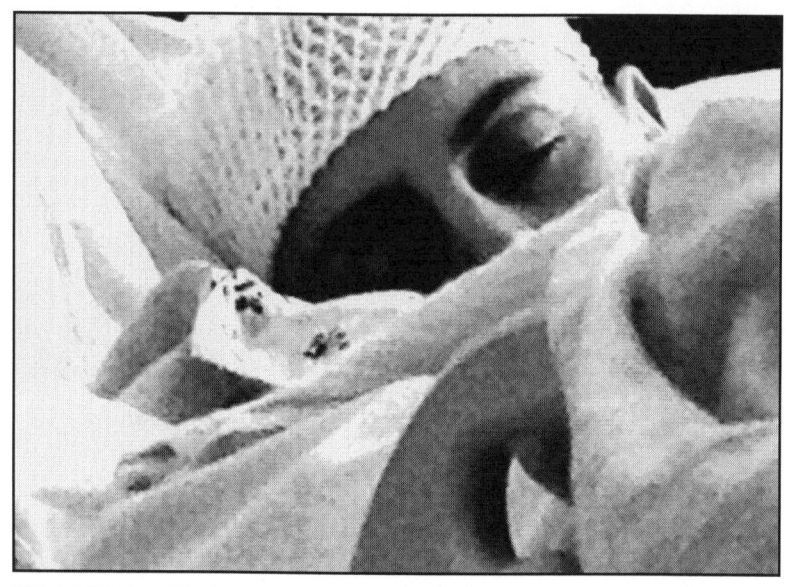

Apparently, I was in a coma for six days, but how is one to gauge the difference between a journey and a long, silent sleep?

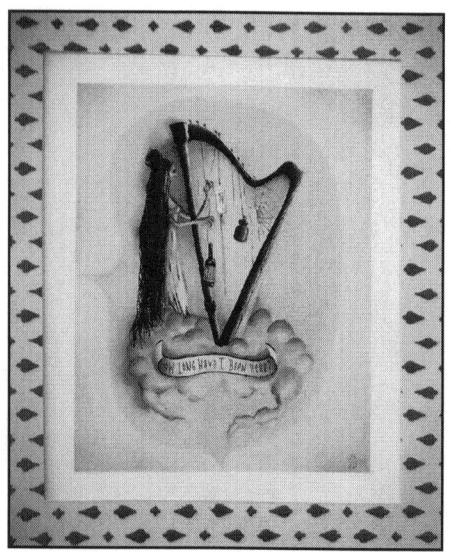

This piece, painted by Georganne Deen, was sold to Danny Elfman in a benefit to raise funds for my medical care while I was in the hospital.

She dreamed this up after hearing about some of my first words after the coma. Upon being asked if there was anything I needed, I apparently replied,

"A Scotch on the rocks."

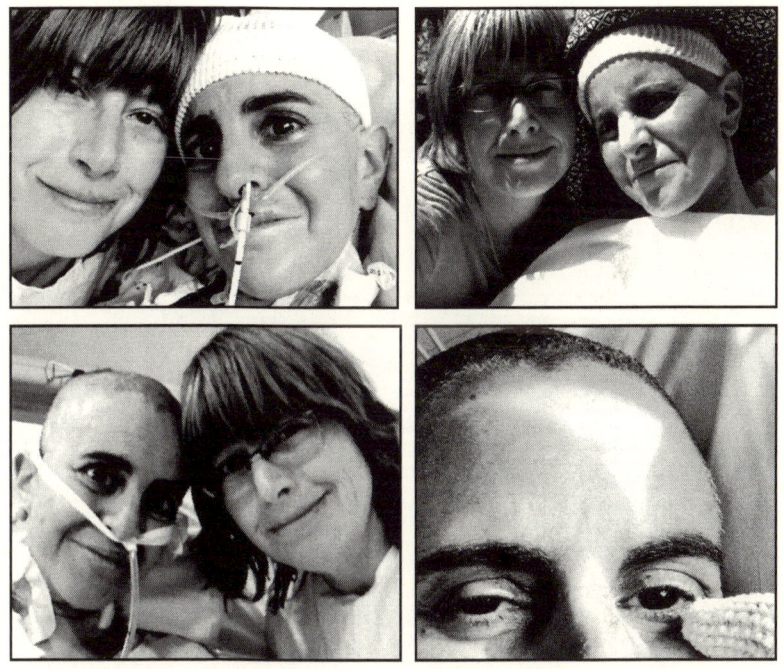

From one moment to the next, my life was profoundly changed.

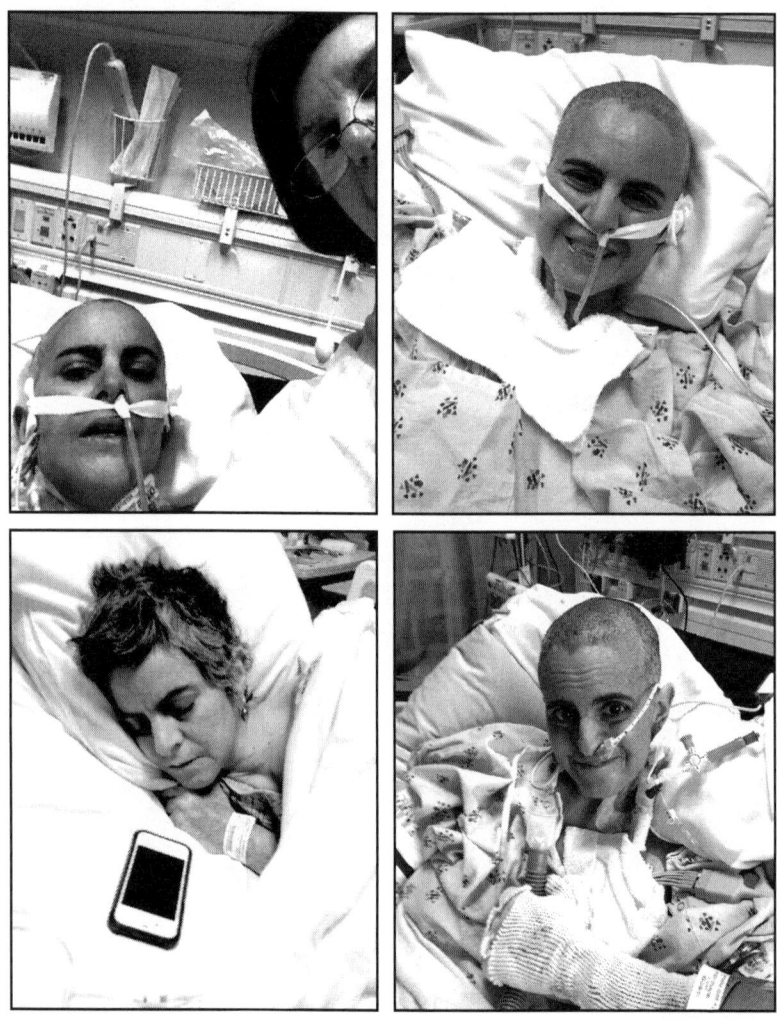

It took me so long to come back to myself. It was months before I registered that I had a personality, ran a store, before I remembered that I had a life. For months, I was only surviving from moment to moment, with no history or ego.

What a journey, this.

No matter how hard the journey, love always prevailed.

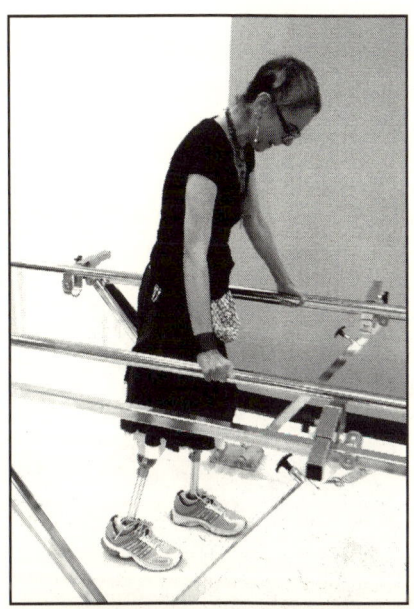

My first steps after almost a year.

I was certain that I would never actually be able to balance without using handrails.

It was painful and terrifying. And exhilarating.

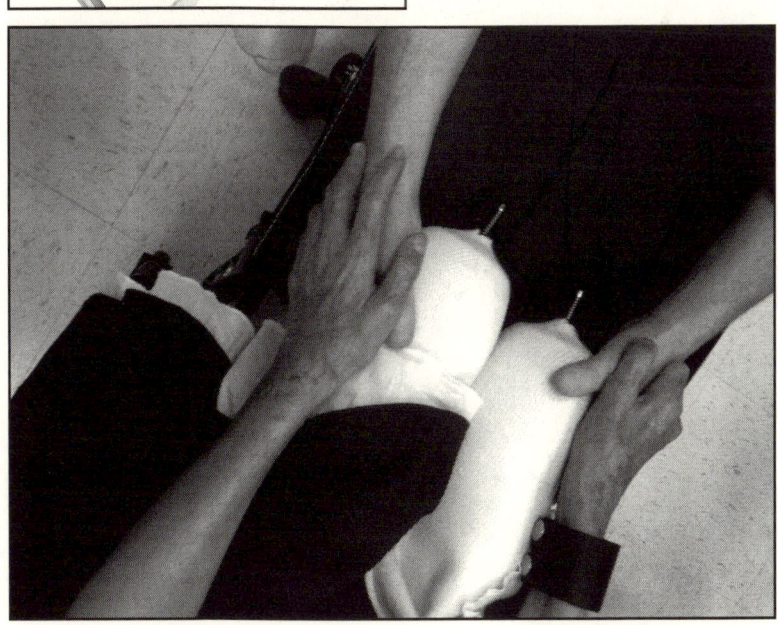

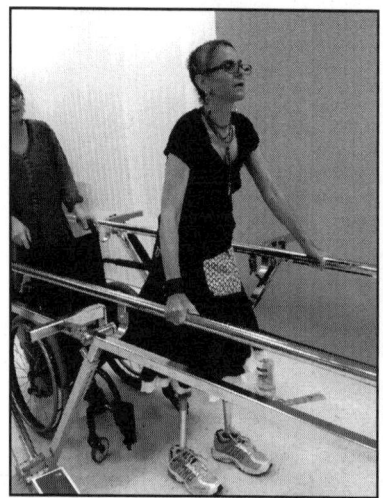
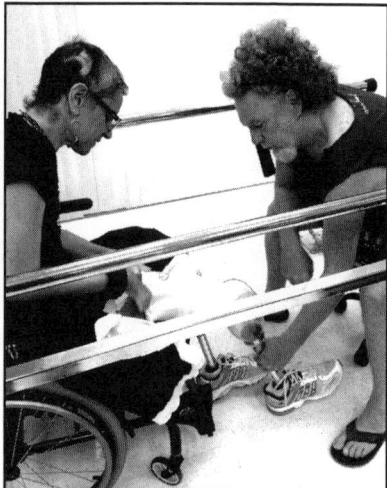
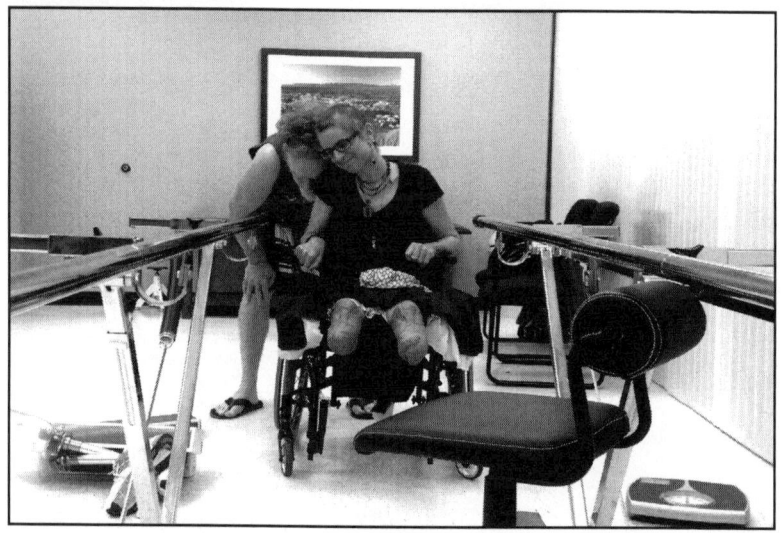

As I took my first steps, we were all crying to the soundtrack of 'These boots are made for walking.'

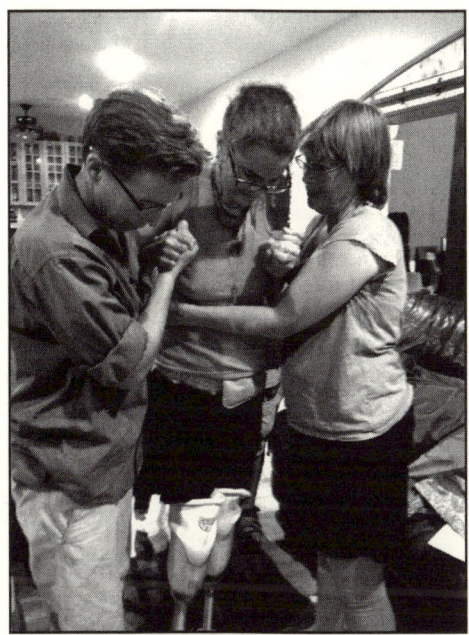

Learning to walk on these stilts is crazy hard.

Having support is how I made it through.

Thank you, sweet community..

Jenny Q

*Even fresh out of the
hospital, I was ready
to get back into my life.*

Our best man, Barnett English.

We postponed our wedding twice.

I was determined to marry Myshkin standing up.

And without nephrostomy tubes!

My siblings, and Yazzy smudging the Circle.

Our community blessed us with their presence and love.

Starting our honeymoon; on the plane to San Miguel de Allende.

This was our first international trip after my body's changes.

Getting back to my life..

*..with ardor
and passion.*

The next generation
of festie kids at
the Joshua Tree
Music Festival.

*My therapist, the cello,
I picked her up after I lost
my fingers, as I could still
hold a bow.*

*Little did I know, I would
find my soul instrument.*

My biggest blessing, my family.

part four

aftermath

jenny

how can i print this?

what a great idea this is..

how cool will it be to reach out to other disabled folks,

arabs, arab queers, trauma survivors?

it has felt so inspiring to think about reaching out and connecting those of us who are Other..

and who doesn't feel like Other? i have met few, if any, who feel like they fit in comfortably with the rest.. with Everybody..

but then the reality hits me of what it means to Come Out so fully..

not only am i disabled and queer, i am arab..

which means not airing all your dirty clothes on the line..

especially not your skivvies.

it's why i have always been careful not to be totally out..

i tried so hard not to be gay. i married a man who later became a dear friend and the father of our treasured child. i have tried and tried to keep my true, all-too-loud self quiet.

it seems impossible for this leo palestinian.

and i can't live a lie.. it goes against my ethic and everything i am trying to teach my daughter.

so i try to avoid particular topics with certain people, namely aunties and arab friends of my folks.

"are you dating again, jenny?"

"no, i am content right now."

no need to tell them that i am happily married..

"why do you live with a woman? it is not safe! you should try and marry again!"

"ok, auntie. i will think on that!"

but the truth is, i am sure very few of my extended family believe me to be straight.

i never wanted to hide who i am, and yet i always wanted to respect my parents and shield them from the shame that comes from a child of theirs being gay.

and yet here i am, speaking out about all of it..

it has haunted me these last months..

every time i'm inspired to write and work on this book, i start to fear the repercussions for my parents..

every auntie and uncle and thirty-sixish first cousins will have access to my dirty laundry, and while they probably wouldn't really care, my parents undoubtedly would.

so what is a disabled arab queer to do?

live the life that pleases her closest loved ones?

keep her voice a whisper?

is it selfish of me to want to shout out and follow my instinct to reach out?

i know what my mama would say.

and i do indeed respect and love her endlessly.

and i do want to please her enough to squash my instinct.

almost.

jenny
reticent

as i get closer and closer to the end of this project, i become more and more insecure about this collection of work..

so many kind, loving words.. so many people pouring out love and affection, it makes me reticent and less and less confident about putting it out there..

don't i look ridiculous making public what is really a series of love letters, intermingled with a story of near-death? don't i seem so damn conceited?

as much as i want to take in people's words and believe them, it is a journey for me to allow them to seep into my deepest core..

oh, and the fear of making myself so vulnerable!

of sharing so much about the wounds i sustained, my changed body and my crazy emotional ride in trying to assimilate..

putting out there for anyone to see what perhaps most sane people would cover up with clothing and never mention..

but while somewhat terrified of sharing so much, i have a certain agenda.

in addition to just being called and drawn to tell my story, i want to expel people's misconception of disabled folks as being "other," to open myself to the curious, and to reach out to others who, like me, sometimes feel alone and isolated in their otherness..

but the truth is that this project is indeed a love story..

the story of a community that is so committed, they reach out to hold each other in times of crisis, they listen and weep and laugh and dance together, they call to the gods to bring back the dead..

yes, this is a story written by a community that is stretched across the globe..

about life in all its hardships, its glory, its sorrow and profound joy..

this story could be about any one of us.. it just happens to be about me.

jenny
collage piece

a good friend made a long journey to come visit.. she hadn't seen me since before i got sick..

when she walked through my door, she reacted like most.. joy, tears, compassion..

before we even sat down, she asked me many questions, and was shocked at how serious my illness had been.. it was a surreal moment to watch her take in my changed physical self..

you see, she had moved to the midwest and hadn't been in touch with our joshua tree community, so while she was aware i was struggling, she had no idea how much.

she wasn't aware that i had lost my legs… she wasn't aware of my missing fingers.. she had no idea i had almost died..

she wanted details, she wanted all my stories, sweet ana..

so we looked at pictures.. pictures i had never seen but knew were in my photo album.. close-up, unforgiving images..

so many photographs were taken on my ipad to track my progress or, goddess forbid, decline..

we sat and looked at these intense images splayed on the television in the middle of my house..

we saw pictures of my back with tubes running straight through the skin and into my kidneys..

oh, and the skin. i had become allergic to the plastic tape they had to use everywhere.. and yet my entire surface had to be kept sterile or else infection would travel to my kidneys.. so the skin was just deteriorating ..bleeding. sloughing. swollen. angry .. really disgusting-looking..

and my yoni! oh, my yoni!..

and the open wounds, the skinless areas..

382

donor skin-graft sites all over my body.. the whole front of my scalp—well, scalped.. my entire back open..

myshkin is a collage artist. all of her record covers are her own collage pieces.. she and yazzy revel in their time creating pieces out of old magazines and books....

for years, i searched and searched for the right tattoo artist to paint my back.. i had already created the image in my head, but i wanted the right person to ink my body..

i kept searching until one day, i saw a young woman with four salvador dali paintings on her back.. the work was stunning..

i had finally found my artist.. she wasn't even twenty-one years old yet.. she wasn't legally allowed in a bar yet, but i was going to trust her with my body's permanent expression..

i had planned that tattoo on my back for more than ten years.. i went to jay'e jones and returned home— after two torturous eight-hour sessions— with a piece that was four times as large as i thought it would be.. beautiful? yes. large? also yes.

a woman tree, her roots traveling down my buttocks and branches, reaching for the moons sitting above her just below my shoulders.. i loved her, and she reminded me to stay grounded.. when i felt scared or flighty, i would meditate on her and reach for the earth with my feet.. and with my arms, i would reach for the moon to find my inspiration..

and the moons on my fingers.. those i miss the most.. ahh, such frivolity, when you think of it..

so much of my art was taken from me.. a twenty-two-year-old tattoo of a meditating woman on one ankle and another piece that wasn't even a year old on the other..

oh, i loved that one.. it was a redwood tree, a favorite totem of mine, going up my leg almost to the knee with roots all down my foot.. and a woman stirring her herbal concoction in her cauldron at the tree's base.. it was my only colorful piece..

see, i chose trees because i was always so fiery, in the air, floating with the breeze and the stars.. reaching for the moon was never a stretch for me. finding my roots was my meditation. and those trees on my body helped me.

years of meditating on my roots helped me find my ground, my center.

and now my symbols are gone. my reminders have vanished. even my feet, our human roots, have been taken. i no longer tread on the earth.

oh, thank you, goddess, for the inspiration to make my practice a meditation of finding the deepest core of the earth, to ground myself. years of practice. a divine gift.

...

in the hospital, i was confused when a group of doctors laughed as one repeatedly spoke of blue moons on my ass. even through the drug and shock haze, i was aware of how inappropriate his choice of words and topic of joke were. but i didn't understand what he was talking about. what was so funny? what were these men chuckling about as they spoke and loomed above me?

it wasn't until after a major surgery that i got the joke. they sliced the moons from my back and placed them on my butt— my ass— to protect the skin that was destroyed.

at first, i was humiliated when i realized the meaning of the joke.

but later, the humiliation dissipated as myshkin spoke of her love of collage.

i was to be her living art piece.

even through the fog, i heard her. how lucky was i?

yes, i have become a collage...

i feel like it's been that way my entire life..

as an arab born in america, i picked and chose the parts of my culture and legacy that suited me...

i always felt like i have been woven together, only now it is visible...

indeed, they have taken the tattoo from my back and used it to patch me up over many parts of my body...

i look and i see bits of blue here and there, the tattooed ink now on my thighs and on my backside and on my legs..

art that was once whole has now been shattered and scattered and woven together to create a new work of art...

it shows the person that i have always been ...

the montage, now visible..

woven together...

a collage...

jenny
brush with death

for days, i was in so much pain..

i hadn't even been home for six months.

and ahh..

i couldn't do anything but moan and cry out and rock back and forth.. i couldn't talk or read or watch a movie because i couldn't focus on anything but getting through each moment..

that november, the one after i lost my legs, i spent so many long days surviving pain because we were all so used to me being in that state.. we just thought that this was my new reality.

it didn't occur to any of us that i should go back to the hospital.

until finally, i did go back. i ended up having to stay thanksgiving week without food as they ran tests and pumped me up yet again with antibiotics..

that was a long week.

but, oh.. when i left, i felt like a person again..

feeling overjoyed to be out of my misery, i traveled with my family that next week to visit my sister for my niece's birthday..

i was so excited to get to do a thing that used to be normal less than a year ago..

but once i got there, the pain started again..

all of a sudden, the party was focused on me, as once again i succumbed to the treachery of this new state of being.

my sister is a doctor and my sister-in-law an acupuncturist, and they were both doing everything they could to help me, while the rest of my family had to watch as i spiraled down..

not only was i experiencing the horror of the physical pain, but i was feeling incredibly guilty for ruining my niece's party..

after an hour of uncertainty on how to proceed, joyce decided to pack me in the car and take me to the emergency room..

by that time, i felt we couldn't get there fast enough..

i knew i was dying..

i started to give joyce instructions on what to do if i didn't make it..

"yazzy's savings are in these accounts.."

"yazzy has to go to college."

"make sure the house is secured for her.."

"protect her, joyce!"

at first, joyce didn't want to hear it, then changed her mind and said, "tell me everything, jenny."

i ended up staying in the hospital that time for three weeks. the doctors told me they were amazed that my kidneys hadn't just burst from the severity of the hydronephrosis i was suffering from.

they were amazed i even survived the night..

and all i could feel was relief that this time, i had felt the brush with death..

now i would know the feeling of dire emergency, and i would recognize the warning if i was about to die.

jenny
patience

patience. i thought i knew patience. i went through nursing school as a single mom, for goddess' sake!

i have so many memories from those times that forged my patience..

..carrying yazzy through the pitch-black desert to drop off at a friend's at five in the morning in order to make my nursing clinicals on time. my baby in my arms sleeping, then half awake and crying, "mama where are we? don't leave me, mama!"

i thought i knew patience.

i went to see my urologist, doctor jordan, after that november scare when my kidneys almost shut down and they reinserted the nephrotomy tubes, despite my loud, angry protests..

i had been looking forward to seeing doc jordan for weeks. how long must these urine bags hang off my body? isn't the colostomy bag enough?

"just a few more months," he told me.

that's a few more months with nephrostomy bags, tubes that run directly out of my back, my skin peeling off in protest against the plastic. every day, it was a struggle just to find clothes that hide the damn bags.

a few more months? how was i gonna get through another day?

jenny

shopping with mysh

how soft some of these experiences make me! how had i been so clueless before!

how did i used to treat people whom i perceived as different from me?

one day, myshkin took me shopping for my store. she drove me to little india to check out some of the places i used to frequent.

i was feeling energetic. spunky. but i was still sick, still in my wheelchair most of the time.

managing to squeeze around the tight spaces of a favorite shop, i made my choices and picked out what i needed, feeling buoyant and empowered.

the clerk came out and i had questions about some of her stock. she listened and she answered myshkin. i asked her some more. again, she answered myshkin. frustrated and holding back tears, i finished asking her what i wanted to know, but she still didn't look at me. she assumed i would not be the one who needed to know the information about the business.

she saw that i am disabled, that i was sitting in a wheelchair, and her inability to talk to me or even look at me answered all the questions i would never ask.

we left and went to another store.

i was devastated. i was furious. how dare she assume that i'm stupid just because i'm legless?! how could she deem my brain was damaged just because my body was?

as hurt as i was, and as angry, i had to ask myself:

have i ever treated anyone differently because of what i perceive their disability to be?

have i made an assumption about someone just because of the way they presented themselves?

that woman had no hard feelings towards me. she was probably just curious about my odd appearance. almost certainly uncomfortable.

ashamed of myself, i had to face the fact that i have probably treated someone the same way in my past.

as hard as some of these experiences are, as uncomfortable as some of these truths make me, i am so grateful for the wisdom they offer.

instruction on how to treat those around me..

indeed, i am becoming softer by the moment.

jenny
arduous growth

sometimes i wonder when the lessons will ever stop..

sometimes i wonder if i am such a young and inexperienced soul that i have to have painful evolutions happening almost all the time..

even in writing this book— a book about a trying journey-- i am experiencing arduous growth..

i want to yell at the sky.. i want to ask,

"will it ever be easy, for just one day?"

"can't i just be lazy and static for one damn minute?"

"i take it back! i would rather sit around and NOT GROW!"

but i know that i won't.

jenny
tough

i always toughed shit out.. i was always the one who would brush away difficult experiences and continue to move forward.

when i first met rosie, we were held up at gunpoint.

there were two men who put a gun to our heads and took our possessions.

i was so nervous, i started giggling hysterically and the younger man, the man with the gun, started shaking and i thought,

'oh my god! he's going to accidentally blow my head off!'

rosie didn't leave her house for three weeks after that.

me? i went on as if nothing ever happened.

i didn't even cry or feel scared afterward.

now? oh my goddess. now?

now, i weep if i feel left out of a conversation.

i yell if i feel wronged.

i got in a fender bender and i was hysterical.

i couldn't fathom driving home afterward.

i couldn't fathom putting my baby in the car with me.

how could i put her in danger?

how could i put her through any more trauma than she has already experienced?

i never used to be fazed by anything. i could always power through.

now, everything is on the surface.

isn't there anything in-between?

jenny
respite

how close have you ever been with someone? i mean someone who is not a mother, father, brother, sister or partner.. someone who is not your child?

we all have friends.. hell, here in joshua tree, we call our close friends "members of our tribe".. without each other, we would not survive this powerful desert..

but how close are we willing to get to another person not bound by blood or commitment? how vulnerable will we become?

kristen, the beloved tribeswoman who introduced myshkin and i in the first place, is a spirit sister.. we knew it the moment we laid eyes on each other.. we met because of someone we both loved in a complex, maybe slightly sordid situation.. that probably deserves its own book..

in that first moment, we knew we were sisters, and that the universe had shimmied and shaken to allow us to be standing in front of each other, at last eye to eye..

this we knew..

but what we didn't know was just how close we were to become..

when i finally came home from the hospital, even as we rejoiced deeply, myshkin, yazzy and i found ourselves in a dire situation. my partner was now in charge of all my care without the medical knowledge to back her up..

she was placing gauze on my open back, checking my wounds for infection, having to move me in order to help me pee and figure out how to teach me to maneuver myself around in a wheelchair without much strength..

yazzy was so happy to have me home, but she was terrified i was going to have to leave again, or wasn't going to survive and she was afraid to touch me, lest she hurt me. she really just needed alone time with the mama she thought she was going to lose, yet nobody was going to allow me to be home without another adult..

it was a hard time..

and now i was really in shock, because while being in the hospital was hard— and all i wanted was to come home— being back in my own home only reminded me of what i could not do.. i don't think i was very graceful during that transitional period..

and this, after myshkin had months of little sleep, of overwhelming fear, of traveling, of surviving on adrenaline..

it was a really hard time..

and though i was hazy from the pain and foggy on the meds, i saw it.. i saw myshkin spiraling down, down.. she was a shell of herself, absolutely maxed out..

and i was frightened that with all this medical care she was giving me, even to my most intimate parts, she would lose her sexual desire for me.. that our relationship would become one of caregiver and dependent.. it was an acute fear..

one day, i looked at myshkin and saw such darkness under her eyes and a look that clearly said, "i am on the brink of a breakdown."

so i called kristen.. i asked her to come and do respite care for me three or four days a week.

and so she came..

kristen came those mornings, physically got me out of bed, undressed me, wrapped me in plastic wrap..

wait.. back up..

yes, kristen had to wrap me up each morning before pushing my wheelchair into my shower and sliding me onto my shower chair..

you see, i had wounds everywhere.. indeed, my back was entirely skinned with the donor sites for my skin grafts.. these would just not heal!

but i also had two nephrostomy tubes and a new colostomy bag which i didn't know much about. because we believed we couldn't get it wet, we thought we had to wrap me up every morning for the rest of my life! i also had a PICC line in my arm that could not get wet..

so she would sit me up in my wheelchair in my bathroom and wrap me up, get a running start to push me up the new ramp— built for me by guy green and barnett english and the community of folks that had readied my house for me—and finally, into the shower.

i also want to interrupt myself to say that kristen herself was a hot mess.. she had been diagnosed with M.S. only a couple of years before and was dealing with a lot of body pain issues herself.. and at that time, she was transitioning into a new way of being, emotionally and physically..

we would say: the gimp leading the gimp..

so this woman in pain, and with a new disability, would shove me up into the shower and slide me over to my chair, terrified that my nephrostomy tubes might get pulled out, and worried about all my business getting wet..

she would shower me, dry me, get me back over to my wheelchair, put my skivvies on me and dress me.. at some point, she would need to look at my yoni to make sure my wound there was okay..

i know, a lot of information..

but this is my point.. we love our friends, we tell them our secrets, ask for their advice and cry on their shoulders.. but how many people do we have in our lives who would come over and care for all parts of us?

kristen's love for me allowed me to become unfathomably vulnerable and trusting..

a genuine, and i think necessary, part of my healing.

jenny
in an emergency

i think the biggest distress that i have experienced with regards to not having legs anymore is the fear that i will not be able to get to yazzy fast enough during an emergency.

one night, while myshkin was at a gig and yazzy and i were at home, in our own beds, we had an earthquake. it wasn't a large one, but it was enough to strike that panic button that goes off in every mother's body during a crisis. it took me a good three seconds before i realized i couldn't just jump out of bed and run to her,

and another three to figure out how long it would take me to get my legs on and get to her.

later that night, i had nightmares of catastrophes happening and me being stuck in concrete or quicksand, and helpless in my ability to protect my daughter.

i think about this often. the fact that i cannot be her ultimate protector in an emergency is the thought that keeps me up at night.

jenny
hard lessons, wicked laughter

there have been so many lessons that have come in such hard and hilarious ways..

i suppose life is what you make of it.. who doesn't know this? my ten-year-old will tell you this.. but sometimes the simple lessons are so much more arduous than others..

...

i was finally well enough to hold a staff meeting.. this in itself was a victory..

i was nervous, yes..

who wouldn't be when addressing the women who had taken care of her business for the better part of a year?

it went wonderfully. i was so happy and we were all feeling so close.. it felt like a success..

...

the kidneys are vital organs.. without a functioning kidney, it is a matter of hours or days before death. doctors, nurses and worried family members intensely monitor urine output when a loved one is near death or has had kidney failure for one reason or another.. it's no joke..

my kidneys were fine.. it was my ureters that were acting up. i guess when i was in the coma, they sustained a loss of blood flow and became attenuated, or thinned, near the bladder and weren't draining like they were supposed to..

i nearly died four months after arriving home from the long hospital stay. my kidneys swelled to extremity because the ureters couldn't drain into the bladder..

that was when the dreaded nephrostomy tubes went in again.. oh goddess, i cannot ever describe the pain and suffering one goes through having to live with those things.. they are tubes that run straight into your back and drain into a urine bag..

yes, folks, i had tubes poking straight through my body and into my kidneys.. and was walking around with two urine bags attached to me..

getting dressed was always a stressful event, as i had to find clothes that hid my colostomy bag, nephrostomy tubes and bags..

and i had two urine bags hanging off my body!

not my favorite time..

…

happy as i was after this meeting, i stood up to give hugs and was momentarily confused by a rush of water pouring out from under my baggy dress.. it took me a full five seconds to realize that a bag had burst and was draining out onto the floor as i was surrounded by my colleagues..

i had felt so great about the professionalism i had displayed at this meeting, only to be standing in my own urine by the end..

i tried to keep my cool as i politely and demurely asked myshkin to help me.. the amazing women around me immediately started wiping up the mess without so much as a visible flinch.. i know i am surrounded by greatness..

no tears came out until i got into the car with myshkin.. only then did i let the reality of the situation fully wash over me..

i knew i needed to talk to patricia.. i knew i needed a good, wicked laugh about this, and that she would be the perfect person for that..

when she came over to take me on a walk the next day, she kindly listened to me, horrified, as i relayed the story to her.. by the end of our walk, we were cackling madly at the hilarity of the lesson.. knowing that humility is a gift, and that we were now free to go through life with lightness..

"so i said something silly at work?" "so i gave the wrong direction to my students at my yoga class this morning?" okay, that may be embarrassing, but did i piss my pants in public today?

life can be as traumatic or as humorous as we choose..

it is often not as intense as it sometimes seems..

life is truly what we make of it..

jenny
permission

i want to give people permission to stare at my body, to get an
eyeful..

jenny
why would i?

why would i talk about my bag? why would i do it?

the thought terrifies me, and yet i feel the same way about hiding my prosthetic legs.

being consumed by shame and embarrassment leads so many to want to conceal the parts of ourselves that make us different.

when i first came home, i felt terrified that anyone would find out i had a colostomy bag or that someone would see it.

but if we all hide, if we can never see each other, we will always feel like the only ones in the world.

i don't want to be the only amputee in the world... i don't want to be the only person with a colostomy bag. it's lonely.

thoughts arise such as:

i won't be accepted in my community!

where will my desirability go?

i still want to be seen as beautiful!

does myshkin see me as desirable?

she says she does. i'm going to believe her.

for today, at least.

i have to.

my heart depends on it.

jenny
ptsd

my therapist told me that i most definitely have PTSD..

she said, "even if you don't have the emotional symptoms of PTSD, after so many surgeries, there is no way you aren't suffering the after-effects of trauma.."

i hadn't talked to her in several months because of the craziness of so many more surgeries and moving back to my home, my work and my community from the insular safety of my parents..

she told me, "after the iatrogenic illness, there is no way you wouldn't be suffering from trauma and post-traumatic stress.."

before i could answer, she said, "you may not be aware of it, but it is indeed happening."

oh, i knew this was happening..

previously in our conversation, i had spoken extensively about the details of my physical health after my latest operations, but i hadn't had a chance to tell her about the mood swings i was experiencing..

i was having these all-encompassing emotions that seemed to be out of my control..

i would be fine one minute, euphoric even, going about my day.. and then something would happen that would trigger me and i would fall onto a pyre of rage or sorrow..

it would feel like flames consuming my body.. my face would turn red and hot..

i would start sweating and then panic from the uncontrollable heat that held me prisoner..

somewhere inside me, i would recognize that there wasn't a rational reason to be feeling the way i did, but that would do nothing to allay the ride..

i was unable to reason myself out of the emotion that was devouring me..

after a few weeks of this emotional instability and psychological night-mare for my whole family, i realized that this must be a result of the trauma, for this was not the jenny i remembered.. i desperately asked those closest to me if i was still the person they knew..

"how could myshkin know if this was the woman she was partnered with? we were a new couple when i got sick!"

my friends assured me that indeed i was a naturally stable person and would return to that state..

but even after realizing that my emotions and reactions were irrational and a part of the recovery, i could not reign them in ....

i just learned to close up and let my feelings wash over me so as not to let them seep out all over myshkin or yazzy.. consequently, they consumed me ..

i didn't get a chance to fill my therapist in on any of that because the hour flew by.. i didn't get a chance to tell her about it, but oh yes, i am aware that i am experiencing PTSD, and that it's rife with emotional symptoms..

myshkin

ptsd

What PTSD looks like to me- she becomes completely inaccessible. It seems she is still able to fake it with everyone else, smiling and light voiced with friends when they appear, but she feels icy to me. It feels like punishment, like I must have done something wrong. My attempts to break through the ice are futile, pawing soft against steel. I see cold fury in her eyes. I am easily hurt so I close up like a sea creature in her shell. I have taken out my helpless hurt on Yazzy, criticizing her, trying to get her to obey me, to feel like I still have some control in this out of control moment. Jenny tells me I am the person she completely trusts, can let down her guard with. But in the icy moment it is hard to feel this as a privilege. Maybe other people see the fury too, but are able to distance Jenny's feelings from their own. I am not so able. Her triggering triggers me, I trigger Yazzy and suddenly it's like we are in a house full of IEDs.

Sometimes I get triggered first. Sometimes Yazzy does. Even now, when it happens less often, I still struggle to find the appropriate response. I want to stay calm, balanced, take my space for some time if I need to and then gently come back to them with an open heart, holding not pushing … that is actually the only thing that ever works. But too often I am thrown into a spiral of indignant anger that I then have to find my own slow way out of it. I am grateful to science, for finding a name for this syndrome, PTSD. It really helps us to not feel lost in crazy.

I reacted to the trauma in other ways as well. Generally independent, intrepid and creative, I found myself pretty adrift for the first years after Jenny's illness. I kept starting things that I didn't finish, falling into patterns of floating, time wasting, non-directional activity. I started losing faith in my possibilities and abilities. A job which took me away from my family and out to the middle of the desert three days a week forced me to spend time alone; to once again feel my value, which finally, and I hope permanently, snapped me out of that particular malaise.

jenny
still trying to figure it out

i had been doing so well.. the doctors kept telling me they were surprised at my recovery.

"amazed!" they would say.

"i can't believe it! what are you doing?! tell me about these herbs!"

i no longer needed certain surgeries, for things were healing up on their own.

my skin was mending so well that my wound specialist and occupational therapist asked what i used so they could pass that information on to their other patients..

i was doing well.

i was excited to get back to work..

i realize now that i was connecting the ability to work with my recovery.

that it would hold some semblance of normality.

and i tried a couple of weeks after i first got out of the hospital..

"i am ready," i told everyone.

i remember sitting in a meeting and everyone looking at me with compassion and love, but with expressions that said, 'what are you doing here?'

i left that meeting after twenty minutes and lay down in pain and defeat.

i found myself yearning for my job back, the world i once knew.

months later, i got what i asked for.

i asked the universe for the reclamation of my business, and whew!

be aware of what you put out because you can get just that..

while i was away at the hospital, many devoted people kept my businesses afloat.

six months after i got home, many of those people were exhausted from taking care of me as much as they did. slowly, they melted away to take back their own lives.

i found myself doing all the books, in charge of all manufacturing and orders in the lab and working three days a week in the shoppe..

six days a week, i was constantly running until i fell into bed, spent.. after all, i was still a mama, a homemaker, a fiancée..

but i got a wake-up call a couple of months later..

after some tests and visits to my docs, i found that some of those surgeries that were no longer needed were on the verge of being needed again.. my kidneys were declining, my grafts were not growing the way they had been, my veins were collapsing under the IV.

i got all this information right before a trip to portland with my family.. while yazzy was at rock-and-roll camp for girls during the day, i had time to reflect on my health and my priorities..

after the hospital, my thoughts had been, "i know i need to focus on my health, but yazzy is number one, and in order to be a good mama i need to provide for her!"

i finally came to the realization that without my health, i wouldn't be able to do anything for her.. it'snot rocket science, i know.. but it was a huge opening for me.. i have always taken very seriously my role as her provider and stable force..

how would i come to balance being a good mama, getting all my work done, being an attentive partner and take care of my health?

i have no idea.. after all this time, i am still trying to figure that out.

jenny
shoes, irrationality and change

so much has changed for me..

no, not just my legs, my hand, my belly.. i feel different.. why can't i be the nice person i always was before..?

i was always so open, accommodating, gentle..

today, i just want to scream, to push away, to thrash around and weep..

giving my shoes away. fuck. this hurts. watching people try on the shoes that i will never again be able to wear. fuck, this hurts.

whenever i can't find something in the house or when i see an object that has been relocated while i was in the hospital, i get so triggered. it makes me crazy inside.

i know it's not rational, but there it is.

it hurts. i get angry that i had to live in a fucking bed while a whole community was inhabiting my house.

how could i ever say something so treacherous when everyone is just trying to support me and my family?

i said it wasn't rational. but there it is.

jenny
tired

i'm so tired..

i'm just so tired...

is it normal to be this tired all the time?

jenny

post traumatic stress syndrome

myshkin urged me to write..

she said, "write this minute so you can catch what you are feeling as it is happening.."

ahh.. that is the hardest time to download, because all i want to do is scream and rail and pound my fists..

i got triggered again today..

it could be anything that triggers me.. it could be a random word taken the wrong way. it could be when i am not able to join in an activity due to my new health state, or it can be nothing at all.. perhaps a cocktail of fatigue and hypersensitivity..

it could be that i had to miss my shoppe shifts because i was in the hospital again, having to rule out some serious condition due to symptoms i was having.. this always creates a ripple of fear and edginess in my household.

on the way to my shoppe one morning, i was so nauseous, hot and achey, that i lasted only twenty minutes before having to reach out, yet again, to have someone cover my shift..

but whatever the reason, i was triggered.

the night of the chili cook-off and stick horse rodeo (no, really) in pioneertown.. i really wanted to go but of course, i was too sick to attend..

a small part of me was relieved at the opportunity to have a couple of hours of alone time. this is something that rarely happens, maybe once every six months or so..

rationally, there was a feeling of gratitude that i could be in bed all by myself.. quiet..

but i started noticing provocative thoughts sneaking up on me.. like a snake slithering towards me. slowly..

i see her, that snake, and tell her, "no, i don't need you tonight.. i need this quiet time.. i am sick.. go away!"

after a few more moments, she is not creeping up on me, this snake.. she is brazen, loud, bold.. i see her approach.. she is saying, "hello, here i come."

"no," i tell her.. "really.. i don't need you to protect me.. i am happy to be left alone tonight."

it doesn't matter what i say.. she continues to come towards me..

the thoughts start to sprout in my head, as herbs do in my garden after a week of watering..

"of course, i am stuck alone again.. of course, everyone will get to go and have fun except for me.."

"no," i tell the snake.. "i need time alone.. what a gift it will be to do whatever i want to do.."

"nobody cares that you will have to stay home.. nobody even offers to hang out with you or ask why you look sad," says the snake.

"you don't understand!" i shout..

no longer is our conversation little insinuations and rebuttals.. no more are there suggestions, quiet snide remarks from this damn snake.. there are only taunts and mockery..

there is a yelling match happening.

"if anyone offered to stay with me, i would tell them to leave, that i just need the space!"

"but they don't care that you can't go. they don't worry that your feelings might be hurt that the party continues whether you are there or not!"

"but of course they care!.. they love me!"

myshkin asks if i am okay and the explosion happens in my head..

there is red, there is noise, there is upheaval..

my head starts to become a small round room, my own self-preservation running in circles and trying to find the exit, any small opening it can escape from.. there is full-blown mocking, yelling, punching, wicked laughter from the reptile..

and whimpering, reasoning, pleading from my heart..

at this point, it is imperative that i don't look in anyone's eyes.. someone might ask again if everything is okay, and i will explode and blame them, or else break down and weep..

which would be so much better if there was anything coherent to explain or any reason at all to feel this way..

this is what i have started to call the Triggering.. if there is a name for it, i can eventually let myshkin know what is happening..

at some point, i can warn her that i am unreasonable and volatile, that i am having an Episode and that if she gets too close, she will be directly in the line of fire..

it is exhausting for all of us.. yaz, mysh and myself.. but i am recognizing it more and more quickly, and able to reach out and ask for help or pardon in less and less time..

i wish i could explain the sensation more succinctly and i am anything but proud of myself for putting my loved ones through such distress, but i am writing this, coming out about this, in hopes of reaching out to all those who experience PTSD, and to their loved ones so affected by it..

to tell them that they are not alone, and that they are not crazy..

myshkin

lawyer after lawyer

As a musician who had been working back in the days when record companies ruled, I had heard tales of the ways labels court artists to get them under contract. This was the exact feeling I got, the day a big fancy Wilshire Boulevard law firm sent a limousine all the way out to Joshua Tree to pick us up and take us to Los Angeles to meet them. They led us into a large, fancy room in a large, fancy office and sat us around a long, oval table. Jenny was still so very sick. She didn't even have prostheses yet, and was in so much pain. At one point during the meeting, Jenny doubled over and the distressed lawyers all left the room so she could recover composure.

They didn't take the case. They said it was too complicated, that the doctors they would pay to have as expert witnesses could not determine clearly enough who had been at fault, that there were too many doctors and institutions involved. One hospital was a state facility whose statute of limitations was therefore six months instead of a year. At six months Jenny was still in rehab, not pursuing lawsuits.

I think most everyone assumed Jenny would have a case in this situation. This is, after all, why doctors pay for such comprehensive malpractice insurance. Because things go wrong, because sometimes it is their fault, because if you go in for a tiny, two stitch surgery, and you come out of it after six months, without legs, it seems like someone would be at fault. And lawyer after lawyer thought so too. But in time they all reached the same conclusion. It was not cut and dried, it was too messy. And since malpractice suits are undertaken on spec and they only get paid if there is a settlement, no one took the gamble. No one took the case. It took a lot out of Jenny, still in deep physical recovery. She felt dirty having to deal with such negativity, and with this weird kind of rejection over and over. And came to realize that she would have to keep working just as hard to make a living, with a fraction of her old physical capacity.

jenny
mood swings

will these mood swings ever go away?

jenny
i am (not so) sorry

i feel apologetic .. i walk around actually feeling apologetic..

i know i am making people feel uncomfortable and i want to tell them that i am sorry for looking the way i do..

i even tell people that i am sorry.. sorry for having lost my legs.. sorry that my hand looks the way it does.. ooh— sorry for the weird hand shake..

i feel bad when i don't mention it... my Ordeal.. when i don't let people know that i was Normal not so long ago.. that i was just like them so recently.

it feels like a mean thing to do.. as though i could make it easier for them and help them feel more comfortable, and yet i choose not to do it..

but it's not really like that.. it's not that i am deciding to make them do the work on their own.. sometimes, i just don't have it in me.. sometimes, i am in a hurry or just have to get things done, or i'm with my daughter, or just too cranky to get into a long explanation…

and that feels as though i am not being nice.. not giving just a bit to ease people's discomfort.. so i find myself apologizing..

more recently, i have been playing with not explaining myself as an experiment.. or a way of screaming, Fuck You! This Happened! I look Weird! Get Over It!!

usually, i just apologize..

myshkin

drugs

Anahita, a local potter, made a gorgeous underwater green ceramic tray with many tiny ceramic cups, and gifted it to Jenny. For pills for now, said the note, but soon you'll be filling it with chocolate. When Jenny came home she had whole swaths of her back in open wounds, tubes coming out of her kidneys, in so much pain. I propped her between six pillows in bed so she would not roll onto her back as she slept. I changed dressings, putting into practice all I had witnessed in the burn unit, worried sick over the persistent skin infections right where those tubes went straight. into. her. kidneys.

She was on ten or fifteen different prescriptions, I had many alarms set throughout the day and night for dosing. She began to wean herself from the pharmaceuticals as soon as she was able. Jenny is not someone that wants to owe her allegiance or health to a pill. Stubborn that way. The toughest was the methadone they had put her on, the first week in the burn unit, as a long acting cushion underneath the spikes and dips of the other pain killers. Methadone is so long acting that no one actually knows its half life. Which makes it long hell to get off of. I do believe everyone expected her to stay on it forever. But after a few months home of ever increasing intestinal pain, midnight trips to the ER, inpatient stays at the hospitals down the hill, and finally being told that the opioids were a part of her problems, she initiated a withdrawal.

Insomnia, depression, discomfort, pain. She didn't want to take antidepressants, the docs didn't see how she could do it without them.

She quit them after a day or two, rode it out like a cowgirl.

jenny
cold turkey

piper kept quoting this song as i was coming off the methadone.. cold turkey by john lennon and yoko ono.

how i didn't anticipate the hardship of coming off this particular drug amazes me, since i know so many people who have gone through opioid withdrawals, both personally and during my time working in an emergency room.

this was the work of the divine, i am sure, because if i had really thought about it, really knew how hard it would be, i might not have attempted it.

you see, when i first came out of the hospital, i had many prescriptions, maybe ten or ten thousand. sweet anahita brought me a handmade, ceramic pill dispenser, a beautiful tray with thirty-one tiny little bowls inside. she left a note that said, "for your prescriptions. one day soon, i hope they will be filled with bits of chocolate."

so many pills that my daily doses didn't fit into the bowls.

i quickly became tired of all the drugs. i would decide on one day or another to stop one of them and tell myshkin, "no, today i am stopping that one."

though i could see it worry her, she never pushed me.

after two months, i only had one daily prescription left.. methadone.

while i knew it was an opioid and that it would be the hardest one to quit, i really had no idea of the depth of suffering i was about to experience.

i decided on a sixteen-day weaning, and on day eight, many friends came over to celebrate the halfway mark. "you can do it!" "look at how brave you are!"

i needed their encouragement because i was having such a hard time of it.

i was getting about half an hour of sleep per night, and this alone was creating trauma.

my stomach was in so much pain.. have you ever seen the movie trainspotting? the bathroom stall scene? opioids slow down peristalsis in your intestines, so when the drug starts leaving your body, your intestines go crazy. try this with a colostomy bag.

oh, and the depression and shock. what i wasn't prepared for was the reality that would hit me once the haze of drugs wore off. i looked down and saw my new body. i looked around and saw my life, my work, my daily activities with my daughter in someone else's hands.

in an attempt to lift my spirits, i was being driven to the beach and into the national park and put into a wheelchair to look at the beauty of the world, to remember why i fought so hard to live. and while trying to smile and appear somewhat normal, i was melting away inside, watching myshkin hike and splash around and climb rocks with yazzy, while i was left to ponder my new life from a chair, an observer, sure that i would never again be a participant.

even while i was aware that everyone else was trying so hard to make my life easier, i couldn't connect, couldn't be that person that everyone remembered.

i couldn't find the light. i couldn't find the prospect of a better day, or really of any hope at all.

piper came over and declared that we were having a harry potter marathon and we proceeded to watch all the films. she told me that i was wearing a horcrux, a ring or talisman that stores part of a person's soul to protect them from death (known as a phylactery outside the world of harry potter) and that it was making me see all black, but i wasn't really seeing the truth. she knew that everything was going to be okay and that she would hold that truth for me.

i had to believe her, had to hold onto that.

there was one day when kimberly came over and just let me put my head in her lap. i lay there for hours— weeping i think.

elise and patricia came by and tried to bring some buoyancy to me. they took me to marshalls to shop, because at eighty pounds, none of my clothes fit me. i saw everyone laughing and having fun. i saw myself join in. but it was from far away that i took in these scenes.

we had a new cat, peter, and he was my protector. if i was in pain, he would hover around me and not let anyone too close. one time, i was in the bathroom with the door closed, so he couldn't get to me when he heard the moans and weeping. he pounded his head on the door over and over, until i could let him in.

one day, i called kimberly and asked if she could come over while i got into the shower. it was one of the first days that i was left alone. i was trying to be responsible by having someone with me while i transferred to my shower chair.

she told me that she would be over in fifteen minutes. by the time she arrived, peter was circling me and i was wailing and sweating and scared at the sheer amount of pain i was feeling. later that day, i was again admitted into the hospital.

these days of withdrawing seemed to go on forever.

after two months, because i started to become frantic that i wasn't feeling any better, myshkin took me to see a psychologist who specialized in opioid withdrawal. he had been working with people for thirty years, had even written a book on the subject.

one of the first questions he asked me was, "are you in pain?"

"not really," was my answer.

after talking for a bit, he said, "you told me at the beginning of our meeting that you are not in any pain, but over the last half hour, you have mentioned pain in your legs, in your intestines, on your open wounds and at your nephrostomy tube sites, as well as your incessant insomnia. do you want me to repeat the question?"

he told me that methadone was created in germany during world war II when opioids had started to run out. they made sure it had lasting efficacy and indeed there is controversy on just how long the half-life is. the doctor said that he believed it to be thirty days, meaning that after a month, half of the amount of the drug is still in your body. "so it could take up to sixty days for your body to feel the true withdrawal of the drug."

the therapist told me that these days, doctors generally only prescribe methadone to people in dire situations, assuming they will stay on it for the rest of their lives.

indeed, myshkin thought i would have to live on painkillers.

as shocking and scary as this was to hear, it was also validating, because i had started to feel crazy, like i would feel this terrible for the rest of my life.

when my dad talked to some of my surgeons about me withdrawing myself, they seemed shocked. "why would she do that?" they asked him.

i quit methadone on october twentieth and started to feel somewhat human again by january. i am so grateful that i didn't know how hard that particular journey was going to be.

jenny
yazzy hit the wall

i awoke this morn filled with heaviness and resolve..
my little girl, the one it's all for, finally hit her wall..
it finally hit her last night..
it was time for us to get help..

jenny
four missing fingers

the idea for this book came many months ago, maybe a year.. yazzy and i were living at my folks'..

i started recording my thoughts..

then i moved back home to joshua tree and started to crawl my way back into my life..

time slips..

now i am looking at the book from a different angle..

it seems like i am looking over my shoulder at the Ordeal behind me..

can i still write from this perspective?

am i still having this experience? is the Ordeal a thing of the past?

ha! then i look down as i struggle to find a new typing style..

tapping on a keyboard with four missing fingers is not easy!!!

though i have been on a healing path and done much recovering, i suppose my experience will be fresh for a long time to come..

will i ever get used to my legs?

jenny
post trauma

oh, ouch goddess! to watch the emotions resurface..

everyone expects me to ride the roller coaster of PTSD, but witnessing yazzy in the heart-wrenching throes of it is torture..

last week, in preparation for the book, piper interviewed yazzy for the first time.. she asked her all kinds of questions including some really hard ones..

after their meeting, the two of them walked into my lab where i was tincturing.

"how was it?" i asked.

"it was fun, mama!" she assured me.

i had asked piper to do it that day because mysh, yazzy and i had a family counseling session scheduled for later that afternoon.

after piper left, i asked yazzy how it really went, and she said, "HARD. piper asked me what i would have done if you really had died."

i told her that must have been tough.

she said, "yeah, mama.. it was terrible!"

later, in therapy, when i brought up the interview, the therapist asked her how it went.

she acted so casual: "oh, it was fun."

i said, "but it was difficult, yes, baby?"

"NO, MOM!" she said.

she works so hard to have a tough exterior, though i do feel blessed that she tells me the real truth— even though she whispers it.

an hour after we got home from the therapy session, she had a spectacular, all-out meltdown.. i mean, she started wailing and didn't stop for an hour. screaming and crying. it was only when i told mysh that i was canceling all plans for that evening, and that yazzy and i were having a night to ourselves, that yazzy calmed down.

she was quiet and stuck to me like glue for the rest of the night. she ended up in my bed at midnight. i cuddled her all night.

then it happened again today when we were on our way to gretchen's art class after school and stopped at the natural sisters' café so i could buy treats for the family.. it was friday, after all..

i could tell yazzy was tired, but when she was rude to mysh and stomped on her foot in frustration, we took her cookie away until after class and dinner. this was less of a punishment than a concern that the sugar would make her feel even more out of control.

the twentyfive-minute drive to class in twentynine palms proved to be a nightmare.. she was hysterical and sobbing about her cookie..

she sounded just like she did when she was three years old.. no amount of reasoning could get through to her..

finally, late or not, i pulled over on the highway and started talking soothingly to her..

i told her i loved her no matter how loud she cried and that i would always be there for her. after a couple of minutes, she acknowledged that she was hungry and agreed to eat her protein snack. we had a calm drive after that as she told me about her day in school..

watching her regress like this is agony, but i am taking it to heart and holding on for dear life to the wisdom someone recently gave me:

this catharsis is heart-opening.

this catharsis is healing.

this catharsis is allowing the trauma out of her body.

jenny
plastic surgeon

ahh, the dark comedy..

yes, it is my way of dealing with hardship when life is particularly difficult..

i imagine a john waters film.. or wes anderson.. someone who can take a treacherous situation and twist it until we are laughing at the absurdity..

this has been my powerful coping method.. screwing my eyes just right so they can see the audience laugh as they munch on their popcorn..

so i went to see a plastic surgeon.. indeed, this was planned before i even left the ICU.. i lost so much tissue at the site of my infection that there was only skin covering my coccyx.. there is still no fat there.. it's not ideal to walk around with no padding over the bottom of your spine..

all my surgeons told me that this plastic surgeon was the best of the best.. that if anyone could work on top of grafted and scarred skin, he could.. my surgeons were the best, and if they were praising him, i knew he would be good..

so i went to the plastic surgeon.. i didn't feel comfortable, but i went.

i was disconcerted to see posters of before and after pictures of breasts and bellies, but i waited for my turn, believing that my cause was different.

when he swooped into the room and hugged me, i was immediately put at ease.

he was a sweetheart!

but this first visit, i was still so sick.. it was six months after my Big Stay in the Hospital and two weeks since my latest three-week stint. i was weak, foggy and vulnerable.

a camera was being focused on my yoni and the image projected on the opposite wall, which i found shocking. i hadn't yet seen my new yoni, and was not aware of the damage it had sustained.

i don't think i even cried that time. i was just stunned deeper into my fog.

he let my parents and i know that it was probably not possible to insert padding into the coccyx area because when the initial surgeries were happening, too much fat had been removed. so much tissue was damaged that the doctors would have had to take all the fat cells out. he explained that if there was at least one layer of adipose tissue left over my tailbone, he could insert more, but if the skin was attached to muscle, there would be nothing he could do.

it was necessary for me to have some diagnostic tests for him to determine if reconstructive surgery was a possibility.

i was too thin and weak for my surgeon to talk seriously of surgery at that time, so he just told me to gain weight, get healthy and come see him in a year.

so i went to see him that next year. the posters in the waiting room really bothered me this time. i realized that over the past year, i had been dreaming that my plastic surgeon could fix me somehow. that he could reconstruct my butt and reshape my belly. that he would be able to make my body a bit of what it had been before.

the posters leered at me. i couldn't with good grace judge anyone who wanted reshaping just to feel more beautiful as long as i was wanting the same thing.

damn it!

this time when i entered the office, he had me undress and stand in front of a large mirror. you know those mirrors in a fitting room that make you look skinny? the ones that make you look fabulous in a dress that really looks pretty terrible on you?

well, i think that this mirror did just the opposite.

i found myself hoping that it did.

i wanted to think that this looking glass was a circus mirror, enlarging you so that you beg for someone to fix you and make beautiful— to at least normal.

i stood there as he picked up skin grafts that had grown loose and let them drop again. over and over. "see what i could do?" (lift) "see the difference?" (drop) "see how the graft has loosened?" (lift) "see how i could fix it?" (drop)

i stood there, trying to cover my body with my gown as he kept lifting it and the skin, explaining how he could fix me.

i was mortified.

but while a good portion of me was experiencing this horror, there was an even larger part chuckling at the dark humor, enjoying the campiness, itching to get home and share with my people the absurdity of this experience.

and i would have let him fix me. if it were possible to pad my coccyx while reshaping it into a somewhat normal form, i would have let him into cut me. except that it would have cost more than i would ever really have. and it would put me in bed again for three months, something my psyche could not handle so soon.

so i left. and i left feeling free, finally letting go of the secret, deeply held desire to be made normal again.

jenny
i came to you whole

i came to you whole
and still you love me?

jenny
yoga on stilts

when i first started writing for this project, i spent a lot of time thinking up possible titles.

the first name that stuck was 'yoga on stilts'..

i was in a yoga class and there was an asana i could not get into..

there have been so many times that i think i will never be able to get into a position and yet, over weeks or months, i do anyway.. miraculously, i find myself doing the impossible..

but on this particular day, i knew i would never be able to achieve a particular pose.. it was a squat all the way down.. without any ankle flexion, my face would crash into the ground..

i tried anyway, until i realized the disaster i would have caused..

then i got angry.. i was seething the whole two minutes that everyone who has fucking ankles got themselves easily (or not so easily) through the asana..

i watched myself and my emotion..

even while i was supremely frustrated, i was amused at myself for getting so pissed off that i couldn't get into one position

during a ninety-minute class

for able-bodied people..

in my converse high tops.. on my stilts..

jenny
ice skating

it never failed.

every time i walked yazzy into the ice-skating rink, i would be overcome by the same peculiar feeling.

i would be taken back to my childhood skating excursions.

but the feeling was more than recollection.

i felt like i was one of the children walking toward the ice on that thick rubber flooring heading to a class.

it was tactile, overwhelming.

then it hit me.

it took multiple trips for me to understand the intensity of the memory.

i am always trying to find ways to describe what it feels like to walk on these prostheses. people are always so curious.

i FEEL like i'm on ice skates, all the time.

but especially when i'm walking through that rubber matting of the rink.

i am above the Earth, always working to keep my legs from falling inwards at the knees because of my distance from the ground.

jenny

cranky as hell

being farther away from the trauma of the Ordeal, i find myself feeling cranky as hell.. it comes out of nowhere and leaves when it is good and ready..

to be fair, it is softening.. i am now able to talk myself out of it quicker than when it started.. but it still descends upon me without notice or reason..

if it were a friend telling me this, i would know how to say all the right things:

"oh.. ptsd is a real and intense experience.."

"give yourself a break!"

"be gentle with yourself, you've had a crazy year!."

but sitting in the middle of it.. being the cranky one, watching the hurt pass through my family's eyes?

it's so much easier to be gentle with a friend than with yourself..

jenny
a slice of my new life

on this day, i am back in my wheelchair again, dammit. my new life is such that, if i have an extra long week, i bust a hole in the fragile new skin of one of my legs..

this week was one of those long and arduous weeks that ended with a trip down to orange county to visit my many doctors and shop for my store-- all at top speed. after driving two and a half hours to get home, a wound appeared when i peeled off my prosthesis.

so i am in my wheelchair again.

i was helping execute a project in yazzy's room, though piper had to take over to wield the hammer since i am so short in my wheelchair.

i wheeled over to the kitchen to start dinner, a trail of yazzy's excited shouts from the remodel project following me, when i got serenaded by mysh, who was in costume and practicing for her burlesque rehearsal tonight..

i wheeled past our dog shadow, as she munches on her dinner, used to the high energy of this family..

jenny
the new me

i keep wanting to write more, but have to keep trying to convince myself that i am not terrified about peering into the last couple of years and shedding light on them without tripping and falling..

into what? despair? depression? reality?

i lie here, recovering after my fiftieth surgery since the Big Ordeal..

finally giving myself the excuse to rest, to slow down, to heal..

only a few days before, doctor lane, my rock-star surgeon, had dissected my previously inserted bovine vaginal graft to better snuggle in my new stem-cell infused porcine graft..

you heard me right, folks.. i now have a tri-species pussy, about as fetish-y as one can ask for.. although probably not appropriate for anyone who is kosher..

yes, i need to keep telling my story from a comic perspective..

if i don't embrace the humor of some of this stuff, i would surely be crouched on the floor, cursing or crying..

it's true, i have always had a flair for the dramatic (being a leo) and for the quirky (being me)..

but i am starting to see the beauty of my new form: my new legs are starting to feel like me, my bag is losing its shame, my fingerless hand becoming endearing.. i am starting to love this new person..

figuring out how to thrive in my new reality is still a journey, but there is a warm light emanating from my thoughts..

somehow, this new year started with the realization that this will not be an easy year, the kind of year i had been hoping for, bringing the kind of ease that everyone has been telling me i deserve now..

it was a slow dawning that in the new year, i will still be working hard on achieving patience, as though i am pushing a heavy, lopsided rock up a hill, trying to find grace;

that it is still my practice to let go of fear, to relax, to breathe and to trust;

and that allowing myself to rest becomes my industriousness..

jenny
library fun

you know that feeling when you're in the middle of a great dream and then you look down and notice that you are naked?

i had that moment with my eyes wide open.

i was getting out of my car at the library.

i was feeling pretty good about myself, as i'd a busy morning, helping a friend with her newborn and doing various things for my shoppe.

i even had the energy to stop at the library and pick up the book i had ordered for yazzy.

follow through.. this is something i struggle with in my disorganized life-- it is what i am working hard on so that yazzy can trust my word.

and i had been getting tired so easily of late. working at the shoppe had left me so fatigued that i was lucky if i made it to the bank twice in a month.. pretty embarrassing for a store owner..

but on this day, i was feeling pretty damn proud of myself.

i parked right in front of the library, and as i stood up, i heard a soft 'plunk.'

i slowly looked down.

there, between my feet, was my colostomy bag.

it only took a few seconds of confusion to recognize that something was terribly wrong..

that the item at my feet should be attached to my body.

i could have really freaked out at that moment, as i was in the middle of downtown joshua tree. but by now, i have been in so many unlikely situations that i calmly bent down, picked up my bag and got back in my car.

i decided that no one could see me as i lifted my shirt and attached the bag back onto my body where it belonged.

then, after sanitizing my hands, i stood up once again and walked into the library.

jenny
my fifty-first surgery

maybe it's because i have been so open about my whole medical journey..

hell, maybe it's because i have always been just so damn open..

but i find it humorous when people ask me, "where was your surgery done?"

at the hospital in orange county, i always answer.

"no, but where on your body?" comes the all-to-often reply..

oh, it was another graft.

"where is the graft?"

let's chat later, i have started saying.

you see, it's my yoni. my pussy. that is where the graft went.

they are rebuilding my vagina, as it was destroyed three years ago.

i really don't have that much shyness in talking about it, but having that conversation in the middle of my shoppe? in line at the crowded health food store?

instead, i have just been saying, "let's have a drink. we'll chat."

jenny
life is full

my life is rich.. my life is so damn sweet..

i recognize this and sit back ..

i look at what i have and sigh with gratitude, with sorrow and with great joy..

but most of all with gratitude..

i have fought hard for this sweetness.. my life has brought many challenges, many gifts and many opportunities.

through the years, i have taken in as many as i could; indulging, over-indulging, savoring..

i have been in all kinds of states: depressed as a teen, high as a kite in my early adulthood, uncertain during divorce, stressed from single parenthood..

immersed in trauma, trauma, trauma, post-trauma..

and life brought joy, tears, belly laughs, awe, all. all..

and these days, i am full. rich. juicy.

stable. emerging and evolving.

day after day. after day.

jenny

is this all just a dream?

i had one of those dreams last night where you wake up feeling confused.

where you're not sure at first where you are, and it takes a few seconds just to recognize your own room?

in my dream, i'm walking with a group of people through a long, industrial, medical hallway. important people are there with me— yazzy, myshkin, my mom, some others. none of them are clear, just the knowledge that the Important Ones are there with me.

we are being led around by some sort of medical assistant in a white lab coat, reassuring me that the doctor is coming, that we will be on our way in no time.. there is an urgency about the whole atmosphere, with more than a touch of franticness.

i know we are waiting for my gynecological reconstructive surgeon. a mouthful, yes, and shocking that there are enough of us in need to warrant a specialist, but my doctor— felicia lane— is wonder-woman, a super rock-star.. i just love this woman— in my life and, apparently, in my dreams as well. she has cut me and pasted me and reassured me and loved me and believed in me more times than i can relay..

we've all watched those doctor shows— if you're a nerd like me, anyway— where the surgeons are gorgeous and brilliant and no more than twenty years old. haven't we all laughed at how unrealistic television can be?

not so with dr. lane. she is that gorgeous, that young and that competent.

okay, maybe not that young. but certainly no older than i am.

in my dream, we finally meet up with her. she pulls me aside and asks me in a very serious tone if i am sure that i want to go through with this...

if i am ready to see my dead body.

i am sure, yes.

she informs me that this sight can shake me from Reality, it can cause confusion if people find out about it. it may jolt me from the Present.

i tell her that i am nervous but ready.

my Important Ones are grouped around me and we start moving down the long, dark hallway, following my doctor.

we enter a room and things slow down. not the urgency, but our progress. there is a shifty vibe in the room.

everyone is milling about and i feel that the doctor is procrastinating.

i am impatient to get there, to see, to get this over with..

so dr. lane walks me into the adjoining room.

there in the corner is form in the shape of a body. i can see it, but there is a very bright light blinding me. i am squinting in an attempt to avoid the glare, but no matter what i do, i am unable to. i still can't see the body.

i walk around the room trying to block it out, but am unable to do that as well.

the is a lamp with a naked bulb in the room and i toss a dark red scarf over it.

the whole room reddens and grows dimmer.

i am able to see.

the first thing i notice is the bright red nail polish on my toes.

i think, "i never wear that color!"

only then do i notice that i have feet!

when i approach, i see that the feet and half-legs are standing up next to my supine form.

my calves and feet are not attached to my body, but there is no blood.

i am looking down at myself now. there are two large bowls beside my body. they are beautiful and covered in mosaics. yellow and red tiles.

"dia de los muertos!" is what pops into my head.

when i look at where my feet were once attached to my body— by now it seems so long ago— i see that there are large hands attached just below my knees.

they are as large as baseball gloves and open in a receptive fashion. they are covered in the same yellow and redmosaiced tiles as the bowls beside my body.

in the same moment, i am overwhelmed by the beauty and overcome with disgust and embarrassment.

"NO!" i yell.

"no! i can't have those gorgeous hands attached THERE! where feet and legs are supposed to be!"

i want them gone before anyone can see them.

it just looks so odd and creepy.

when i awoke and reoriented, my first thought was,

"oh goddess, this IS just a dream, isn't it?

i really did die in that hospital bed, didn't i?"

i woke myshkin and asked her if i was alive.

jenny

alternate words

my goddess.. it seems so far away from my ordeal..

so often, i am incredulous that this even happened..

did this happen to me?

where are my legs?

i lost my legs??!

damn, i never believed i was artistic or creative,

but look what i conjured up for my body! who but an artist could have
dreamed this body up?

sometimes, when i'm not tired, when i am not feeling insecure,

when i am not in pain..

i look at my body and revel in the beauty of the unimaginable..

i actually enjoy the legs, the quilted skin grafts— and yes— the colostomy bag.

i actually revel in this body..

in this interesting new body

alternate words for interesting..

alluring

amusing

arresting

attractive

beautiful

captivating

charismatic

compelling

curious
delightful
elegant
enchanting
exceptional
exotic..

myshkin
the wedding

We had sent out a 'save the date' invitation to a wedding, spring 2015. But Jenny was still too sick. Once again, she was wiser than I when it came to timing. She kept telling me she didn't want to marry me in a wheelchair with tubes coming out of her back. I wanted to do it as soon as we could but she was convinced it was too early to do it right, so we postponed for a year. The next four seasons were filled with ongoing medical, legal and business struggles, getting a grip on bills and work and Jenny learning to walk again. By the time March of 2016 came, we were so much further down so many roads.

And we did do it right. Thanks to our best man Barnett and his crew of volunteers, our yard was cleaned up, a stage built, the paths and Joshua trees painted with colored light. Then commenced four days of celebrations at our house, from a Thursday night dance party under the stars, DJ'd by Sailor and Jessie Mae, with much Grateful Dead put in for Jenny and her old friends, to an artsy Friday mural painting on the dancing Ganesha that Maryrose had prepared for us, and playing all the old songs on strings and drums that night, to a Sunday brunch tango lesson in the gentle spring sunshine. On Saturday, we created an utterly unique ceremony around music, art and ritual, and our circle of amazing people. Jenny wore a skirt and a tie and the gorgeous legs that Georganne had painted for her. Yazzy looked like a princess or a fairy godmother in a long, pink ballgown. Our friends created music for us: a remixed Pachelbel's Cannon in D, Vic sang Nina Simone, Robbi and Kripa made some Kirtan magic for a part of the ritual I dreamed up with Jenny and I getting wrapped in a long red scarf, that I wanted to go on forever. We had Arabic and Dutch influence, marrying our cultures along with our spirits. People spoke and sometimes wept their blessings for us, folks devoured a roasted lamb in about thirty minutes, Gene and Piper's band serenaded us into the dark. We had friends and family from everywhere, my cousin Marleen winning the prize for coming all the way from Zimbabwe. And we were finally able to celebrate and express our gratitude for our far flung and desert communities, who held us together so well in the darkest of times.

There is something I haven't talked about in these writings that I have been trying to figure out how to say. It has to do with gratitude. It's something I would never have felt without Jenny. It is about how all of this medical craziness we have gone through together feels somehow like blessing. And I say this knowing full well I'm not the one trying to get around on stilts and missing so much of my former self.

But there is this heightened sense of living and opening to the infinite that comes when you are in the midst of crisis, which is maybe largely adrenaline, maybe not. But there is something deeper and longer lasting too, having come out the other side. I do not think I would feel this way if Jenny had not traversed this journey with so much joy and grace. Or it would have been different anyway. This deeper knowing of self and of life, of strength in the danger zone, of the high wire dance in which we find our most beautiful balance—this is the gift that landed on us, that we now get to continue giving, to each other.

yazzy and trinidee interview

with yazzy, trinidee, myshkin and jenny

J - Do you remember when you first heard the news about Mama being sick?

Y - No

T - Like at Lola's? We made art for you and sent it to the hospital.

Y - That was not the first time I heard.

J - Yeah, you first heard when you were spending the night at Lola's?

Y - Oh yeah.

J - OK. Who told you?

Y - Myshkin did.

J - Myshkin called you?

Y - Mmhmm.

J - Did you know why you were at Barnett's house?

Y - No.

J - Remember I was kinda sick? I was in a lot of pain.

Y - No …. you wouldn't tell me.

J - But you knew I was sick?

Y - I thought you had the flu.

J - So when Mysh called you, was Barnett with you?

Y - Barnett was on the phone with Myshkin, then he gave me the phone.

J - What did Myshkin say?

Y - I can't remember.

M - I think it was a really short conversation. I told you that Mama was in the hospital, but everything was going to be OK.

Y - Oh yeah, and that I had to stay at Lola's for like another week. I was like, 'What?!'

T - Maybe my dad told me. He said you got sick from doctors using a dirty tool.

J - He told you that?

T - Yeah.

J - And so, Mysh said you were gonna have to stay with Lola for a while and you were like, 'What the heck?'

Y - I was like, 'Why?'

J - You were upset because you had already been there for two days?

Y - Yeah, I was there for like four days all together. You said it was beause you didn't want to risk me getting the flu. That's what you told me.

J - Does that sound right, Mysh? I don't remember that time very well.

M - I don't remember the flu bit. I think we just didn't want to scare you.

Y - Yeah, 'cause I was seven.

J - So right after that, what did you do?

Y - I went to bed. All I thought was that you just had the flu and had to go to the hospital.

...

J - What was the hardest part about not having Mama home?

Y - When I was sick. Because no one else knew when I was sick. Only you know when I am going to have a fever, before I have one. So, they said, 'You don't have a fever. It's time to go to school.' And then I'd be at school and be like, 'Ow, my head.'

J - Because you don't actually get hot with a fever until later.

Y - Yeah, until later.

J - Oh, Habibti.

...

J- Who did you confide in?

Y - No one.

J - You didn't talk to anyone about your fears?

Y - No one.

J - Not Trin?

Y - No. Or well ..

T - Maybe a little.

Y - I would just say, 'Yeah, my mom's in the hospital.'

J - Were you really scared?

Y - Yeah, definitely 'cause everyone was like, "She's gonna die."

J - Who was saying that?

Y - Everyone. Everyone except Myshkin.

T - Not me.

J- You believed I would be OK, Trin?

T- Yeah.

J - So you overheard people saying that I wasn't going to make it?

Y - Yeah and then they'd see me and be like, 'Oh, hi Yazzy!'

Y - And a friend at school was like, 'What are you gonna do if your mom dies?' And I was like, 'I'm gonna live with my dad.' And she was like, 'No, you're gonna live with me.' And I was like, 'No, I'm gonna live with my dad!'

And that created a big argument, we had a big argument.

J - And when you went on Thursday nights to Lola's, did Barnet talk to you or anything?

Y - He would ask if I was OK.

J - A few adults said that when they would ask how you were doing, you would just say, 'Fine.'

Y - I would say, 'Good.'

T - You were trying to stay as happy as possible, huh?

J - But was it that you just didn't know how to talk to people about such a scary situation, because you usually confide in Mom?

Y - Maybe. But I didn't really want to talk about it.

J - Because..

Y - Well..

J - It was too scary?

Y - Yeah.

J - To think about?

Y - Yeah.

T - It's like when people put something negative in the air. It's just like my dad is always saying. 'Don't talk about moving ever, or we are going to end up having to move.'

Y - Yeah.

J - So, did it feel like, 'I just don't want to talk about it,' but you were thinking about it internally and didn't want to talk about it?

Y - It was more like I just pushed it away. It was gone.

J - So you were going about your day not actually thinking about it? Wow. But it's a common thing kids do.

M- It's a coping mechanism.

Y - Yeah.

J - But I'm glad you talk about it now because when that kind of stuff happens and you don't talk about it, it stays in your cells and in your guts.

Y - Yeah.

...

J - Did anything help your fear?

Y - No.

J - No? The fear was there all the time? Where did you feel it? In your belly?

Y - No, not that I can remember. It was like three or four years ago.

T - Like, sometimes when I'd come over, I remembered the feeling of Jenny being here. Without her being here, it was like a lower spirit around the house, 'cause there was not as much joy going around. 'Cause you're always, like, super energetic.

Y - Except when she's mad.

J - That's still a lot of energy. (laughter)

Y - Not good energy, but energy. (laughs)

J - Are there certain moments that stick out in your memory during this time?

T - Yeah, definitely one for me. It was when you and me and Lola and Madison were all making little rag dolls, and sent them to the hospital.

J - What about you, Punk?

Y - When the nurses were like, 'Yeah she's gonna die, she's totally gonna die, but we'll just keep working so maybe she doesn't.' And I was like right behind them.

J – What?

M- That's wild. I wonder whether you mistook them or ..

Y - They were standing outside her room looking at, at my mom, and they were just like, (whispers) yeah...

M - At UCI?

Y - Yeah, none of the other hospitals would let me go in. Sixteen and older, burn unit..

...

J - I'm curious about the first time you saw me in the hospital.

Y - I don't remember.

...

M - The second time, you were awake and they were feeding you Jello, Jenny.

Y - Yes. And I got to have Jello!

M - I think for the first time.

Y - That was the first time in my life that I ever had Jello. And it was so good.

J - Yeah, I kind of remember.

M - It was your first food out of the coma.

Y - And you were just eating it..

...

J - OK, so any other memories that you have?

Y - No.

T - Like the book thing in the shop? Everyone writing notes to you in books to bring to your hospital room.

Y - Yeah, I remember that.

J - And making cards?

Y and T - Yeah.

M - Do you remember how your Baba would take you to UCI on Sundays and then I would drive you home?

Y - I was too young to remember. I was just too young

…

J- What is the worst memory you have?

Y - Probably the 'she's gonna die' thing. Yeah. Oh, and the time when they wouldn't let me come in your room. I was standing there crying. And finally they said OK.

T - My worst memory is when my dad talked to me and I was really worried that if you didn't live, Yazzy would be heartbroken for life.

J - That's intense. Do you have any memory of trying to talk to Yazzy about it?

T - I might have tried a few times, but you always changed the subject.

Y - Yeah. I don't think you tried. I think you tried once.

T - I think I tried once. And then you changed the subject.

Y - I just had a hard time talking about it, like I said. I just put all the thoughts over there. (motions beside herself)

…

J - Is there anything cool that you can think of about this experience?

Y - Yeah. We get the best parking! (laughs)

J - What else is cool?

Y - Your legs are awesome. I love your new ones. I mean, your legs are awesome and your prostheses are awesome and it's awesome. You get to have a wheelchair and I get rides on it.

J - What about you, Trin. Anything cool about this experience for you?

T - You came back as a different person.

J - In what way?

T - You were just more energized and happier about life, that you lived through the whole experience. You're more… you cherished life more.

Y - Yeah you were like, 'this could happen to anybody at any time.'

T - My dad told me that only ten percent of the people ..

Y - With sepsis. I think it's less than that.

T - Yeah, only a little bit live and you were one of them.

Y - Yep. You were one of that little percent.

...

J - So, what lessons did you learn that you might take into your adulthood?

T - That you should cherish life.

Y - Yeah, that's just what I was about to say. Cherish life.

T - Just make it count 'cause who knows, next thing you might be in the hospital.

Y - Yeah.

T - Like you're in the car all happy, headed to a wedding and then you get hit by a car.

Y - Yeah. Anything could happen, so cherish life.

...

J - Anything else?

Y - Don't judge other people.

T - Yeah, like before you got out of the hospital, I didn't hang out with disabled people often, and then while you were in the hospital, I became friends with Samantha, a deaf girl at school.

Y - Samantha was my best friend in third grade.

T - And then the other day in my class, in drama, this disabled woman with a service dog came in. She had, I don't know what disorder it was, but her neck always moved, it twitched around, but I didn't care. I thought she was just a normal person. Other people looked at her weird and I didn't.

Y - If I see someone disabled, I smile at them. If they don't smile back its ok, but if they do, I think its a good thing. I'm like, 'My mom is an amputee!'

J - So you guys feel closer to disabled people now?

Y - Yeah, definitely.

...

J - I still feel like we missed a lot of time together. Any last words?

T - I'm just glad that you survived.

Y - I'm so happy you are back home with me.

jenny
light and light

today, i got to spend the day with sophia, kimberly's newborn.

i held and held that five-day-old while she slept in the stars

and found her way slowly into her body.

i watched her face and saw it.

i remembered.

i remembered being in the coma. i remembered being in the stars.

being in the stars and being aware of my body,

but far away

i wasn't attached. i was aware that my body was struggling,

was suffering immense pain..

i was aware of the distress,

but i was soft and peaceful and joyous in the stars.

light and light.

sofia's peaceful face brought me back to the place between places,

the place that is nowhere,

but indeed everything..

my soul and body needed to merge..

i knew i would integrate and i did, slowly.

one tiny bit at a time, no stress, no worry, peaceful, slow.

there was no pressure or fear or even sadness at this difficult job i needed to do.

i was at once totally at peace in the stars, an observer of my process and aware of my physical body.

today, i remembered this— knew this-- as i stared down at sofia's perfect little face.

i watched as her breathing normalized--

breaths first quick, shallow, then a bit deeper.

now again shallow..

testing the form, toes in the water..

her eyes crinkle shut, then open, then softly close..

hands waving, resting on her face, waving again.

lips pucker, then the rooting, searching, then a smile..

i knew she was sleeping in the stars.. slowly, surely, peacefully stepping into this new, physical body that would be hers.

and goddess, with all my fiber, i remembered.

with all my being, i knew-

that from the stars we are born,

and to those stars, we return.

Contributors

Jenny Q

Myshkin Warbler

Barnett English

Tania Hammidi

Photo by Love Alban

Lynne Thelen

Ted Quinn

Michelle Qaqundah

Maryrose Crook

Kripa and Robbi Rob

Suad & Boulos Qaqundah   Felicia Banks   Jessie Mae Vancraeynest

Kali Poulin   Stella Ru   Melissa Meyers

Katie Lussier   Eva Soltes   Erik Kramer-Webb

Joyce Qaqundah

Sue Burns

Marilyn Moshos

Michelle Baum

Elise

Lena Moffet

Cheryl Montelle

Susan & David Jordan

Willow Tocatta

Patricia Thompson   Maya Tocotta   Rodney Soderberg

Georganne Deen   Karen Hayes   Lisa Starr

Liesl   Anita Prezell   Jimmy Qaqundah

Christa Cranston

Selah Green

Ronda Mueller

Allison Simonis

Karin Pine

Julia Ehret

Paula Rivera

Johnny Qaqundah

Matt Perry

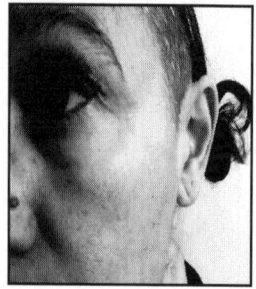

Julie Tolentino *Nina Mihranian* *Trinidee Cappel*

Yazzy Qaqundah